OLD-IRISH PARADIGMS

AND SELECTIONS FROM
THE OLD-IRISH GLOSSES

With notes and vocabulary by
JOHN STRACHAN
Fourth Edition, revised by
OSBORN BERGIN

ROYAL IRISH ACADEMY
DUBLIN
(1949)

Reprinted 1998

Royal Irish Academy,
19 Dawson Street, Dublin 2.

ISBN   0 901714 35 6

© Royal Irish Academy 1949
   Fourth edition, reprinted 1970, 1984, 1989, 1995, 1998

Printed in Ireland by Colour Books Ltd.

PREFACE TO THE FOURTH EDITION

THIS edition has been further revised and enlarged. New sections have been added to the Paradigms, illustrating the declension of article+noun+adjective, and the use of the infixed pronoun. Some of the verbal paradigms have been arranged in a fuller and clearer form. In the Selections the spelling of the Latin has as a rule been normalized. Where the text of the Glosses has been emended, the manuscript readings are given in foot-notes. Though these may seem out of place in an elementary book, I hope they will be helpful to students who intend to pass on to the study of Early Irish manuscripts. Mere extensions, however, have not been marked by special type. Many of the Notes have been re-written, and Additional Notes appended. References to the Glosses have been added to the Vocabulary.

Advanced students can now consult Thurneysen's *Grammar of Old Irish*, the new edition, in English, of his *Handbuch*.

For several corrections I have to thank Dr. R. I. Best and Rev. Prof. F. Shaw, S.J., and especially Prof. E. Knott who has read the Selections, Notes and Vocabulary in proof.

OSBORN BERGIN.

PREFACE TO THE THIRD EDITION

THE *Selections* first appeared in 1904, and the *Paradigms* in 1905. In 1909, after Professor Strachan's death, a new edition was issued in one volume. In the present edition both parts have been revised, and sections on the comparison of adjectives and on personal pronouns added.

The *Paradigms* were originally ' put together to serve as the skeleton for a course of lectures on Old-Irish Accidence '. In his preface to the *Selections* Professor Strachan wrote :

' The arrangement of the glosses calls for some explanation. It has been found that to students, particularly to students who are already familiar with the modern language, the Old Irish noun and pronoun present no great difficulties. On the other hand, the complicated verbal system is very puzzling to the beginner. This book has, therefore, been so arranged that the student who has mastered the nominal inflexion may learn the verb gradually, tense by tense.

' In the notes much will be found that would more properly be relegated to the grammar. Of recent years, however, much progress has been made in the study of Old Irish grammar, and, as yet, no grammar has appeared in which these recent discoveries have been embodied. It is hoped that the references which are given will lead the student to consult the original authorities. A translation of the Irish may be found in the *Thesaurus Palaeohibernicus.*'

As the authorities to which Professor Strachan referred have proved inaccessible to most beginners, such references have, as a rule, been omitted in this edition. Advanced students will now find them in Thurneysen's *Handbuch des Altirischen* and in Pedersen's *Vergleichende Grammatik der keltischen Sprachen.*

OSBORN BERGIN.

March 1929.

LIST OF WORKS REFERRED TO
AND ABBREVIATIONS

Acr. = Glosses on S. Augustine's Soliloquia, Carlsruhe (Thesaurus Palaeohibernicus, ii. pp. 1-9).

Bcr. = Glosses on Beda, Carlsruhe (Thesaurus Palaeohibernicus, ii. pp. 10-30).

Contt. = Contributions to Irish Lexicography.

Corm = Sanas Cormaic, ed. Meyer.

Ériu, Royal Irish Academy, Dublin.

Félire Óengusso.

Im. Br. = Imram Brain, ed. Meyer.

KZ. = Kuhns Zeitschrift für vergleichende Sprachforschung.

LB. = Leabhar Breac, Royal Irish Academy.

Lib. Ardm. = Book of Armagh (Thesaurus Palaeohibernicus, i. pp. 494-8 ; ii. pp. 238-42).

Ml. = The Milan Glosses on the Psalms (Thesaurus Palaeohibernicus, i. pp. 7-483).

LL = Book of Leinster.

LU = Lebor na Huidre.

Sg. = Glosses on Priscian, S. Gall (Thesaurus Palaeohibernicus, ii. pp. 49-244).

Táin Bó Cúalnge.

Thesaurus Palaeohibernicus, (Thes. Pal.) ed. Stokes and Strachan : Cambridge, 1901, 1903.

Tur. = The Turin Glosses on S. Mark (Thesaurus Palaeohibernicus, i. pp. 484-94).

Wb. = The Würzburg Glosses on the Pauline Epistles (Thesaurus Palaeohibernicus, i. pp. 499-712).

VG. = Vergleichende Grammatik der keltischen Sprachen.

ZCP. = Zeitschrift für celtische Philologie.

OTHER ABBREVIATIONS

A. *or* acc. = accusative
abs. = absolute
act. = active
Add. = Addenda
adj. = adjective
art. = article
cf. = compare
comp. = compound
compar. = comparative
conj. = conjunction
cons. = consuetudinal
D. *or* dat. = dative
e.g. = for example
emph. = emphatic
Eng. = English
f. *or* fem. = feminine
fr. = from
fut. = future
G. *or* gen. = genitive
gl. = gloss *or* glosses
id. = the same
i.e. = that is
impers. = impersonal
impf. = imperfect
ind. *or* indic. = indicative
inf. *or* infix. = infixed
intrans. = intransitive
ipv. = imperative
ɫ. = nó ' or ', Lat. uel
lit. = literally

m. *or* masc. = masculine
Mid. Ir. = Middle-Irish
Mod. Ir. = Modern Irish
MS. = manuscript reading
MSS. = manuscripts
neg. = negative
n. *or* neut. = neuter
O. Ir. = Old-Irish
N. *or* nom. = nominative
p. = page
part. = participle
pass. = passive
perf. = perfect
pl. = plural
poss. = possessive
pp. = pages
prep. = preposition
pres. = present
pret. = preterite
pron. = pronoun
rel. = relative
sec. = secondary
sg. = singular
subj. = subjunctive
suff. = suffixed
trans. = transitive
V. *or* voc. = vocative
vb. = verb
verb. = verbal
verb. necess. = verbal of necessity

CONTENTS

OLD-IRISH PARADIGMS

THE ARTICLE

	Masculine	*Feminine*	*Neuter*
N.	in, int	ind',[1] in', int[2]	a n-
A.	in n-, lasin n- etc.	in n-, lasin n-, etc.	a n-, lassa n- etc.
G.	ind', in', int[2]	inna, na	ind', in', int[2]
D.	dond', don', dont[2]	dond', don',	dond', don', dont[2]
	cossind', cossin', etc.	cossind', cossin', etc.	cossind', cossin', etc.

PLURAL

N.	ind', in', int[2]	inna, na	inna, na
A.	inna, na	inna, na	inna, na
	lasna, etc.	lasna, etc.	lasna, etc.
G.	inna n-, na n-	inna n-, na n-	inna n-, na n-
D.	donaib	donaib	donaib
	cosnaib, etc.	cosnaib, etc.	cosnaib, etc.

DUAL

N.	in dá'	in dí'	in dá n-
A.	in dá'	in dí'	in dá n-
G.	in dá'	in dá'	in dá n-
D.	don dib n-	don dib n-	don dib n-

[1] ' indicates that the form lenites. [2] before ś.

THE NOUN

A.—VOCALIC STEMS

1. Stems in -o-

fer m., man.

Singular	Plural	Dual
N. fer	fir	dá ḟer
V. á ḟir	á ḟiru	
A. fer n-	firu	dá ḟer
G. fir	fer n-	dá ḟer
D. fiur	feraib	dib feraib

ball m., limb.

Singular	Plural	Dual
N. ball	boill, baill	dá ball
V. á boill, baill	á baullu, á bullu	
A. ball n-	baullu, bullu	dá ball
G. boill, baill	ball n-	dá ball
D. baull, bull	ballaib	dib mballaib

dliged n., law.

Singular	Plural	Dual
N.V.A. dliged n-	{ dliged { dligeda	dá ndliged n-
G. dligid	dliged n-	dá ndliged
D. dligud	dligedaib	dib ndligedaib

cenél n., race.

Singular	Plural	Dual
N.V.A. cenél n-	cenél, cenéla	dá cenél n-
G. { ceníuil, { cenéuil, cenéoil	cenél n-	dá cenél
D. ceníul, cenéul	cenélaib	dib cenélaib

NOTE.—In the d. sg. -**u**- infection is not always found, e.g.

n.acc, **salm, galar, folt.** So adjectives in **-ach** always have **-ach.**

Further examples of this declension are :

crann, n., tree, g. **cruinn,** d. **crunn.**

nert n., strength, g. **neirt,** d. **neurt.**

leth, n., half, g. **leith,** d. **leuth.**

ech, m., horse, g. **eich,** a. pl. **echu.**

son m., sound, g. **suin,** d. **sun,** a. pl. **sunu.**

lebor, lebur m., book, g. **libuir,** d. **libur,** a. pl. **libru.**

biad n., food, g. **biid,** d. **biud.**

diall n., declension, g. **diill,** d. **diull.**

fíach m., debt, g. **féich,** d. **fíach.**

íasc m., fish, g. **éisc,** d. **íasc.**

día m., God, g. **dé,** d. **día,** a. **día n-,** n. pl. **dé,** a. **deu, deo,** g. **día n-,** d. **déib.**

bél m., lip. g. **béoil, béuil,** d. **béul,** a. pl. **béulu.**

nél m., cloud, g. **níuil,** a. pl. **níulu.**

scél, n., story, g. **scéuil.**

fér n., grass, g. **féuir.**

én m., bird, g. **éuin, éoin,** d. **éun.**

trén m., strong man, g. **tréuin, tríuin,** d. **tríun,** a. pl. **tríunu.**

céol n., music, g. **cíuil.**

demun m., devil, g. **demuin,** is in the plural inflected like an **-i-** stem, g. **demnae,** a. **demnai.**

2. Stems in -ā-, all feminine.

túath, people.

Singular	*Plural*	*Dual*
N.V. **túath**	**túatha**	**dí thúaith**
A. **túaith n-**	**túatha**	**dí thúaith**
G. **túaithe**	**túath n-**	**dá thúath**
D. **túaith**	**túathaib**	**dib túathaib**

cíall, sense

Singular	*Plural*	*Dual*
N.V. cíall	cíalla	dí chéill
A. céill n-	cíalla	dí chéill
G. céille	cíall n-	dá chíall
D. céill	cíallaib	dib cíallaib

NOTE 1.—Nouns in **-acht** have in the d. sg. **-acht,** in the a. **-acht n-,** e.g. **doínacht,** manhood, d. **doínacht,** a. **doínacht n-.**

NOTE 2.—In verbal nouns the dative form is often used for the nominative, e.g. **gabál** and **gabáil,** taking g. **gabálae,** d. **gabáil.**

NOTE 3.—Some nouns in the singular alternate between the **-ā-** and the **-n-** declension ; in the plural they follow the **-ā-** declension. Such are—**bendacht,** blessing, g. **bendachtae** and **bendachtan** ; similarly **dúthracht,** desire, **fortacht,** help, **maldacht,** curse.

NOTE 4.—**persan,** person, has in the n. pl. **persin.**

NOTE 5.—**ben,** woman, is declined : n. v. sg. **ben,** a. **mnaí n-** (archaic **bein**), g. **mná,** d. **mnaí,** n. v. a. pl. **mná,** g. **ban n-,** d. **mnáib,** n. a. du. **dí mnaí,** g. **dá ban,** d. **dib mnáib.**

Further examples of this declension are :
> **cland,** offspring, g. **clainde.**
> **dígal,** vengeance, g. **díglae.**
> **lám,** hand, g. **lámae.**
> **delb,** form, g. **delbae.**
> **pían,** punishment, g. **péne.**
> **croch,** cross, g. **cruchae,** d. **cruich, croich.**
> **long,** ship, g. **lungae.**

3. Stems in -io-
céile m., fellow.

Singular	Plural	Dual
N. céile	céili	dá chéile
V. á chéili	á chéiliu	
A. céile n-	céiliu	dá chéile
G. céili	céile n-	dá chéile
D. céiliu	céilib	dib céilib

daltae m., fosterling.

Singular	Plural	Dual
N. daltae	daltai	dá daltae
V. á daltai	á daltu	
A. daltae n-	daltu	dá daltae
G. daltai	daltae n-	dá daltae
D. daltu	daltaib	dib ndaltaib

cride n., heart.

Singular	Plural	Dual
N.V.A. cride n-	cride	dá cride n-
G. cridi	cride n-	dá cride
D. cridiu	cridib	dib cridib

NOTE 1.—**aue** m., grandson, makes n. sg. **aue**, g. **aui**, d. **auu**, n. du. **aue**, n. pl. **aui**, a. **auu**, d. **auib**.

NOTE 2.—**duine** m., man, is irregular in the plural : n.v.a. **doíni**, g. **doíne n-**, d. **doínib**.

4. Stems in -iā-, all feminine.

guide, prayer.

Singular	*Plural*	*Dual*
N.V. guide	guidi	dí guidi
A. guidi n-	guidi	dí guidi
G. guide	guide n-	dá guide
D. guidi	guidib	dib nguidib

ungae, ounce.

Singular	*Plural*	*Dual*
N.V. ungae	ungai	dí ungai
A. ungai n-	ungai	dí ungai
G. ungae	ungae n-	dá ungae
D. ungai	ungaib	dib n-ungaib

5. Stems in -i-

súil f., eye.

Singular	*Plural*	*Dual*
N.V. súil	súili	dí ṡúil
A. súil n-	súili	di ṡúil
G. súlo, súla	súile n-	dá ṡúlo, ṡúla
D. súil	súilib	dib súilib

cnáim m., bone.

Singular	*Plural*	*Dual*
N.V. cnáim	cnámai	dá chnáim
A. cnáim n-	cnámai	dá chnáim
G. cnámo, cnáma	cnámae n-	dá chnámo, chnáma
D. cnáim	cnámaib	dib cnámaib

muir n., sea.

Singular	Plural	Dual
N.V.A. muir n-	muire	dá muir n-
G. moro, mora	muire n-	dá moro, mora
D. muir	muirib	dib muirib

NOTE 1.—Apart from **muire** there are few examples of the neut. pl.; **druimm**, g. **drommo,** back, has a. pl. **drummai.**

NOTE 2.—Some borrowed words show no ending in the g. sg. Such are : **abbgitir,** alphabet, **argumint,** argument, **firmimint,** firmament, **comparit,** comparative, **posit,** positive, **superlait,** superlative, **tabernacuil,** tabernacle, **testimin,** text.

6. Stems in -ī-, all feminine.

inis, island.

Singular	Plural	Dual
N.V. inis	insi	dí inis
A. insi n-	insi	dí inis
G. inse	inse ,n-	dá inse
D. insi	insib	dib n-insib

blíadain, year.

Singular	Plural	Dual
N.V. blíadain	blíadnai	dí blíadain
A. blíadnai n-	blíadnai	dí blíadain
G. blíadnae	blíadnae n-	dá blíadnaib
D. blíadnai	blíadnaib	dib mblíadnaib

NOTE.—Some nouns follow this declension only in the g. sg., e.g. **méit,** size, g. **méite,** d. **méit** ; **canóin,** canon, g. **canóne,** d. **canóin.**

Further instances of this declension are :

adaig, night, g. **aidche.**
Brigit, g. **Brigte.**
móin, bog, g. **mónae.**

rígain, queen, g. **rígnae.**
sétig, wife, g. **séitche.**

7. Stems in -u-

guth m., voice.

Singular	Plural	Dual
N.V. **guth**	gothae, gotha gothai	dá guth
A. **guth n-**	guthu	dá guth
G. **gotho, gotha**	gothae n-	dá gotho, gotha
D. **guth**	ngothaib	dib ngothaib

rind n., star.

Singular	Plural	Dual
N.V.A. **rind n-**	rind	dá rind n-
G. **rendo, renda**	rendae n-	dá rendo, renda
D. **rind**	rendaib	dib rendaib

Further examples of this declension are :

bith m., world, g. **betho, betha**, d. **biuth**.
bir, biur n., spit, g. **bero, bera**, d. **biur**, n.a. pl. **beura**.
daur, oak, g. **daro, dara**.
dorus, n., door, n.a. pl. **dorus** and **doirsea**.
fid m., wood, g. **fedo, feda**.
gin m., mouth, g. **geno, gena**, d. **giun**.
mess m., judgement, g. **messo, messa**.
mid m., mead, g. **medo, meda**.
mind n., diadem, n.a. pl. **mind**, d. **mindaib**.
suth m., offspring, g. **sotho, sotha**.
molad m., praise, g. **molto, molta**.
foilsigud m., manifestation, g. **foilsigtheo, foilsigthe**.

The fem. **deug**, drink, and **mucc**, pig, follow the declension of -ā- stems ; g. **dige, muicce**, d. **dig, muicc**.

8. Stems in a diphthong.

bó f., cow.

Singular	Plural	Dual
N.V. bó	baí	dí baí
A. boin n-	bú	dí baí
G. bou, bó	báo n-, bó n-	dá bó
D. boin	buaib	dib mbuaib

B.—CONSONANTAL STEMS

9. Stems in a guttural.

(a) cathir f., city.

Singular	Plural	Dual
N. cathir	cathraig	dí chathraig, chathir
V. á chathir	á chathracha [1]	
A. cathraig n-	cathracha	dí chathraig, chathir
G. cathrach	cathrach n-	dá chathrach
D. cathraig caithir	cathrachaib	dib cathrachaib

Similarly :

> nathir f., snake, g. nathrach
> sail f., willow, g. sailech
> Findubair f., g. Findubrech
> Lugaid m., g. Luigdech

---

[1] In consonantal stems the vocative has in the singular the same form as the nominative, in the plural the same form as the accusative. Hence it is unnecessary to give it in the following paradigms.

(b)   **aire** m., noble.

Singular	Plural	Dual
N. aire	airig	dá airig, aire
A. airig n-	airecha	dá airig, aire
G. airech	airech n-	dá airech
D. airig	airechaib	dib n-airechaib

Similarly :

> **Ainmire,** g. **Ainmirech**
> **are** m., temple of the head, g. **arach**

Similarly, but with **-u-**, **-o** in the nominative :

> **Cúanu** m., g. **Cúanach**
> **Echu** m., g. **Echach.**
> **céo** m., mist, g. **ciach.**
> **éo** m., salmon, g. **iach.**

(c)   **rí** m., king.

Singular	Plural	Dual
N. rí	ríg	dá ríg
A. ríg n-	ríga	dá ríg
G. ríg	ríg n-	dá ríg
D. ríg	rígaib	dib rígaib

Similarly **brí,** hill, a. **brig n-,** g. **breg,** d. **brig, brí.**

(d)   **lie** m., stone.

Singular	Plural	Dual
N. lie	lieic	dá lieic
A. lieic n-	leca	dá lieic
G. liac	liac n-	dá liac
D. lieic	lecaib	dib lecaib

10. Stems in a dental.

(a)   **cin** m., fault.

Singular	*Plural*	*Dual*
N. cin	cinaid	dá chinaid, chin
A. cinaid n-, cin n-	cinta	dá chinaid, chin
G. cinad	cinad n-	dá chinad
D. cinaid, cin	cintaib	dib cintaib

Further examples are :

> **cing** m., warrior, g. **cinged.**
> **eirr** m., fighter in a war-chariot, g. **erred.**
> **seir** f., heel, g. **sered.**
> **traig,** foot, g. **traiged,** a. pl. **traigthea.**
> **luch,** mouse, g. **lochad,** a. pl. **lochtha.**

(b)   **tene** m., fire.

Singular	*Plural*	*Duel*
N. tene	tenid	dá thenid, thene
A. tenid n-	teintea	dá thenid, thene
G. tened	tened n-	dá thened
D. tenid, tein	teintib	dib teintib

arae m., charioteer.

Singular	*Plural*	*Dual*
N. arae	araid	dá araid, arae
A. araid n-	arada	dá araid
G. arad	arad n-	da arad
D. araid	aradaib	dib n-aradaib

Further examples are :

> **ascae** m., rival, g. **ascad.**
> **tengae** m., tongue, g. **tengad.**
> **niae** m., nephew, g **niad.**

Similarly :

    cré f., clay, a. **crieid n-**, g. **criad**, d. **crieid**.

    dé, smoke, g. **diad**.

    gléo, fight, a. **glieid n-**, g. **gliad**, d. **glieid, gléo.**

(c) fili m., poet, a. **filid n-**, g. **filed**, d. **filid**, n. pl. **filid**, a. **fileda**, etc. So **oígi** m., guest, g. **oíged** ; **druí** m., wizard, g. **druad**.

(d) bethu m., life, a. **bethaid n-**, g. **bethad**, d. **bethaid, bethu.** So many abstract nouns in **-tu**, e.g. **foirbthetu** m., perfection, g. **foirbthetad** ; in these nouns in the acc. and dat. both **-taid** and **-tu** appear. Similarly **bibdu** m., culprit, g. **bibdad** ; **coimmdiu** m., lord, g. **coimded**.

(e)   **carae** m., friend.

Singular	*Plural*	*Dual*
N. carae	carait	dá charait
A. carait n-	cairtea	dá charait
G. carat	carat n-	dá charat
D. carait	cairtib	dib cairtib

So are declined the tens ; **fiche** m., twenty, g. **fichet** ; similarly, but with **-o, -a** in the nom., **trícho, trícha** m., thirty, g. **tríchot, tríchat**, etc.

Similarly, but with **-a** in the nom., **fíada** m., lord, g. **fíadat**.

Similarly, but with **-u** in the nom., **dínu**, lamb, d. **dínit**, **Núadu**, g. **Núadat**.

dét n., tooth.

Singular	*Plural*	*Dual*
N.A. dét n-	dét	dá ndét n-
G. dét	dét n-	dá ndét
D. déit	détaib	dib ndétaib

So **lóchet** n., lightning.

(a)   **11. Stems in a nasal.**

                brithem m., judge.

Singular	Plural	Dual
N. brithem	brithemain	dá brithemain
A. brithemain n-	brithemna	dá brithemain
G. brithemon	brithemon n-	dá brithemon
D. brithemain,	brithemnaib	dib mbrithemnaib
brithem		

Further examples are :

> escung, eel, g. escongan.
> derucc, acorn, g. dercon.
> Miliucc m., g. Milcon.
> talam m., earth, g. talman (but d. talam.)
> triath, sea, g. trethan.

aisndís f., exposition, g. aisndísen, has a. aisndís n-,
   d. aisndís.

anim f., soul, a. anmain n- and anim n-, g. anmae, d.
   anmain and animm, n. pl. anmain, a. anmana, etc.

braó, bró f., quern, a. bróin n-, g. broon, brón.

cú, m. hound, a. coin n-, g. con, d. coin, n. pl. coin, a. cona,
   etc.

(b)   **béim** n., blow.

Singular	Plural	Dual
N.A. béim n-	béimmen	dá mbéim n-
G. béimme	béimmen n-	dá mbéimmen
D. béimmim,	béimmenaib	dib mbéimmenaib
béim		

ainm n., name.

Singular	Plural	Dual
N.A. ainm n-	anman, anmann	dá n-ainm n-
G. anmae	anman n-	dá n-anman
D. anmaim	anmanaib	dib n-anmanaib

arbor n., corn, inflects like ainm, except in n.a. sg., g. arbae, d. arbaim.

(c)   menmae m., mind.

Singular	Plural	Dual
N. menmae	menmain	dá menmain (?)
A. menmain n-	menmana	dá menmain (?)
G. menman,	menman n-	dá menman
menmmann		
D. menmain	menmanaib	dib menmanaib

With -u in the nom. :

fíadu m., witness, a. fíadain n-, g. fíadan, d. fíadain, etc.

Mumu f., Munster, a. Mumin n-, g. Mumen, Muman, d. Mumin, Mume, Mumu.

Albu f., Britain, Scotland, g. Alban, d. Albain, Albae.

(d)   toimtiu f., meaning, opinion.

Singular	Plural	Dual
N. toimtiu	toimtin	dí thoimtin (?)
A. toimtin n-	toimtena	dí thoimtin (?)
G. toimten	toimten n-	dá thoimten
D. toimtin, toimte,	toimtenaib	dib tpimtenaib
toimtiu		

Further examples are :

genitiu f., genitive, g. geniten, n. pl. genitne, Sg. 200[a]14. noídiu f., infant, g. noíden.

Tailltiu f., g. Taillten.

(e)   **gobae** m., smith.

Singular	*Plural*	*Dual*
N. gobae	gobainn	dá gobainn
A. gobainn n-	goibnea (?)	dá gobainn
G. gobann	gobann n-	dá gobann
D. gobainn	goibnib (?)	dib ngoibnib (?)

Similarly, but with **-u** in the nom. :

     áru f., kidney, g. **áraṇn,** d, pl. **áirnib.**

     Anu, g. **Anann.**

     Cúalu, g. **Cúalann.**

     oblu f. consecrated host, g **oblann.**

Similarly further :

     brú f., belly, g. **bronn,** d. **broinn, brú.**

     rétglu, star, g. **rétglann.**

(f) íriu f., land, a. **írinn n-,** g. **írenn,** d. **íriṇn, íre.**

In the same way :

     Bricriu m., g. **Bricrenn.**

     Derdriu f., g. **Derdrenn.**

     Ériu f., Ireland, g. **Érenn,** d. **Érinn, Ére.**

     imbliu, navel, g. **imblenn.**

Similarly, but with **-e** in the nom., **díle,** deluge, g. **dílenn.**

12. Stems in -r

athair m., father.

Singular	*Plural*	*Dual*
N. athair	aithir	dá athair
A. athair n-	aithrea, athra	dá athair
G. athar	aithre n-	dá athar
D. athair	aithrib. athraib	dib n-aithrib
		dib n-athraib

In the same way **bráthair,** brother, **máthair,** mother.

siur f., sister, makes a. **sieir n-,** g. **sethar,** d. **sieir,** n. pl. **sethir,** a. pl. **sethra.**

13. Stems in -s, neuter.

tech n., house.

Singular	Plural	Dual
N.A. **tech, teg**	**tige, taige**	**dá tech n-**
G. **tige, taige**	**tige n-**	**dá tige**
D. **tig, taig**	**tigib**	**dib tigib**

Further instances are :

    glún, knee, g. **glúne.**
    glenn, valley, g. **glinne.**
    leth, side, g. **lethe.**
    slíab, mountain, g. **slébe.**
    dún, fort, g. **dúine.**
    mag, plain, g. **maige.**
    nem, heaven, g. **nime.**
    og, egg, g. **ugae,** d. **uig.**
    síd, elfmound, g. **síde.**
    tír, land, g. **tíre.**

áu, ó, ear, g. **aue,** d. **áui, oí,** n. pl. **óe,** d. **auib,** n. du. **dá n-ó.**

Some neut. **o**-stems in **-ach, -ech** are declined in the pl. like **tech** : **tossach,** beginning, g. **tossaig,** but n. pl. **tosge ; étach,** garment, g. **étaig,** n. pl. **étaige.**

A masculine stem in **-s** is **mí,** month.

Singular	Plural	Dual
N. **mí**	**mís**	**dá mí**
A. **mís n-**	**mísa**	**dá mí**
G. **mís**	**mís n-**	**dá mí**
D. **mís**	**mísaib**	——

ADJECTIVAL DECLENSION

1. Stems in -o-, -ā-

becc, little.

SINGULAR

Masculine	*Feminine*	*Neuter*
N. becc	becc	becc n-
V. bicc	becc	becc n-
A. becc n-	bicc	becc n-
G. bicc	bicce	bicc
D. biucc	bicc	biucc

PLURAL

Masculine	*Feminine*	*Neuter*
N. bicc	becca	becca
V.A. biccu, becca	becca	becca
G. becc n-	becc n-	becc n-
D. beccaib	beccaib	beccaib

NOTE 1.—In the v.a. pl. m., when the adjective is used sub-stantively, the ending is always -u.

NOTE 2.—When the n. sg. of a noun is used for v. (see note p. 9), a qualifying adjective is also n. sg. : **a rí már,** O great king.

NOTE 3.—Adjectives have no special dual forms. The plural is used instead : **da ṅ-ainmm cosmaili** ' two similar nouns ' Sg. 28ª7.

2. Stems in -io-, -iā-

buide, yellow.

SINGULAR

Masculine	Feminine	Neuter
N. buide	buide	buide n-
V. buidi	buide	buide n-
A. buide n-	buidi n-	buide n-
G. buidi	buide	buidi
D. buidiu	buidi	buidiu

PLURAL

N.V.A. buidi
G. buide n-
D. buidib

amrae, wonderful.

SINGULAR

Masculine	Feminine	Neuter
N. amrae	amrae	amrae n-
V. amrai	amrae	amrae n-
A. amrae n-	amrai n-	amrae n-
G. amra	amrae	amrai
D. amru	amrai	amru

PLURAL

N.V.A. amrai
G. amrae n-
D. amraib

NOTE.—In the v.a. pl. m., when the adjective is used substantivally, the ending is -u : buidiu, amru. In the n.v.a. pl. neut. there is no specially substantival form.

Like **buide** are declined the pronominal adjectives **uile,** all,
aile, other (except that the n.a. sg. neut. is **aill), al-aile,**
the other (except that the n.a. sg. neut. is **al-aill),** g. pl.
ala n-aile.

3. Stems in -i-

maith, good.

SINGULAR

Masculine	*Feminine*	*Neuter*
N.V. maith	maith	maith n-
A. maith n-	maith n-	maith n-
G. maith	maithe	maith
D. maith	maith	maith

PLURAL

N.V.A. **maithi**
G. **maithe n-, maith n-**
D. **maithib**

sainemail, excellent

SINGULAR

Masculine	*Feminine*	*Neuter*
N.V. sainemail	sainemail	sainemail n-
A. sainemail n-	sainemail n-	sainemail n-
G. sainemail	sainemlae	sainemail
D. sainemail	sainemail	sainemail

PLURAL

N.V.A. **sainemlai**
G. **sainemlae n-, sainemail n-**
D. **sainemlaib**

coir, coair, fitting.

SINGULAR

Masculine	Feminine	Neuter
N.V. coir	coir	coir n-
A. coir n-	coir n-	coir n-
G. coir	córae	coir
D. coir	coir	coir

PLURAL

N.V.A. córai
G. córae n-, coir n-
D. córaib

NOTE 1.—In the g. sg. the form is also used substantivally e.g. **in diuit** Sg. 221^{b}1.

NOTE 2.—In the n.a. pl. neut. **fudumne** appears substantivally Wb. 5^{c}16, 8^{b}6, but **fudumnai** Ml. 81^{a}4, cf. Ml. 81^{c}15, 118^{a}9.

NOTE 3.—In the g. pl. when the adjective is used substantivally the longer forms are employed; otherwise the shorter form is already in O. Ir. almost universal.

NOTE 4.—In the plural **ísel, úasal, díles,** and **daingen** are inflected like -i- stems : n. pl. **ísli, úaisli, dílsi, daingni.**

4. Stems in -u-

The material is insufficient for a complete paradigm. In the plural they are declined like -i- stems.

dub, black.

SINGULAR

Masculine	Feminine	Neuter
N. dub	dub	dub n-
A. dub n-	duib n-	dub n-
G. duib	dubae	duib
D. dub	duib	dub

PLURAL

N.A. **dubai**
G. (later **dub**)
D. **dubaib**

Similarly **follus,** clear, g. sg. m. n. **follais,** f. **foilse ;**
pl. n.a. **foilsi,** d. **foilsib.**

5. Stems in a consonant.

An instance is **té,** hot, N. Pl. F. **téit.**

Paradigms of Article, Noun, and Adjective.[1]

:n **lebor cétnae,** the same book.

SINGULA :	PLURAL
N. **in lebor cétnae**	**ind libuir chétnai**
A. **in lebor cétnae**	**inna libru cétnai**
G. **ind libuir chétnai**	**inna llebor cétnae**
D. **dond libur chétnu**	**donaib lebraib cétnaib**

in ben gel, the bright woman.

SINGULAR	PLURAL
N. **in ben gel**	**inna mná gela**
A. **in mnaí ngil**	**inna mná gela**
G. **inna mná gile**	**inna mban ngel**
D. **don mnaí gil**	**donaib mnáib gelaib**

a slíab n-ard, the high mountain.

SINGULAR	PLURAL
N.A. **a slíab n-ard**	**inna slébe arda**
G. **int šlébe aird**	**inna slébe n-ard**
D. **dont šléib ard**	**donaib slébib ardaib**

[1] Only the sg. and pl. are given.

COMPARISON OF ADJECTIVES

The Equative

dían, swift : dénithir.
léir, diligent : lérithir.
demin, certain : demnithir.
suthain, lasting : suthainidir.
erlam, ready : erlamaidir.

The Comparative

sen, old : siniu.
dían, swift : déniu.
fáilid, glad : fáiltiu.
oll, great : uilliu.
ard, high : ardu.
lobor, weak : lobru.
tromm, heavy : trummu.
brónach, sad : brónchu.
cumachtach, mighty : cumachtchu.
ansae, difficult : ansu.
toísech, chief, first : toísigiu, toísechu, toísegu,
    prior.

The Superlative

cóem, dear : cóemem.
toísech, chief : toísigem, toísechem.
follus, clear : faillsem.
ansae, difficult : ansam.

In the Milan Glosses the suffix is sometimes doubled :
(h)úasal, noble : húaislem and húaislimem ; fírián, righteous : fíriánamam.

IRREGULAR COMPARISON

	Equative	Comparative	Superlative
il, many	lir	lia	
lethan, broad	lethidir	letha	
már, mór, great	móir	mó, móo, móa, máo, móu, máa, má	máam, mám, moam
oac, óac, young		óa	óam
sír, long		sia, sía	síam
trén, strong	tresithir	tressa	tressam
remor, fat	remithir, remidir		
accus, ocus, near		nessa, nesso	nessam
bec(c), small		lugu, laigiu, laugu	lugam, lugimem
maith, dag-, deg-, good		ferr	dech, deg
olc, droch-, bad		messa	messam

DECLENSION OF THE NUMERALS
óen, oín, one.

This is commonly uninflected, entering into composition with a following noun.

da, dá, two.

	Masculine	Feminine	Neuter
N.A.	**da'**	**dí'**	**da n-**
G.	**da'**	**da'**	**da n-**
D.	**dib n-**	**dib n-**	**dib n-**

When unaccompanied by a noun, **a dáu, a dó.**

tri, three.

Masculine	Feminine	Neuter
N. tri	téoir, téora	tri'
A. tri	téora	tri'
G. tri n-	téora n-	tri n-
D. trib	téoraib	trib

When unaccompanied by a noun, **a trí.**

cethir, four.

Masculine	Feminine	Neuter
N. cethir	cethéoir, cethéora	cethir'
A. cethri	cethéora	cethir'
G. cethre n- (?)	cethéora n-	cethre n- (?)
D. cethrib	cethéoraib	cethrib

When unaccompanied by a noun, **a cethir.**

cóic, five, and **sé,** six, eclipse in the genitive.

For **fiche,** twenty, **trícha,** thirty, etc., see above, p. 12.

cét n., hundred, is a noun and is declined like a neuter **-o**-stem : n.a. **cét n-,** G. **céit,** n. ⌐l. **cét,** etc.

míle f., thousand, is declined like **guide,** p. 6.

PERSONAL PRONOUNS
A.—Emphasizing Pronouns

Singular	Plural
1. -sa, -se	-ni
2. -so, -su, -siu	-si
3. *m.* -som, -sem, -sium	
f. -si	} -som
n. -som, -sem	

Attached to personal pron. : **messe,** etc. Attached to prep. + suff. pron. : **dím-sa, úadi-si, friu-som,** etc. Attached to noun preceded by poss. pron. : **mo thorbe-se, a persan-som,** etc. Emphasizing infix. pron. : **du-m-em-se,** etc. Attached to verb as subject : **bíuu-sa, gúidme-ni, ad-rothreb-si,** etc. Attached to predicate of copula : **am cimbid-se, nídad foirbhthi-si, romtar bidbdaid-som,** etc.

B.—Stressed Forms

Singular	*Plural*
1. **mé,** emph. **messe**	**sní,** emph. **snisni, sníni, sisni, sinni**
2. **tú,** emph. **tussu**	**sí,** emph. **sib, sissi**
3. *m.* **é, hé,** emph. **(h)ésom**	
f. **sí**	**é, hé**
n. **ed, hed**	

These are used (*a*) absolutely, (*b*) as predicate with copula (sometimes understood), (*c*) as subject only after interrog. pron., e.g. **ce hé** 'who is he ?'; never as object.

C.—Pronouns Suffixed to Verbs

Singular	*Plural*
1. **-um**	**-unn**
2. **-ut**	**-uib**
3. *m. n* **-i**	
f. **-us**	**-us**

These are used to express the object after the 3 sg. absolute forms of simple active verbs, e.g. **sástum,** ' satisfies me ' (**sásaid**) ; **beirthi** ' bears it ' (**berid**) ; **léicsius,** ' he let her, or them, go ' (**léicis**).

After the absolute 1 sg. in **-a,** 1 pl. in **-mi,** and 3 pl. in **-it,** a 3 sg. m. and n. is sometimes found, e.g. **promfit** ' I will try it ' (**promfa**) ; **guidmit** ' we pray for it ' (**guidmi**) ; **gontit** ' they slay him ' (**gonait**).

D.—INFIXED PRONOUNS

	A	B	C
Sg. 1.	m(m)'	dom', tom', dam', tam'	dom', dam',
2.	t'	tot', tut'	dot', dat', dit'
3. *m.*	an°[1]; after ní, n°	tn°	idn°, didn°, dn°
f.	sn°, s	da, ta	da
n.	a'; after ní,'	t'	id', did', d'
Pl. 1.	n(n)	don, ton, tan	don, dun, dan
2.	b	dob, dub, tob	dob, dub, dab
3.	sn°, s	da, ta	da

Class A is used after prepositions and particles originally ending in vowels : **ro, no, do, di, fo, ar, imm, ní. ro, no, do, di,** and **fo** lose their vowel before **an°, a'.** Before prons. beginning with consonants **ar** has the form **aru, aro, ari, ara ; imm** has the form **immu, mmi.**

Class B is used after **etar** and **for** ; combined with the dental of the pronoun **fri(th)** becomes **frit-** and **con- (com)** becomes **cot-** ; **ad-, aith-, ess-, in- (ind-)** all become **at-.**

Class C is used (*a*) after prep. + rel. ; **dia n-** ' from whom, from which ', **lassa n-,** ' by whom, by which ', etc. (and **i n-,** ' in which ', the rel. being understood) ; hence after the conjunctions **dia n-,** ' if ', **ara n-,** ' in order that ', **co n-,** ' so that '.

(*b*) in rel. clauses when rel. is subject.

(*c*) after rel. **n.**

(*d*) after the interrogative particle **in n-.**

NOTE 1.—In 1 and 2 Sg. and Pl. Class A is common in rel. clauses : **intí no-t ail** or **intí no-dat ail,** ' he who nourishes

---

[1] **n°** denotes a nasalizing **n.**

thee '; **in tan no-t ail** or **in tan no-n-dat ail,** ' when he nourishes thee '.

NOTE 2.—Class B remains in rel. clauses : **is hé cotammidethar** ' it is he who controls them '; but in sg. 3 m. and n. it is generally replaced by Class C : **atn-opair** ' he offers him '; **ad-idn-opair** ' who offers him '.

Infixed pronouns after ná, nád.

Singular	*Plural*
1. **náchim', nácham'**	**náchin, náchan**
2. **náchit', náchat'**	**náchib, náchab**
3. *m.* **nách n°**	
f. **nácha**	**nácha**
n. **nách', náchid'**	

NOTE.—Sg. 1 and 2 **náchi-** in Wb., **nácha-** in Ml.

Paradigms of Verbs with Infixed Pronouns

caraid, loves		**ní ben,** does not strike.	
me	**nom chara**	**ním ben**
thee	**not chara**	**nít ben**
him	**na cara**	**ní mben**
her	**nos cara**	**nís mben**[1]
it	**na chara**	**ní ben**
us	**non cara**	**nín ben**
you	**nob cara**	**nib ben**
them	**nos cara**	**nís mben**[1]

[1] or **nís ben**

	ad-cí, sees.	**ní accai (aicci)** does not see.
me	**atom-chí**	**ním accai**
thee	**atot-chí**	**nít accai**
him	**at-cí**	**ní n-accai**
her	**ata-cí**	**nís n-accai**
it	**at-chí**	**ní accai**
us	**aton-cí**	**nín accai**
you	**atob-cí**	**níb accai**
them	**ata-cí**	**nís n-accai**

	co n-accae (so that) he saw.	**intí do-eim,** he who protects.
me	**condom accae**	**do-dom-eim**[1]
thee	**condot accae**	**do-dot-eim**
him.	**con(d)id n-accae**	**do-dn-eim**
her	**conda accae**	**do-da-eim**
it	**con(d)id accae**	**do-d-eim**
us	**condon accae**	**do-don-eim**
you	**condob accae**	**do-dob-eim**
them	**conda accae**	**do-da-eim**

	in tan ro-n-ánaic, when he reached.	**intí nád chúalae,** he who has not heard
me	**ro-n-dom-ánaic**[2]	**náchim chúalae**
thee	**ro-n-dot-ánaic**	**náchit chúalae**
him	**ro-n-dn-ánaic**	**nách cúalae**
her	**ron-da-ánaic**	**nácha cúalae**
it	**ro-n-d-ánaic**	**náchid chúalae**
us	**ro-n-don-ánaic**	**náchin cúalae**
you	**ro-n-dob-ánaic**	**náchib cúalae**
them	**ro-n-da-ánaic**	**nácha cúalae**

[1] or sg. 1 **do-m-eim,** 2 **do-t-eim** ; pl. 1 **do-n-eim,** 2 **do-b-eim** (Class A). [2] or sg. 1 **ro-m-ánaic,** 2 **ro-t-ánaic** ; pl. **ro-n-ánaic, ro-b-ánaic** (Class A).

E.—Prepositions with Suffixed Pronouns
I. Prepositions with Dative.

a, out of.

Sg.			Pl.	
1.			1.	
2.		essiut	2.	
3.	*m. n.*	ass, as[1]	3.	essib
	f.	eissi, esse		

di, from.

Sg.			Pl.	
1.		dím	1.	dín(n)
2.		dít	2.	díb, díib
3.	*m. n.*	de	3.	diib, díib, díb
	f.	dí		

do, to.

Sg.			Pl.	
1.		dom, dam	1.	dún(n)
2.		duit, dait, deit, dit	2.	dúib
3.	*m. n.*	dó,[2] dáu, dóu	3.	doaib, doib, dóib,
	f.	dí		duaib

fíad, in presence of.

Sg.			Pl.	
1.		fíadam	1.	
2.		fíadut	2.	fíadib
3.	*m. n.*	fíada -o	3.	fíadaib

íar, after.

Sg.			Pl.	
1.			1.	
2.		íarmut	2.	
3.	*m. n.*	íarum	3.	íarmaib

ís, below.

Sg.			Pl.	
1.		íssum	1.	íssunn
3.	*m.*	íssa	3.	íssaib

[1] Archaic es. [2] With emph. pron. dossom.

ó, úa, from.

Sg.				Pl	
1.			(h)úaimm[1]	1.	(h)úain(n), (h)úan(n)
2.			(h)úait	2.	(h)úaib
3.	*m.*	*n.*	(h)úad, (h)úaid	3.	(h)úaidib
	f.		(h)úadi		

oc, at.

Sg.				Pl.	
1.			ocum	1.	occunn
2.			ocut	2.	occaib
3.	*m.*	*n.*	oc(c)o, oc(c)a	3.	occaib
	f.		occ(a)i, oc(c)ae		

ós, úas, over, above.

Sg.				Pl.	
1.			úasum	1.	úasunn
2.			úasut	2.	
3.	*m.*	*n.*	úaso, úasa	3.	ósib, úassaib
	f.		úaise		

re, before.

Sg.				Pl.	
1.			rium	1.	riun
2.			riut	2.	
3.	*m.*	*n.*	riam	3.	remib
	f.		remi		

II. Prepositions with Accusative.

amal, like, as.

Sg.				Pl.	
1.			samlum	1.	
2.			samlut	2.	
3.	*m.*	*n.*	samlaid	3.	samlaib

[1] Archaic sg. 1 óim, 2 óit, 3 m. ood, pl. 1 ón, 3 ódib.

cen, without.

Sg.			Pl.	
1.			1.	
2.	cenut		2.	cenuib
3. *m. n.*	cenae		3	cenaib

co, to.

Sg.			Pl.	
1.	cuccum		1.	cucunn
2.	cuc(c)ut		2.	cuc(c)uib
3. *m. n.*	cuc(c)i		3.	cuccu
f.	cuicce, cuccae			

eter, between.

Sg.			Pl.	
1.	etrum, etrom		1.	etron(n), etrunn
2.	etrut		2.	etruib
3. *m. n.*	etir, itir		3.	etarru, etarro

frí, against.

Sg.			Pl.	
1.	fri(u)mm		1.	frinn
2.	fri(u)t		2.	frib
3. *m. n.*	fris(s)		3.	friu
f.	frie			

im. about.

Sg.			Pl.	
1.	immum		1.	immunn
2.	immut		2.	immib
3. *m. n.*	imbi		3.	impu, impo
f.	impe			

la, with, by.

Sg.			Pl.	
1.	lem(m), lim(m), lium(m)		1.	linn, lenn
2.	lat(t)		2.	lib
3. *m. n.*	leiss, les(s), lais(s)		3.	leu, leo, lethu
f.	lee, laee, læ			

sech, past.

Sg.				Pl.		
	1.		sechum		1.	sechunn
	2.		sechut		2.	sechaib
	3.	*m. n.*	sechae		3.	seccu
		f.	secce			

tar, dar, across, over.

Sg.				Pl.		
	1.		torum		1.	torunn
	2.		torut		2.	toraib
	3.	*m. n.*	tarais		3.	tairsiu
		f.	tairse			

tri, tre, through.

Sg.				Pl.		
	1.		trium		1.	triunn
	2.		triut		2.	triib
	3.	*m. n.*	triit		3.	treu, tréu, treo
		f.	tree			

III. Prepositions with Dative and Accusative.

ar, for, before.

Sg.				Pl.		
	1.		airium, erum		1.	erunn, eronn
	2.		airiut, erut, aurut		2.	airib, eruib
	3.	*D. m. n.*	airiu		3. *D.*	airib
		A. m. n.	airi		*A.*	airriu, erriu, erru
		f.	airre, erre			

fo, under.

Sg.				Pl.		
	1.		foum		1.	founn
	2.		fout		2.	
	3.	*D. m. n.*	fou, fó		3. *D.*	foib
		A. m. n.	foí		*A.*	foo
		f.	foæ			

for, on.

Sg. 1.	form, forum	*Pl.* 1.	fornn, forunn
2.	fort	2.	fuirib, fo(i)rib
3. *D. m. n.* for[1]		3. *D.*	for(a)ib
A. m. n. foir, fair		*A.*	forru
f. forrae			

i, in, into.

Sg. 1.	indium(m)	*Pl.* 1.	indiunn
2.	indiut	2.	indib
3. *D. m. n.* and		3. *D*	indib
f. indi		*A.*	intiu
A. m. n. ind			
f. inte			

F.—féin, self.

Sg. 1.	féin	fadéin	céin	cadéin
2.	féin	fadéin		
3. *m. n.*	féin, fessin	fadéne		
	fesine	fadeisin	cesin	cadésin
f.	feisine, féisne	fadisin		
	féissin			
Pl. 1.	fesine	fanisin		canisin
2.	féisne, fésin	fadéisne		
		fadisin		
3.	féssine, féisne	fadeisne		cadesne
	feissin	fadésne		cadésin
		fadesin		

The absence of the mark of length is no sure evidence that the vowel **e** of any particular form was actually short; it always bears the stress.

[1] Very rare ; almost always replaced by **foir, fair**.

VERBAL INFLEXION

The Present Stem

From the present stem are formed the present indicative, the imperfect indicative, and the imperative. The following represent the types of the present active:

> **A (1) berid,** carries.
>
> (2) **benaid,** strikes, **ara-chrin,** perishes.
>
> (3) **gaibid,** takes.

> **B (1) marbaid,** kills.
>
> (2) **léicid,** leaves.

In the deponential inflexion A (1) and (2) are not represented. To A (3) belong deponents like **midithir,** judges, **do-moine-thar,** thinks, **-cuirethar,** places, **-cluinethar,** hears. Of B (1) **labrithir,** speaks, is an example. B (2) contains many denominatives in **-igidir,** e.g. **foilsigidir,** manifests.

Active and Passive

In the imperfect indicative, the past subjunctive, the secondary future, the 3 sg. imperative, and the 2 pl. of all moods and tenses deponent verbs have the same endings as active.

The passive has forms only for the third persons singular and plural. The other persons are expressed by means of the 3 sg. with infixed pronouns, e.g. **no-m berar,** I am carried, **no-n berar,** we are carried, etc.

Present Indicative.

A (1)

SINGULAR

Absolute	Conjunct
1. biru	-biur
2. biri	-bir
3. berid, berith	-beir
Rel. beres	
Pass. berair	-berar
Rel. berar	

PLURAL

1. bermai	-beram
Rel. bermae	
2. beirthe	-berid
3. berait	-berat
Rel. bertae	
Pass. bertair	-bertar
Rel. bertar	

A (2)

SINGULAR

Absolute	Conjunct
1. benaim	-benaim
2. benai	-benai
3. benaid	-ben
Rel. benas	
Pass. benair	-benar
Rel. benar	

PLURAL

Absolute	*Conjunct*
1. benmai	-benam
Rel. benmae	
2. bentae	-benaid
3. benait	-benat
Rel. bentae	
Pass. bentair	-bentar
Rel. bentar	

A (3)

SINGULAR

Absolute	*Conjunc*
1. { gaibiu	-gaibiu
{ gaibim	-gaibim
2. gaibi	-gaibi
3. gaibid	-gaib
Rel. gaibes	
Pass. gaibthir	-gaibther
Rel. gaibther	

PLURAL

Absolute	*Conjunct*
1. gaibmi	-gaibem
Rel. gaibme	
2. gaibthe	-gaibid
3. gaibit	-gaibet
Rel. gaibte	
Pass. gaibtir	{ -gaibter
	{ -gaibetar
Rel. gaibter	

B (1)

Absolute	*Conjunct*
1. { marbu	-marbu
{ marbaim	-marbaim
2. marbai	-marbai
3. marbaid	-marba
Rel. marbas	
Pass. marbthair	-marbthar
Rel. marbthar	

1. marbmai	-marbam
Rel. marbmae	
2. marbthae	-marbaid
3. marbait	-marbat
Rel. { marbtae	
{ marbate	
Pass. { marbtair	-marbtar
{ marbaitir	-marbatar
Rel. { marbtar	
{ marbatar	

B (2)

Absolute	*Conjunct*
1. { léiciu	-léiciu
{ léicim	-léicim
2. léici	-léici
3. léicid	-léici
Rel. léices	
Pass. léicthir	-léicther
Rel. léicther	

PLURAL

Absolute	*Conjunct*
1. léicmi	-léicem
Rel. léicme	
2. léicthe	-léicid
3. léicit	-léicet
Rel. { léicte / lécite	
Pass. { léictir / lécitir	-léicter / -lécetar
Rel. léicter	

NOTE 1.—Sg. 1. The ending **-o** is also found, e.g. **arcu, arco,** I beseech. In A (1) there is also an absolute ending **-im,** e.g. **melim,** I grind. In A (2) there appears also e.g. **for-fiun,** exanclo. No definite rules can be laid down for the use of the different forms ; in time the **-im** forms get the upper hand.

NOTE 2.—Sg. 2. The short form like **-bir** is found only in a few verbs. Most verbs have **-i** also in the conjunct forms.

NOTE 3.—In A (1) the last consonant of the root is palatal in 2 and 3 sg. and 2 pl., non-palatal in 1 and 3 pl. and passive. Hence the alternation between *ĭ* and *ĕ* in **cingid** ' steps ', **cinges, -cing** : pl. 1 **cengmai,** 3 **cengait** ; **ibid** ' drinks ', **ibes, -ib** : pl. 3 **ebait, -ebat,** pass. **ebair, -ebar.**

Imperative

SINGULAR

	A (1)	A (2)	A (3)	B (1)	B (2)
1.	biur				
2.	beir	ben	gaib	marb	léic
3.	bered	benad	gaibed	marbad	léiced
Pass.	berar	benar	gaibther	marbthar	léicther

PLURAL

1. beram	benam	gaibem	marbem	léicem
2. berid	benaid	gaibid	marbaid	léicid
3. berat	benat	gaibet	marbat	léicet
Pass. bertar	bentar	gaibter	marbatar	léicter

NOTE 1.—Except in 3 sg. the endings are the same as those of the conjunct present indicative. Cf. 1 sg. **tíag** (p. 90) ' let me go ', ' I will go '; **fuircim** ' let me find ' (**fo-ric**).

NOTE 2.—Verbs of class A (1) with ĭ in the root show the same alternation as in the present indicative, e.g. **ithid** ' eats ', ipv. sg. 2 **ith**, 3 **ithed**, pl. 1 **etham**, 2 **ithid**, 3 **ethat**.

NOTE 3.—The ipv. of compound verbs is always stressed on the first syllable except when an infixed pronoun is used, e.g. **do-ic, tic** ' comes ', ipv. sg. 3 **ticed**, but **do-m-iced** ' let him come to me.'

Imperfect Indicative

SINGULAR

A (1	A (2)	A (3)
1. no berinn	no benainn	no gaibinn
2. no bertha	no benta	no gaibthea (?)
3. no bered	no benad	no gaibed
Pass. no berthe	no bentae	no gaibthe

B (1)	B (2)
1. no marbainn	no léicinn
2. no marbtha	no léicthea
3. no marbad	no léiced
Pass. no marbthae	no léicthe

PLURAL

	A (1)	A (2)	A (3)
1.	no bermis	no benmais	no gaibmis
2.	no berthe	no bentae	no gaibthe
3.	no bertis	no bentais	no gaibtis
Pass.	no bertis	no bentais	no gaibtis

	B (1)	B (2)
1.	no marbmais	no léicmis
2.	no marbthae	no léicthe
3.	no marbtais	no léictis
Pass.	no marbtais	no léictis

NOTE.—When any other conjunct preverb is used the **no** is absent : **ní berinn, co mberinn,** etc. In relative inflexion the consonant following **no** is lenited or nasalized. The same rules apply to the past subjunctive and to the secondary future.

DEPONENT
Present Indicative
A (3)
SINGULAR

	Absolute	*Conjunct*
1.	midiur	-midiur
2.	mitter	-mitter
3.	midithir	-midethar
Rel.	midethar	
Pass.	mittir	

PLURAL

Absolute	*Conjunct*
1. **midimmir**	**-midemmar**
Rel. **midemmar**	
2. **mitte**	**-midid**
3. **miditir**	**-midetar**
Rel. **midetar**	
Pass. **miditir**	**-midetar**

Similarly, but with conjunct endings only :

SINGULAR

Conjunct	*Conjunct*
1. **-cuiriur**	**-cluiniur**
2. **-cuirther**	**-cluinter**
3. **-cuirethar**	**-cluinethar**
Pass. **-cuirther**	**-cluinter**

PLURAL

1. **-cuiremmar**	**-cluinemmar**
2. **-cuirid**	**-cluinid**
3. **-cuiretar**	**-cluinetar**

NOTE.—In independent position **-cuirethar** is replaced by **fo-ceird**. In the absence of any other conjunct particle **ro-** is prefixed to **-cluinethar**.

B (1)

SINGULAR

Absolute	*Conjunct*
1. **labrur**	**-labrur**
2. **labrither**	**-labrither**
3. **labrithir**	**-labrathar**
Rel. **labrathar**	

PLURAL

Absolute	*Conjunct*
1. **labrimmir**	**-labrammar**
Rel. **labrammar**	
2. **labrithe**	**-labraid**
3. **labritir**	**-labratar**
Rel. **labratar**	

B (2)

SINGULAR

1. **foilsigim**	**-foilsigur**
2. **foilsigther**	**-foilsigther**
3. **foilsigidir**	**-foilsigedar**
Rel. **foilsigedar**	
Pass. **foilsigthir**	**-foilsigther**
Rel. **foilsigther**	

PLURAL

1. **foilsigmir**	**-foilsigmer**
Rel. **foilsigmer**	
2. **foilsigthe**	**-foilsigid**
3. **foilsigitir**	**-foilsigetar**
Rel. **foilsigetar**	
Pass. **foilsigtir**	**-foilsigter**
Rel. **foilsigter**	

NOTE.—In the absolute form of the 1 sg. of the derivative verbs in **-ig-** the active inflexion is regular.

Imperative

SINGULAR

	A (3)	A (3)	B (1)	B (2)
2.	**cluinte**	**cuirthe**	**labrithe**	**foilsigthe**
3.	**cluined**	**cuired**	**labrad**	**foilsiged**
Pass.	**cluinter**	**cuirther**		**foilsigther**

PLURAL

2. cluinid	cuirid	labraid	foilsigid
3. cluinetar	cuiretar	labratar	foilsigetar
Pass. cluinter	cuirter		foilsigter

NOTE.—The deponent inflexion is found in 1 sg. **águr,** 1 pl. **ágamar, cuiremmar, finnamar,** but the active ending in 1 pl. **seichem** Wb. 25ᶜ6.

Imperfect Indicative

A (3)	A (3)	B (1)	B (2)
1. ro-cluininn	no cuirinn	no labrainn	no foilsiginn
etc.	etc.	etc.	etc.

The inflexion is the same as in active verbs.

SUBJUNCTIVE MOOD

There are two modes of forming the subjunctive mood : (1) the -ā- subjunctive, (2) the -s- subjunctive.

-ā- subjunctive

ACTIVE AND PASSIVE

Present Subjunctive

A (1)

SINGULAR

Absolute	*Conjunct*
1. bera	-ber
2. berae	-berae
3. beraid	-bera
Rel. beras	
Pass. berthair	-berthar
Rel. berthar	

PLURAL

Absolute	*Conjunct*
1. bermai	-beram
Rel. bermae	
2. berthae	-beraid
3. berait	-berat
Rel. bertae	
Pass. bertair	-bertar
Rel. bertar	

NOTE.—Some verbs with **a** in the radical syllable of the indicative have **e** in the radical syllable of the subjunctive, e.g. **at-baill, at-bail,** dies : subj. **at-bela.**

A (2)

The material is insufficient for a complete paradigm. The following are occurring forms from **crenaid,** buys, **benaid,** cuts, (in the past subjunctive also from **ro-cluinethar,** hears).

SINGULAR

Absolute	*Conjunct*
1. ——	-créu
2. ——	-crie, criae
3. ——	-crïa
	-fo-bia
	-ind-ar-be
Pass. crethir	-crether, du-fo-bither

PLURAL

1. ——	crïam
2. ——	——
3. ——	crïat
	eter-di-bet
Rel. crete	
Pass. cretir	——

A (3)

	SINGULAR	
Absolute		*Conjunct*
1. gaba (?)		-gab, -gaib
2. gabae		-gabae
3. gabaid		-gaba
Rel. gabas		
Pass. gabthair		-gabthar
Rel. gabthar		

	PLURAL	
1. gabmai		-gabam
Rel. gabmae		
2. gabthae		-gabaid
3. gabait		-gabat
Rel. gabtae		
Pass. gabtair		-gabtar
Rel. gabtar		

B (1)

	SINGULAR	
1. marba		-marb
2. marbae		-marbae
3. marbaid		-marba
Rel. marbas		
Pass. marbthair		-marbthar
Rel. marbthar		

	PLURAL	
1. marbmai		-marbam
Rel. marbmae		
2. marbthae		-marbaid
3. marbait		-marbat
Rel. marbaite		
Pass. { marbtair	-marbtar
{ marbaitir	-marbatar
Rel. { marbtar	
{ marbatar	

B (2)

SINGULAR

Absolute	*Conjunct*
1. léicea	-léic
2. léice	-léice
3. léicid	-léicea
Rel. léices	
Pass. léicthir	-léicther
Rel. léicther	

PLURAL

1. léicmi	-léicem
Rel. léicme	
2. léicthe	-léicid
3. léicit	-léicet
Rel. léicte, léicite	
Pass. léictir, lécitir	-léicter, lécetar
Rel. léicter	

Past Subjunctive

SINGULAR

A (1)	A (2)	A (3)
1. no berainn		no gabainn
2. no bertha		no gabtha
3. no berad	⎰ no criad ⎱ itir-di-bed	no gabad
Pass. no berthae	no crethe	no gabthae

B (1)	B (2)
1. no marbainn	no léicinn
2. no marbtha	no léicthea
3. no marbad	no léiced
Pass no marbthae	no léicthe

PLURAL

A (1)	A (2)	A (3)
1. no bermais	ro-cloimmis	no gabmais
2. no berthae		no gabthae
3. no bertais	⎧ no cretis ⎨ itar-di-bitis ⎩ ro-cloitis	no gabtais
Pass. no bertais	no cretis	no gabtais

B (1)	B (2)
1. no marbmais	no léicmis
2. no marbthae	no léicthe
3. no marbtais	no léictis
Pass no marbtais	no léictis

DEPONENT

Present Subjunctive

A (3)

SINGULAR

Conjunct	Conjunct
1. -menar	-corar
2. -mentar	-coirther
3. -menathar, -adar	-corathar
Pass. -mentar	

PLURAL

1. -menammar, -menmar	-corammar
2. -menaid	-coraid
3. -menatar	-coratar
Pass.	-coirter

Cf. the indicatives, -cuiriur, -moiniur, etc.

Absolute subj. forms of **gainithir**, is born, were probably sg. 1. **genar**, 2. **gentar**, 3. **genaithir**, rel. **-athar**, pl. 1. **genaimmir**, rel. **-ammar**, 2. **gentae**, 3. **genaitir**, rel. **-atar**.

B (1)

SINGULAR

Absolute	*Conjunct*
1. labrar	-labrar
2. labrither	-labrither
3. labrithir	-labrathar
Rel. labrathar	

PLURAL

1. labrimmir	-labrammar
Rel. labrammar	
2. labrithe	-labraid
3. labritir	-labratar
Rel. labratar	

B (2)

SINGULAR

Absolute	*Conjunct*
1. foilsiger	-foilsiger
2. foilsigther	-foilsigther
3. foilsigidir	-foilsigedar
Rel. foilsigedar	
Pass. foilsigthir	-foilsigther
Rel. foilsigther	

PLURAL

1. foilsigmir	-foilsigmer
Rel. foilsigmer	
2. foilsigthe	-foilsigid
3. foilsigitir	-foilsigetar
Rel. foilsigetar	
Pass. foilsigtir	-foilsigter
Rel. foilsigter	

Past Subjunctive

	A (3)	A (3)	B (1)	B (2)
Sg. 1.	-menainn	no corainn	no labrainn	no foilsiginn
	etc.	etc.	etc.	etc.

-s- Subjunctive

ACTIVE AND PASSIVE

Examples, **guidid**, prays, and **téit**, goes.

Present Subjunctive

SINGULAR

Absolute	*Conjunct*
1. gessu (?)	-ges
2. gessi	-geiss
3. geiss	-gé
Rel. ges	
Pass. gessair	-gessar
Rel. gessar	

PLURAL

1. gesmi	-gessam
Rel. gesme	
2. geste	-gessid
3. gessit	-gessat
Rel. gestae	
Pass. gessitir	-gessatar
Rel. gessatar	

SINGULAR

Absolute	*Conjunct*
1. **tíasu**	**-tías**
2. **tési**	**-téis**
3. **téis**	**-té, téi**
Rel. **tías**	
Pass. **tíasair**	**-tíasar**
Rel. **tíasar, tíastar**	

PLURAL

1. **tíasmai**	**-tíasam**
Rel. **tíasmae**	
2. **téiste** (?)	**-tésid**
3. **tíasait**	**-tíasat**
Rel. **tíastae**	

NOTE 1.—Further examples of the conjunct form of sg. 3 act. are (*a*) **in-gré** (**in-greinn**), **fo-ló** (**fo-loing**) ; (*b*) **do-coí** (=*de-co-vetst, perf. ind. **do-coid**), **ar-coí** (**ar-coat**), **ad-sléi** (**ad-slig**).

NOTE 2.—In the 3 sg. pass. the ending **-tar** is the more common.

Past Subjunctive

SINGULAR

Absolute	*Conjunct*
1. **no gessinn**	**no téisinn**
2. **no gesta**	**no tíasta**
3. **no gessed**	**no téised**
Pass. **no gestae**	**no tíastae**

PLURAL

Absolute	*Conjunct*
1. no gesmais	no tíasmais
2. no gestae	no tíastae
3. no gestais	no tíastais
Pass. no gestais	no tíastais

NOTE.—Roots in **-eng-** show the same variation between *é* and *ia* as **tíagu**, e.g. **cingid**, steps, 3 pl. rel. **cíastae, lingid,** springs, 3 sg. rel. **lías.**

DEPONENT

Examples, **ro-fitir,** knows, supplied by **midithir,** judges.

Present Subjunctive

SINGULAR

Absolute	*Conjunct*
1. messur	-fessur
2. messer	-fesser, -fésser
3. mestir	-festar, -fíastar
Pass. mestir	-festar
Rel. mestar	

PLURAL

1. messimir	-fessamar
Rel. messamar	
2. meste	-fessid
3. messitir	-fessatar
Rel. messatar	
Pass. messitir	-fessatar
Rel. messatar	

Past

ro-fessinn, no messinn, etc., as in the active.

The Future

Of the future there are three types—(1) the **-f-** or **-b-** future.
(2) the reduplicated and **-ē-** future, (3) the **-s-** future.

-f- Future

Active and Passive

B (1)

Singular

Absolute	*Conjunct*
1. **marbfa**	**-marbub**
(ainfa)	**-mairbiub**
	⎡ **-bendachub** ⎤
	⎣ **ad-elliub** ⎦
2. **mairbfe**	**-mairbfe**
(íccfe)	
(follnaibe)	
3. **marbfid** (?)	**-marbfa**
(pridchibid)	**-mairbfea**
	⎡ **-soírfa** ⎤
	⎣ **-soírfea** ⎦
Rel. **marbfas** (?)	
mairbfes (?)	
(prithchibes)	
Pass. **marbfidir**	**-marbfaider**
(promfidir)	**-mairbfider**
	⎡ **-sechmalfaider** ⎤
	⎢ **-ícfider** ⎥
	⎣ **-pridchabthar** ⎦
Rel. **marbfaider,** etc.	

PLURAL

Absolute	Conjunct
1. marbfimmi	-marbfam
	-mairbfem
	⎰-tinscanfam⎱
	⎱do-aidlibem⎰
Rel. marbfimme	
2. marbfithe (?)	-marbfid (?)
3. marbfait	-marbfat
mairbfit	-mairbfet
⎰molfait⎱	⎰-toscélfat⎱
⎱géillfit⎰	⎱-béithfet⎰
Rel. marbfite (?)	
(comallaibte)	
Pass. marbfitir (?)	-marbfaiter
(comallaibtir)	mairbfetar
	⎧-ícfaiter) ⎫
	⎨-soírfetar ⎬
	⎩for-ceinfiter⎭
Rel. marbfaiter, etc.	

B (2)

SINGULAR

Absolute	Conjunct
1. léicfea	-léiciub
2. léicfe	-léicfe
3. léicfid	-léicfea
Rel. léicfes	
Pass. léicfidir	-léicfider
	⎰do-díuscibther⎱
	⎱for-brisbedar ⎰
Rel. léicfedar	

PLURAL

Absolute	*Conjunct*
1. léicfimmi	-léicfem
Rel. léicfimme	
2. léicfide	-léicfid
3. léicfit	-léicfet
	(du-róscibet)
Rel. léicfite	
Pass. léicfitir	-léicfiter, -fetar
	⎰ad-rímfetar⎱
	⎱du-róscaibtar⎰
Rel. léicfiter	

Secondary Future

SINGULAR

B (1)	B (2)
1. no mairbfinn (?)	no léicfinn
2. no mairbfeda	no léicfeda
(no ainfeda)	no léicfed
3. no marbfad	
no mairbfed	
⎰no soírfad⎱	
⎱no soírfed⎰	
Pass. no mairbfide (?)	no léicfide
(no comallaibthe)	(-tochuiribthe)

PLURAL

B (1)	B (2)
1. no mairbfimmis (?)	no léicfimmis
2. no mairbfithe (?)	no léicfide
3. no marbfaitis	no léicfitis
Act. and pass. no mairbfitis	
⎰no labrafaitis⎱	
⎱for-ceinnfitis⎰	

NOTE.—Verbs of class B (1) form their futures largely like

those of class B (2). The forms given from **marbaid** have been invented to illustrate the variety of inflexion ; the forms actually found in the O.-Ir. Glosses are added in brackets.

NOTE 2.—Like class B (2) are inflected also some verbs belonging to class A (1) and A (3).

DEPONENT

No complete paradigm can be reconstructed.

Future

SINGULAR

A (3) *Conjunct*	B (1) *Conjunct*	B (2) *Absolute*	*Conjunct*
1. do-cuirifar ad-áichfer	-molfar	gaimigfer	-scíthigfar
2. ——	——	mescaigfider	——
3. ad-áichfedar	——	——	——
Pass. ——	——	húaibrigfidir	fo-cridich-fider

PLURAL

1. ——	-labrafammar	——	——
3. ar-muinfetar du-roimnibetar -áichfetar	fo-celfatar	——	——
Pass. ——	——	——	-míchlo-thaigfetar

Secondary Future

As in the Active.

Reduplicated Future and -ē- Future.

REDUPLICATED FUTURE

The inflexion is the same as that of the -ā- subjunctive.

The following paradigms may be reconstructed with pro-
bability to illustrate the two types of this future :—

(a) canaid, sings.

Future

SINGULAR

	Absolute	*Conjunct*
1.	cechna	-cechan
2.	cechnae	-cechnae
3.	cechnaid	-cechna
Rel.	cechnas	
Pass.	cechnaithir	-cechnathar
Rel.	cechnathar	

PLURAL

1.	cechnaimmi (?)	-cechnam
Rel.	cechnaimme (?)	
2.	cechnaithe (?)	-cechnaid
3.	cechnait	-cechnat
Rel.	cechnaite (?)	
Pass.	cechnaitir (?)	-cechnatar
Rel.	cechnatar	

Secondary Future

	Singular	*Plural*
1.	no cechnainn	no cechnammis (?)
2.	no cechnatha (?)	no cechnaithe (?)
3.	no cechnad	no cechnaitis (?)
Pass.	no cechnaithe (?)	no cechnaitis (?)

Further examples are :—

daimid, grants : fut. sg. 1 **-didem,** sg. 2 **fo-didmae,**
pl. 3 **fo-didmat** ; fut. sec. sg. 3 **fo-didmed.**

caraid, loves : fut. sg. 3 **-cechra,** pl. 3 **cechrait, -cechrat.**

-cíu, see : fut. sg. 3 **du-écigi** ; fut. sec. sg. 3 **-acciged,**
pl. 3 **ad-cichitis.**

do-goa, chooses : fut. sg. 1 **do-gega,** pl. 3 **do-gegat ;** fut.
sec. sg. 3 **do-gegad,** pl. 1 **do-gegmais.**
ibid, drinks : fut. sg. 1 **-íb,** pl. 3 **íbait.**
Examples of deponent forms are :—
gainithir, is born : fut. sg. 3 **gignithir, -gignethar ;**
fut. sec. sg. 3 **no gigned.**
ad-gládathar, addresses : fut. sg. 1 **ad-gegaldar,** sg. 3
ad-gegaldathar.

(b) renaid, sells
Future
SINGULAR

Absolute		*Conjunct*
1. ——		**-ririu**
2. **rire** (?)		**-rire** (?)
3. **ririd**		**-riri**
Rel. **rires**		
Pass. **rirthir**		**-rirther**
Rel. **rirther**		

PLURAL

1. **rirmi** (?)		**-rirem**
Rel. **rirme** (?)		
2. **rirthe** (?)		**-ririd**
3. **ririt**		**-riret** (?)
Rel. **rirte** (?)		

Secondary Future
The instances which occur are given below.
Further examples are :—
benaid, cuts : fut. sg. 3 **-bia, du-fobi,** pl. 3 **-biat,** pass.
sg. 3 **-bether ;** fut. sec. sg. 3 **no biad,** pass. **fo-indarpaide.**
ara-chrin, perishes : fut. pl. 3 **ara-chíurat.**
glenaid, sticks : fut. pl. 3 **gíulait ;** fut. sec. sg. 3 **no
gíulad.**

lenaid, adheres : sg. 2 **lile** (?), sg. 3 **lilith, -lili,** rel. **liles,** pl. 3 **lilit.**

ro-cluinethar, hears : fut. sg. 3 **ro-cechladar.**

ro bebe, has died : fut. pl. 3 rel. **bebte.**

-ē- FUTURE

berid, carries

Future

SINGULAR

	Absolute	*Conjunct*
1.	béra	-bér
2.	bérae	-bérae
3.	béraid	-béra
Rel.	béras	
Pass.	bérthair	-bérthar
Rel.	bérthar	

PLURAL

1.	bérmai	-béram
Rel.	bérmae	
2.	bérthae	-béraid
3.	bérait	-bérat
Rel.	bértae	
Pass.	bértair	-bértar
Rel.	bértar	

Secondary Future

	Singular	*Plural*
1.	no bérainn	no bérmais
2.	no bértha	no bérthae
3.	no bérad	no bértais
Pass.	no bérthae	no bértais

-s- Future

The future is the subjunctive with reduplication.

Active and Passive

guidid, prays

Future

SINGULAR

Absolute	*Conjunct*
1. gigsea	-gigius
2. gigsi	-gigis
3. gigis	-gig (?)
Rel. giges	
Pass. gigsithir (?)	-gigsethar (?)
Rel. gigestar	

PLURAL

1. gigsimmi	-gigsem
Rel. gigsimme	
2. gigeste	-gigsid
3. gigsit	-gigset
Rel. gigsite	
Pass. gigsitir	gigsiter
Rel. gigsiter	

NOTE.—Examples of the conjunct form of the 3 sg. act. are **-mema** (**maidid,** bursts) and **-sil** (**sligid,** hews).

Secondary Future

Singular	*Plural*
1. no gigsinn	no gigsimmis
2. no gigesta	no gigeste
3. no gigsed	no gigsitis
Pass. no gigeste	no gigsitis

DEPONENT

Examples, **ro-fitir,** knows, supplied by **midithir,** judges.

Future

SINGULAR

	Absolute	*Conjunct*
1.	messur	-fessur
2.	messer	-fesser
3.	miastir	-fiastar, -festar
Rel.	miastar	
Pass.	miastair	-fiastar
Rel.	miastar	

PLURAL

1.	messimmir	-fessammar
Rel.	messammar	
2.	miastae (?)	-fessid
3.	messitir	-fessatar
Rel.	messatar	

Secondary Future

ro-fessinn, etc., as in the active.

THE PRETERITE AND PERFECT

Of this tense there are three types : (1) the **-s-** preterite and perfect, (2) the **-t-** preterite and perfect, (3) the reduplicated preterite and perfect. In the passive, however, there is only one mode of formation, namely by means of a suffix **-to-,** as in the past participle passive in Latin. Except in a few verbs in which the preterite and perfect come from different roots, e.g. **luid,** he went, **do-coid,** he has gone, the perfect is the preterite with the addition of one of the perfective particles, of which the most common is **ro,** e.g. **gabais,** he took, **ro gab,** he has taken. In this case the verb has always the conjunct endings.

-s- Preterite and Perfect

ACTIVE AND PASSIVE

gaibid, takes

SINGULAR

	Absolute	*Conjunct*
1.	gabsu	-gabus
2.	gabsai	-gabais
3.	gabais	-gab
Rel.	gabas (?)	
Pass.	gabthae	-gabad
Rel.	gabthae	

PLURAL

1.	gabsaimmi (?)	-gabsam
Rel.	gabsaimme	
2.	——	-gabsaid
3.	gabsait	-gabsat
Rel.	gabsaite	
Pass.	gabthai[1] (?)	-gabtha
Rel.	gabthai[1] (?)	

léicid, leaves

SINGULAR

	Absolute	*Conjunct*
1.	léicsiu	-léicsius
2.	léicsi	-léicis
3.	léicis	-léic, -léici
Pass.	léicthe	-léiced
Rel.	léicthe	

[1] There are no examples from sufficiently old MSS. to establish with certainty the final vocalism of these forms.

PLURAL

Absolute	Conjunct
1. léicsimmi (?)	-léicsem
Rel. léicsimme	
3. ——	-léicsid
3. léicsit	-léicset
Rel. léicsite	
Pass. léicthi (?)	-léicthea
Rel. léicthi (?)	

NOTE 1.—Of a 3 sg. rel. there is no instance in the oldest Irish texts ; cf. **sóeras** Hy. I. 25, **foídes** Hy. I. 33.

NOTE 2.—There are no instances of the 2 pl. abs. ; it might perhaps be conjectured that they were **gabsithe, léicsithe.**

DEPONENT

labrithir, speaks

Singular	Plural
1. ro labrasur	ro labrasammar
2. ro labraiser	ro labraisid
3. ro labrastar	ro labrasatar

foilsigidir, manifests

Singular	Plural
1. ro foilsigsiur	ro foilsigsemmar
2. ro foilsigser	ro foilsigsid
3. ro foilsigestar	ro foilsigsetar
Pass. ro foilsiged	ro foilsigthea

NOTE.—In the O.-Ir. Glosses the only instance of an absolute form of the 3 sg. is **cíchnaigistir** g. striderat Sg. 152[b]2 ; in later texts the conjunct form is used. An absolute form of the 3 pl. does not occur in the O.-Ir. Glosses ; in later texts the conjunct form is used.

-t- Preterite and Perfect
berid, bears
SINGULAR

	Absolute	Conjunct
1.	——	-biurt
2.	——	-birt
3.	birt	-bert
Rel.	bertae	
Pass.	brethae	-breth
Rel.	brethae	

PLURAL

1.	——	-bertammar
2.	——	-bertid
3.	——	-bertatar
Rel.	bertatar	
	bertar	
Pass.	brithi (?)	-bretha

orgaid, slays
SINGULAR

	Absolute	Conjunct
1.	——	-ort or -urt (?) [1]
2.	——	-uirt [2]
3.	oirt	-ort
Rel.	ortae	
Pass.	ortae	-ort
Rel.	ortae	

PLURAL

1.	——	-ortammar
2.	——	-ortid
3.	——	-ortatar
Rel.	ortatar	
Pass.	ortai (?)	-orta

[1] Cf. *fris-comurt*, Wb. 33ª12.　　　[2] Cf. *con-tochmairt*, Ml. 17ª2.

Note 1.—Examples of sg. 1 with the accent on the radical syllable are **do-biurt** ZCP. iv. 43, YBL 31^{b}35, **con-gult** LL. 31^{b}21. When the accent falls on a preceding syllable the vowel is regularly **u**, e.g. **as-ruburt**, I have said, **do-ringult**, I have promised.

Note 2.—Of the 3 pl. abs. no example is found in the Glosses; in later texts **bertatar,** etc., appears. In several of the persons the old form is yet unknown.

Further instances are :—**gairid**, calls : **-gart ; fo-geir,** warms : **fo-gert ; dairid,** uaccam init : **-dart ; marnaid,** betrays : **-mert ; ailid,** rears : **-alt ; at-bail,** dies : **at-rubalt ; celid,** hides : **-celt ; gelid,** grazes : **-gelt ; melid,** grinds : **-melt ; -em- (di-em-,** protect, etc.) : **-ét ; -sem- (do-fuissim,** creates, etc.) : ***-sét ; aigid,** drives : **-acht ; aingid,** protects : **anacht ; at-reig,** arises : **at-recht do-érig,** deserts : **do-réracht ; saigid,** aims at : **-siacht.**

Reduplicated preterite and perfect.

There are two types, (*a*) reduplicated forms, e.g. **cechain,** sang, (*b*) forms without reduplication and with a long vowel before a single consonant, e.g. **gáid,** prayed, **fo-caird,** cast.

Active and Passive

(a) canaid, sings.

Preterite

Singular	*Plural*
1. cechan	cechnammar
2. cechan	-cechnaid
3. cechain	cechnatar
Rel. cechnae	
Pass. cétae, -cét	cétai (?), -céta

NOTE.—In the sg. the abs. and conj. forms are identical (but there is a 3 sg. rel. in a -*e*, -*ae*). In the pl. 1 and 3 abs. forms in -*ir* are sometimes found, on the model of the deponent, e.g. **fíchimmir** and **fíchimmar, memdaitir** and **memdatar.** No absolute form of pl. 2 is attested.

Perfect

SINGULAR

Deuterotonic	*Prototonic*
1. **ro cechan**	**-roíchan**
2. **ro cechan**	**-roíchan**
3. **ro cechain**	**-roíchain**
Pass. **ro cét**	**-rochet**

PLURAL

1. **ro cechnammar**	**-roíchnammar**
2. **ro cechnaid**	**-roíchnid**
3. **ro cechnatar**	**-roíchnatar**
Pass. **ro céta**	**-rocheta**

Further examples are :—

> **claidid,** digs : **cechlaid.**
> **maidid,** bursts : **memaid.**
> **sennid,** plays : **sephainn.**
> **sligid,** hews : **selaich.**
> **rigid,** stretches : **reraig.**
> **snigid,** drops : **senaig.**
> **gonaid,** wounds : **geguin.**
> **do-goa,** chooses : **do-roígu.**
> **cingid,** steps : **cechaing.**
> **lingid,** leaps : **leblaing.**
> **dingid,** oppresses : **dedaig.**

dlongid, splits : **dedlaig.**

lenaid, follows : **lil,** pl. 3 **-leldar.**

renaid, sells : **rir.**

-gnin, knows : sg. 1. 2. **-gén,** sg. 3 **-géuin, -géoin.**

crenaid, buys : sg. 1. 2. **-cér,** sg. 3 **-cíuir.**

glenaid, adheres : sg. 3 **gíuil** rel. **gíulae.**

ara-chrin perishes : sg. 3 **ara-ruichíuir,** pl. 3 **-arr-chéoratar.**

ro-cluinethar, hears : sg. 1. 2. **ro-cúala,** sg. 3 **ro-cúalae.**

(b) guidid, prays

SINGULAR

	Absolute	*Conjunct*
1.	**gád**	**-gád**
2.	**gád**	**-gád**
3.	**gáid**	**-gáid**
Rel.	**gáde**	
Pass.	**gessae**	**-gess**
Rel.	**gessae**	

PLURAL

1.	**gádammar**	**-gádammar**
Rel.	**gádammar**	
2.	——	**-gádid**
3.	**gádatar**	**-gádatar**
Rel.	**gádatar**	
Pass.	**gessai** (?)	**-gessa**
Rel.	**gessai** (?)	

Further examples are :—

       rethid, runs : **ráith.**

       techid, flees : **táich.**

       fo-ceird, casts : **fo-caird.**

DEPONENT

gainithir, is born

Singular	Plural
1. génar	génammar
2. génar	-génaid
3. génair	génatar

ro-fitir, knows

Singular	Plural
1. ro-fetar	ro-fitemmar, ro-fetammar
2. ro-fetar	ro-fitid
3. ro-fitir	ro-fitetar, ro-fetatar
Pass. ro-fess	ro-fessa

Further examples :—

daimid, grants (ad-daim, concedes, fo-daim, suffers) : sg. 3 -dámair, pl. 3 -damnatar, -damdatar.
con-ic, is able : sg. 3 con-ánacuir.
midithir, judges : sg. 3 mídair.
-moinethar (do-moinethar, thinks, etc.) : sg. 3 -ménair.

PASSIVE PARTICIPLE AND VERBAL OF NECESSITY

Examples :—

	Passive Participle	Verbal of Necessity
do-formaig, increases	tórmachtae	tórmachtai
orgaid, slays	ortae	ortai
celid, hides	clithe	clethi
as-beir, says	eperthe	eperthi
benaid, cuts	bíthe	bethi
-cuirethar, puts		coirthi
canaid, sings	céte	céti

	Passive Participle	*Verbal of Necessity*
for-cain, teaches	**foircthe**	{ **foircthi** { **forcanti**
do-eim, protects	**díte**	**díti**
guidid, prays	**gesse**	**gessi**
claidid, digs	**claisse**	**classi**
scaraid, parts	**scarthe**	**scarthi**
molaidir, praises	**moltae**	**moltai**
léicid, leaves	**léicthe**	**léicthi**

MISCELLANEOUS PARADIGMS

The Substantive Verb

PRESENT INDICATIVE

SINGULAR

1.	**at-tóo, at-tó**	**-táu, -tó**
2.	**a-taí**	**-taí**
3.	**at-táa, at-tá**	**-tá, -táa**

Impers. Pass. **-tathar.**

PLURAL

1.	**at-taam**	**-taam**
2.	**a-taaid, ataaith**	**-taid**
3.	**at-taat**	**-taat**

The uncompounded abs. sg. 3 **tá(i)th** is found with suffixed pronouns, ' there is to me '=' I have,' etc.

	Singular	*Plural*
1.	**táthum**	**táithiunn, táithunn**
2.	**táthut**	**táthuib**
3. m.	**táthai**	
f.	**táthus**	

The rel. sg. 3 **daas** (=**taas** after rel. **n-**) is found in **ol-daas in-daas** 'than (is),' and in the idiom **cid daas** ' what ails him,' (sg. 1 **cid no tó**, 2 **cid no taí**).

The usual rel. form is the impersonal **fil, feil, fail,** or **file ; fil** also serves as the general conjunct form, except (a) after an infixed pronoun expressing a dative relation, e.g. **ní-m thá**, ' I have not,' but **ní-m fil**, ' I am not ' ; (b) after a relative governed by a preposition, e.g. **lassa tá,** ' with which is '; so after **i n-** ' in which,' **i táa**, ' in which is.'

CONSUETUDINAL PRESENT
SINGULAR

	Absolute	*Conjunct*
1.	**bíuu**	**-bíu**
2.		**-bí**
2.	**bíid**	**-bí, -rubai**
Rel.	**bíis, bís**	
Impers. Pass.	**bíthir**	**-bíther, -rubthar**

PLURAL

1.	**bímmi**	**-biam**
Rel.	**bímme**	
3.	**bíit**	**-bíat, -rubat**
Rel.	**bíte**	

IMPERATIVE

	Singular	*Plural*
2.	**bí**	**biid, bíth**
3.	**bíid, bíth**	**biat**

IMPERFECT INDICATIVE

	Singular	*Plural*
1.	**no bíinn**	**no bímmis**
3.	**no bíth**	**no bítis**
Impers. Pass.	**no bí·he**	

Present Subjunctive

SINGULAR

	Absolute	*Conjunct*
1.	béo, béu	-béo
2.	bee	-bé
3.	beith, beid	-bé, -roib
Rel.	bess	
Impers. Pass.	bethir	-bether

PLURAL

1.	bemmi	-bem, -robam
2.	bethe	-beid, -robith
3.	beit	-bet, -robat
Rel.	bete	

Past Subjunctive

	Singular	*Plural*
1.	no beinn	no bemmis
2.	no betha	no bethe
3.	no beth, -bed	no betis, -roibtis
	-robad	
Impers. Pass.	-bethe	

Future

SINGULAR

	Absolute	*Conjunct*
1.	bia	
2.	bie	
3.	bieid, bied	-bia
Rel.	bias	
Impers. Pass.	bethir	-bether

PLURAL

Absolute	*Conjunct*
1. bemmi	-biam
2. bethe	-bieid, -bied
3. bieit	-biat
Rel. bete	

SECONDARY FUTURE

Singular	*Plural*
1. no beinn	no bemmis
3. no biad	no betis

PRETERITE

Singular	*Plural*
1. bá	bámmar
2. bá	-baid
3. boí, baí	bátar, bátir
Rel. boíe	bátar
Impers. Pass. bothae, -both	

PERFECT

SINGULAR

Deuterotonic	*Prototonic*
1. ro bá	-roba, -raba
2. ro bá	-raba
3. ro boí	-robae, -rabae
Impers. Pass. ro both	

PLURAL

1. ro bámmar	-robammar
2. ro báid	-robaid
3. ro bátar	-robatar, -rabatar

Verbal of Necessity : **buthi, buithi.**

Verbal Noun : **both, buith** gen. **buithe** f.

COPULA

* denotes forms after which lenition might be expected, but where no decisive instances occur.

	Sg. 1.	Sg. 2.	Sg. 3.	Pl. 1.	Pl. 2.	Pl. 3.
PRES. IND. abs.	am	at, it	is	ammi, ammin, immi	adib, idib, adi	it
neg.	nita', nida'	nita'	ní	nitan', nidan'	nítad*, nidad*	nitaat', nitat', nidat'
with con-, etc.	conda'		condid, conid, diandid, diant, connách	condam'		
con- with neg.						
{ rel.	no-n-da'	no-n-da'	as', nád, nand, nant, nách	no-n-dan'	no-n-dad*	ata', at*, natat', nandat'
{ neg.						
with ce, etc.			ceso', cesu', ciaso', ciasu', maso', masu', cenid, manid		cenotad*	ceto', cetu', matu'
neg.						
CONS. PRES.			-bi, -pi			
PRÆS. SUBJ.	ba, -ba'	ba, -ba, be	ba, -ba, -bo, -p, -b	-ban'	bede, -bad*	ropat'

					-bad*	-bat'[1]
PAST. SUBJ.	-benn, -bin	-ptha	rop, ropo, -dip, -dib, cid, ced, mad, bes', bas'	bemmis, -bimmis		cit, mat, bete', beta', -bat' / betis, bitis, -btis, -ptis, cetis, matis
IPV.	ba'		bed', bad', -bad'	baán, ban'	bed', bad', -bad'	bat', -bat'
FUT.	be	be	bid, -ba, -pa, bes', bas'	bimmi, bemmi, bami		bit, -bat* / beta', bat*
SEC. FUT.			robad', bed', -bad'			beitis, roptis
PAST	basa, -psa		ba, -po', -bo', -pu', -bu'			batir, batar, -btar
PERF.	ropsa, robsa, -rbsa	ropsa	ropo', robo', ropu', robu', -rbo', -rbu'	robummar, -rbommar		roptar, robtar, -rbtar

[1] No lenition in Wb., but there are only a few occurrences.

as-beir, says

PRESENT INDICATIVE

SINGULAR

Deuterotonic	*Prototonic*
1. **as-biur**	**-epur**
2. **as-bir**	**-epir**
3. **as-beir**	**-epir**
Pass. **as-berar, as-berr**	**-eperr**

PLURAL

1. **as-beram**	**-eprem**
2. **as-berid**	**-eprid**
3. **as-berat**	**-epret**
Pass. **as-bertar**	**-epertar**

With infixed ro sg. 1 **-érbur**, 3 **as-robair.**

IMPERATIVE

Singular	*Plural*
1.	**eprem**
2. **epir**	**eprid**
3. **epred**	**epret**

IMPERFECT INDICATIVE

SINGULAR

Deuterotonic	*Prototonic*
1. **as-berinn**	**-eprinn**
2. **as-bertha**	**-epertha**
3. **as-bered**	**-epred**
Pass. **as-berthe**	**-eperthe**

PLURAL

1. **as-bermis**	**-epermis**
2. **as-berthe**	**-eperthe**
3. **as-bertis**	**-epertis**
Pass. **as-bertis**	**-epertis**

PRESENT SUBJUNCTIVE

Deuterotonic	SINGULAR	*Prototonic*
1. **as-ber**		**-eper**
2. **as-berae**		**-epre**
3. **as-bera**		**-eprea**
Pass. **as-berthar**		**-eperthar**

	PLURAL	
1. **as-beram**		**-eprem**
2. **as-beraid**		**-eprid**
3. **as-berat**		**-epret**
Pass. **as-bertar**		**-epertar**

With infixed **ro**, sg. 1 **-érbar**, 3 **-érbara** ; pl. 2 **érbaraid** ; Pass. **-érbarthar.**

PAST SUBJUNCTIVE

Deuterotonic	SINGULAR	*Prototonic*
1. **as-berainn**		**-eprinn**
2. **as-bertha**		**-epertha**
3. **as-berad**		**-epred**
Pass. **as-berthae**		**-eperthae**

	PLURAL	
1. **as-bermais**		**-epermais**
2. **as-berthae**		**-eperthae**
3. **as-bertais**		**-epertais**
Pass. **as-bertais**		**-epertais**

With infixed **ro**, sg. 3 **as-robrath**, **-érbarad** ; pl. 3 **as-robartis.**

FUTURE

Deuterotonic	SINGULAR	*Prototonic*
1. **as-bér**		**-epér**
2. **as-bérae**		**-epérae**
3. **as-béra**		**-epéra**
Pass. **as-bérthar**		**-epérthar**

PLURAL

Deuterotonic	Prototonic
1. as-béram	-epéram
2. as-béraid	-epéraid
3. as-bérat	-epérat
Pass. as-bértar	-epértar

SECONDARY FUTURE

SINGULAR

Deuterotonic	Prototonic
1. as-bérainn	-epérainn
2. as-bértha	-epértha
3. as-bérad	-epérad
Pass. as-bérthae	-epérthae

PLURAL

1. as-bérmais	-epérmais
2. as-bérthae	-epérthae
3. as-bértais	-epértais
Pass. as-bértais	-epértais

With infixed **ro**, sg. 3 **-érbarad**.

PRETERITE

SINGULAR

Deuterotonic	Prototonic
1. as-biurt (?)	-epurt (?)
2. as-birt	-epirt
3. as-bert	-epert
Pass. as-breth	-epred

PLURAL

1. as-bertmar	-epertmar (?)
2. as-bertaid	-epertaid (?)
3. as-bertatar	-epertatar (?)
Pass. as-bretha	-epertha

PERFECT

SINGULAR

Deuterotonic	*Prototonic*
1. **as-ruburt**	**-érburt**
2. **as-rubairt**	**-érbairt**
3. **as-rubart**	**-érbart**
Pass. **as-robrad**	**-érbrad**

PLURAL

1. **as-rubartmar**	**-érbartmar**
2. **as-rubartaid**	**-érbartaid**
3. **as-rubartatar**	**-érbartatar**

Verbal of Necessity : **eperthi.**
Verbal Noun : **epert.**

do-beir, gives, brings

PRESENT INDICATIVE

SINGULAR

Deuterotonic	*Prototonic*
1. **do-biur**	**-tabur**
2. **do-bir**	**-tabair**
3. **do-beir**	**-tabair**
Pass. **do-berar, doberr**	**-tabarr, -tobarr**

PLURAL

1. **do-beram**	**-taibrem**
2. **do-berid**	**-taibrid**
3. **do-berat**	**-taibret**
Pass. **do-bertar**	**-tabartar**

Perfective Present corresponding to **do-ratus,** sg. 3 **do-rati,**
-tarti, pl. 3 **-tartat ;** corresponding to **do-uccus,** sg. 3
do-uccai, -tuccai ; pass. sg. **-tucthar.**

IMPERATIVE

	Singular	Plural
1.		taibrem
2.	tabair	tatbrid
3.	taibred	taibret
Pass.	tabarr	

NOTE.—There is also an Imperative from the perfect stem
to-ucc-, sg. 2 **tuic** Wb. 10ᵃ30; pl. 1 **tucam**; 2. **tucaid**;
3 **tuicet**; pass. sg. **tucthar,** pl. **tucaiter.**

IMPERFECT INDICATIVE

SINGULAR

	Deuterotonic	Prototonic
1.	do-berinn	-taibrinn
2.	do-bertha	-tabartha
3.	do-bered	-taibred
Pass.	do-berthe	-tabarthe

PLURAL

1.	do-bermis	-tabarmis
2.	do-berthe	-tabarthe
3.	do-bertis	-tabartis
Pass.	do-bertis	-tabartis

PRESENT SUBJUNCTIVE

SINGULAR

	Deuterotonic	Prototonic
1.	do-ber	-tabar
2.	do-berae	-taibre
3.	do-bera	-taibrea
Pass.	do-berthar	-tabarthar

PLURAL

1.	do-beram	-taibrem
2.	do-beraid	-taibrid
3.	do-berat	-taibret
Pass.	do-bertar	-tabartar

Past Subjunctive

SINGULAR

Deuterotonic	Prototonic
1. do-berainn	-taibrinn
2. do-bertha	-tabartha
3. do-berad	-taibred
Pass. do-berthae	-tabarthae

PLURAL

1. do-bermais	-tabarmais
2. do-berthae	-tabarthae
3. do-bertais	-tabartais
Pass. do-bertais	-tabartais

Subjunctive, corresponding to Perfect **do-ratus.**

Present

SINGULAR

Deuterotonic	Prototonic
1. do-rat	-tart
2. do-ratae	-tartae
3. do-rata	-tarta
Pass. do-rattar	-tartar

PLURAL

1. do-ratam	-tartam
2. do-rataid	-tartaid
3. do-ratat	-tartat
Pass. do-rataiter	-tartaiter

Past

SINGULAR

Deuterotonic	Prototonic
1. do-ratainn	-tartainn
2. do-ratta	-tarta
3. do-ratad	-tartad
Pass. do-rattae	-tartae

PLURAL

Deuterotonic	Prototonic
1. do-ratmais	-tartmais
2. do-rattae	-tartae
3. do-rattais	-tartais, -tartaitis
Pass. do-rattais	-tartais

SUBJUNCTIVE, CORRESPONDING TO PERFECT **do-uccus.**

PRESENT

SINGULAR

Deuterotonic	Prototonic
1. do-uc	-tuc
2. do-uccae	-tuccae, -tuicce
3. do-ucca	-tucca
Pass. do-uchtar	-tucthar, -tuicther
etc.	etc.

PAST

Sg. 1. do-uccinn		-tuccinn
2. do-uctha		-tuctha
etc.		etc.

NOTE.—The prototonic forms are frequently used for the deuterotonic.

FUTURE

SINGULAR

Deuterotonic	Prototonic
1. do-bér	-tibér
2. do-bérae	-tibérae
3. do-béra	-tibéra
Pass. do-bérthar	-tibérthar

PLURAL

1. do-béram	-tibéram
2. do-béraid	-tibéraid
3. do-bérat	-tibérat
Pass. do-bértar	-tibértar

SECONDARY FUTURE
SINGULAR

Deuterotonic	*Prototonic*
1. do-bérainn	-tibérainn
2. do-bértha	-tibértha
3. do-bérad	-tibérad
Pass. do-bérthae	-tibérthae

PLURAL

1. do-bérmais	-tibérmais
2. do-bérthae	-tibérthae
3. do-bértais	-tibértais
Pass. do-bertais	-tibértais

PRETERITE
SINGULAR

Deuterotonic	*Prototonic*
1. do-biurt	-tuburt (?)
2. do-birt	-tubirt (?)
3. do-bert	-tubart, -tubert
Pass. do-breth	-tobrad, tabrath

PLURAL

1. do-bertmar	-tubartmar (?)
2. do-bertid	-tubartaid (?)
3. do-bertar, do-bertatar	-tubartatar,
	-tubertatar
Pass. do-bretha	-tubartha (?)

1. PERFECT = I have given.
SINGULAR

Deuterotonic	*Prototonic*
1. do-ratus	-tartus
2. do-ratais	-tartais
3. do-rat	-tarat
Pass. do-ratad	-tartad

PLURAL

Deuterotonic	*Prototonic*
1. **do-ratsam**	**-tartsam**
2. **do-ratsaid**	**-tartsaid**
3. **do-ratsat**	**-tartisset, -tartsat**
Pass. **do-ratta**	**-tarta**

2. PERFECT=I have brought.

SINGULAR

Deuterotonic	*Prototonic*
1. **do-uccus**	**-tuccus**
2. **do-uccis**	**-tuccis**
3. **do-uic, do-uc, do-uccai**	**-tuicc, -tuic, -tucc**
Pass. **do-uccad**	**-tuccad, -tuiced**

PLURAL

1. **do-uicsem**	**-tucsam**
2. **do-ucsid**	**-tucsaid**
3. **do-ucsat**	**-tucsat**
Pass. **do-uctha**	**-tuctha**

NOTE.—The prototonic forms are frequently used for the deuterotonic.

Verbal of Necessity : **tabarthi.**

Verbal Noun : **tabart.**

do-gní, does.

PRESENT INDICATIVE

SINGULAR

Deuterotonic	*Prototonic*
1. **do-gníu**	**-dén(a)im**
2. **do-gní**	**-dén(a)i**
3. **do-gní**	**-dén(a)i**
Pass. **do-gníther**	**-déntar**

PLURAL

Deuterotonic	*Prototonic*
1. do-gníam	-dénam
2. do-gníith	-dénid
3. do-gníat	-dénat
Pass. do-gníter	-dénatar

With infixed ro, sg. 1 -dernaim, 3 do-rónai, -dernai ;
Pl. 1 do-rónam, 3 -dernat ; pass. sg. 3 -derntar.

IMPERFECT INDICATIVE
SINGULAR

Deuterotonic	*Prototonic*
1. do-gníinn	-déninn
2. do-gnítha (?)	-dénta (?)
3. do-gníth	-dénad
Pass. do-gníthe	-déntae

PLURAL

1. do-gnímmis	-dénmis
2. do-gníthe	-dénte
3. do-gnítis	-déntis
Pass. do-gnítis	-déntis

IMPERATIVE

Singular	*Plural*
1.	dénam
2. déne	dén(a)id
3. dénad	dénat
Pass. déntar	dénaiter

PRESENT SUBJUNCTIVE
SINGULAR

Deuterotonic	*Prototonic*
1. do-gnéo	-dén
2. do-gné	-dénae
3. do-gné	-déna
Pass. do-gnether	-déntar

PLURAL

	Deuterotonic	*Prototonic*
1.	do-gnem	-dénam
2.	do-gneid	-dénaid
3.	do-gnet	-dénat
Pass.	do-gnetar	-dénatar

With infixed -ro-

SINGULAR

	Deuterotonic	*Prototonic*
1.	do-rón	-dern
2.	do-rónae	-dernae
3.	do-róna	-derna
Pass.	do-róntar	-derntar

PLURAL

1.	do-rónam	-dernam
2.	do-rónaid	-dernaid
3.	do-rónat	-dernat

PAST SUBJUNCTIVE

SINGULAR

	Deuterotonic	*Prototonic*
1.	do-gneinn	-déninn
2.	do-gnetha	-dénta
3.	do-gneth	-dénad
Pass.	do-gnethe	-dénte

PLURAL

1.	do-gnemmis	-dénmis
2.	do-gnethe	-dénte
3.	do-gnetis	-déntais
Pass.	do-gnetis	-déntais

With infixed -ro-
SINGULAR

Deuterotonic		*Prototonic*
1. do-róininn		-dernainn
2. do-rónta		-dernta
3. do-rónad		-dernad
Pass. do-róntae		-derntae

PLURAL

1. do-rónmais		-dernmais
2. do-róntae		-derntae
3. do-róntais		-derntais
Pass. do-róntai		-derntais

FUTURE
SINGULAR

Deuterotonic	*Prototonic*
1. do-gén	-digén
2. do-génae	-digne
3. do-géna	-dignea
Pass. do-géntar	-digentar

PLURAL

1. do-génam	-dignem, -digénam
2. do-génaid	-dignid
3. do-génat	-dignet
Pass. do-génatar (?)	-digniter (?)

With infixed -ro-, pl. 3 -dergenat.

SECONDARY FUTURE
SINGULAR

Deuterotonic	*Prototonic*
1. do-génainn	-digninn
2. do-génta	-digenta
3. do-génad	-digned
Pass. do-génte	-digente

PLURAL

Deuterotonic	*Prototonic*
1. do-génmis	-digénmis
2. do-génte	-digénte
3. do-géntis	-digéntis
Pass. do-géntis	-digéntis

With infixed **-ro-**, pl. 1 **do-rigénmais**, 2 **do-rigénte.**

PRETERITE

SINGULAR

Deuterotonic	*Prototonic*
1. do-génus (?)	-dignius (?)
2. do-génais (?)	-dignis (?)
3. do-gén(a)i	-digni
Pass. do-gníth	-dénad (?)

PLURAL

1. do-génsam (?)	-digensam (?)
2. do-génsaid (?)	-digensaid (?)
3. do-génsat	-digensat
Pass. do-gnítha	-dénta (?)

PERFECT

SINGULAR

Deuterotonic	*Prototonic*
1. { do-rignius / do-rigénus	{ -deirgénus / -dernus (once Ml.)
2. do-rignis	-dergénis (?)
3. { do-rigéni / do-rigni	{ -dergéni / -dergini / -deirgni
Pass. do-rónad	-dernad

PLURAL

Deuterotonic	*Prototonic*
1. do-rigénsam	-dergénsam (?)
2. do-rigénsaid	-dergénsaid (?)
3. do-rigénsat	-dergénsat
Pass. do-rónta	-dernta

Verbal of Necessity : **dénti.**

Verbal Noun : **dénum, dénom,** G. **dénma.**

ad-cí, sees

PRESENT INDICATIVE

SINGULAR

Deuterotonic	*Prototonic*
1. ad-cíu	-aicciu, -accu, -accim
2. ad-cí	-aci, -accai
3. ad-cí	-aicci, -accai
Pass. ad-cíther	-accastar

PLURAL

1. ad-ciam	-accam
2. ad-ciid	-accid
3. ad-ciat	-accat, -aiccet
Pass. ad-cíter	

Perfective Present Sg. 1 **-airciu,** Pass. : **ad-rodarcar.**

IMPERFECT INDICATIVE

Sg. 3 **ad-cid, aiccid,** pl. 3 **ad-cítis, aiccitis**

PRESENT SUBJUNCTIVE

SINGULAR

Deuterotonic	*Prototonic*
1. ad-cear	-accar
2.	-aiccither, -aiccther
3. ad-cether	-accathar, -accadar
Pass.	-accastar

PLURAL

Deuterotonic	*Prototonic*
1.	-accamar
2. ad-ceid	-aiccid
3. ad-ceter	-accatar
Pass. ad-ceter	

PAST SUBJUNCTIVE
SINGULAR

Deuterotonic	*Prototonic*
1. ad-ceinn	-accinn
2. ad-cetha	
3. ad-ceth, ad-ced	-aicced, -accad
Pass. ad-cethe	

PLURAL

1.	-aiccimis
2. ad-cethe	
3. ad-cetis	-accaitis, -aiccitis

FUTURE
SINGULAR

Deuterotonic	*Prototonic*
1. ad-cichiu	-acciu
3. ad-cichi (?)	-accigi
Pass. ad-cichestar, ad-cigestar	

PLURAL

3. ad-cichset	-aiccichet
Pass. ad-cichsiter	

SECONDARY FUTURE
SINGULAR

3. ad-ciched	-a(i)cciged

PLURAL

3. ad-cichitis	-accigtis

PRETERITE AND PERFECT

PROTOTONIC

Singular	Plural
1. -acca	-accamar
2. -acca	-accaid (?)
3. -accae	-accatar

The affirmative preterite is formed by prefixing the conjunction **co n-** (lit. ' so that '), which is here unmeaning : **ní acca** ' I did not see ' and ' I have not seen,' but **co n-acca** ' I saw.' The affirmative perfect, deuterotonic only, is formed from a different root.

Singular	Plural
1. **ad-condarc**	**ad-condarcmar**
2. **ad-condarc**	**ad-condarcaid**
3. **ad-condairc**	**ad-condarcatar**

The passive preterite and perfect is **ad-cess, -accas,** pl. **ad-cessa, -accassa** ; the preterite also **co n-accas, co n-aices,** pl. **co n-accassa, co n-aicesa.**

Verbal Noun : **aicsiu, aicsin.**

téit, goes.

PRESENT INDICATIVE

SINGULAR

Absolute	Conjunct
1. **tíagu**	**-tíag**
2. **tégi**	**-téig**
3. **téit**	**-tét**
Rel. **téte**	
Pass. **tíagair**	**-tíagar**
Rel. **tíagar**	

PLURAL

1. tíagmai		-tíagam
Rel. tíagmae		
2.		-téit
3. tíagait		-tíagat
Rel. tíagtae		

Perfective present : sg. 1 -dichthim, -digthim, 3 do-cuat, -dichet.

IMPERATIVE

	Singular	Plural
1.	tíag	tíagam
2.	eirg	ergid
	ná téig	
3.	tét	tíagat
Pass.	tíagar	

SUBJUNCTIVE

tíasu, etc., see above, p. 50

IMPERFECT INDICATIVE

	Singular	Plural
1.	no téginn	no téigmis
3.	no téged	no téigtis
Pass.	no téigthe	

Perfective: sg. 3 -dichtheth

SUBJUNCTIVE, CORRESPONDING TO THE PERFECT

PRESENT

SINGULAR

	Deuterotonic	Prototonic
1.	do-cous	-dichius, -digius, dechos
2.	do-cois	-dichis, -digis, -dechais
3.	do-coí	-dich, -dig, -decha
Pass.		-dichestar

PLURAL

1. do-coísem	-dechsam
2. do-coísid	-digsid
3. do-coíset	-dichset, -dɪgset -dechsat

PAST
SINGULAR

Deuterotonic	*Prototonic*
1. do-coísinn	-dechsainn
2. do-coísta	-digesta
3. do-coísed	-dichsed, -digsed, -dechsad

PLURAL

1. do-coísmis	-dichesmis (?)
2. do-coíste	-dicheste (?), dechaiste
3. do-coístis	-digsitis, -dechsaitis

NOTE.—There is also a sec. fut. do-coísed, LU 5919, do-cóestis, 5370, with the sense of ' it, they, would be (would have been) able to go.'

FUTURE
SINGULAR

Absolute	*Conjunct*
1. rega	-rig, -reg
2. regae	-regae
3. regaid	-riga, rega
Rel. rigas, regas	
Pass. rigthir, regthair	-regthar
Rel. regthar	

PLURAL

1. rigmi, regmai	-regam
Rel. regmae (?)	
2. regthae (?)	-regaid
3. regait	-regat
Rel. regtae	

SECONDARY FUTURE

Singular	Plural
1. no regainn	no regmais
2. no regtha	no regthae
3. no regad, no rigad	no regtais

PRETERITE

Singular	Plural
1. lod	lodmar
2. lod	
3. luid	lotar, lotair
Rel. luide	
Pass. ethae	

PERFECT
SINGULAR

Deuterotonic	Prototonic
1. do-coad, do-cood	-dechud
2. do-cood	-dechud
3. do-coïd, do-cuaid	-dechuid
Pass. do-coas, do-cuas	-dechas

PLURAL

1. do-commar	-dechummar
3. do-cotar, do-cuatar	-dechutar

Verbal Noun : **techt**, f., gen. **techtae** ; **dul**, m., gen. **dula**.

do-tét, comes.
PRESENT INDICATIVE
SINGULAR

Deuterotonic	Prototonic
1. do-tíag	-taíg, táeg
2. do-téig	-taíg
3. do-tét	-taít, -táet
Pass. do-tíagar	

PLURAL
1. **do-tíagam**   **-taígam** (?)
2. **do-tét** (?)
3. **do-tíagat**   **-taígat**
Pass. **do-tíagtar**
Perfective Present : sg. 3 **-tuidchet**, pl. **do-digthet.**

IMPERATIVE

Singular	*Plural*
2. **tair**	**taít, táet**
3. **taít, táet**	**taígat, táegat**

IMPERFECT INDICATIVE

SINGULAR

Deuterotonic	*Prototonic*
1. **do-téginn**	**-taíginn** (?)
3. **do-téged**	**-taíged** (?)

PLURAL

1. **do-téigmis**	**-taígmis** (?)
3. **do-téigtis**	**-taígtis**

PRESENT SUBJUNCTIVE

SINGULAR

Deuterotonic	*Prototonic*
1. **do-tías**	**-táes**
2. **do-téis**	**-táis**
3. **do-té**	**-taí**
Pass. **do-tíasar**	

PLURAL

1. **do-tíasam**	**-táesam**
2. **do-tésid**	**-taísid**
3. **do-tíasat**	**-táesat**

Past Subjunctive
SINGULAR

Deuterotonic	*Prototonic*
1. **do-tésinn**	**-taísinn**
3. **do-tésed**	**-taísed**

Subjunctive, Corresponding to the Perfect
Present
SINGULAR

Deuterotonic	*Prototonic*
2. **do-dichis** (?)	**-tuidchis**
3. **do-dich** (?)	**-tuidig**
do-decha	

PLURAL

3. **do-dechsat**	**-tuidchisset**

Past
SINGULAR

3. **do-dichsed**	**-tuidchissed**

Future
SINGULAR

Deuterotonic	*Prototonic*
1. **do-reg**	
3. **do-rega, do-riga**	**-terga, -tirga**
Pass. **do-regthar**	

PLURAL

1. **do-regam**	**-tergam**
2. **do-regaid**	**-tergaid**
3. **do-regat**	**-tergat**

Secondary Future

Sg. 3 **do-regad,** or **do-rigad, -tergad,** etc.

PRETERITE
SINGULAR

Deuterotonic		*Prototonic*
1. do-lod		
2. do-lod		
3. do-luid		-tul(a)id
Pass. do-eth		

PLURAL

1. do-lodmar		
2. do-luidid		
3. do-lotar		-tuldatar, -tultatar

PERFECT
SINGULAR

Deuterotonic	*Prototonic*
1. do-dechad	-tuidched
2. do-dechad	-tuidched
3. do-chuid	-tuidchid
Pass. do-dechas	-tuidches

PLURAL

1. do-dechommar	-tuidchommar
3. do-dechutar	-tuidchetar

Verbal Noun : **tuidecht.**

do-ic(c), comes.

In this verb and the following the deuterotonic forms are commonly replaced by the prototonic, except when an infixed pronoun or rel. **n** is inserted.

PRESENT INDICATIVE
SINGULAR

Deuterototonic	*Prototonic*
1.	-ticim
2.	-tici
3. do-ic	-tic
Pass. do-ecar	-tecar

PLURAL

Deuterotonic	Prototonic
1. do-ecam	-tecam
2. do-icid	-ticid
3. do-ecat	-tecat

IMPERFECT

SINGULAR

Deuterotonic	Prototonic
1. do-icinn	-ticinn
3. do-iced	-ticed

PLURAL

3.	-tictis

IMPERATIVE

Singular	Plural
1.	tecam
2. tair	ticid
3. ticed	tecat

PRESENT SUBJUNCTIVE

SINGULAR

Deuterotonic	Prototonic
1. do-ís	-tís
2. do-ís	-tís
3. do-í	-tí
Pass. do-ísar	-tísar

PLURAL

1. do-ísam	-tísam
2. do-ísid	-tísid
3. do-ísat	-tísat

Past Subjunctive

Singular

Deuterotonic	*Prototonic*
1. do-ís(a)inn	-tís(a)inn
2. do-ísta	-tísta
3. do-ísed	-tísed

Plural

1. do-ísm(a)is	-tísm(a)is
3. do-íst(a)is	-tíst(a)is

Future

1. do-icub	-ticub
2. do-icf(a)e	-ticf(a)e
3. do-icfa	-ticf(e)a
Pass.	-ticf(a)ider

Plural

1. do-icfam	-ticfam
3. do-icfet, do-icfat	-ticfet, -ticfat

Secondary Future

Singular

Deuterotonic	*Prototonic*
1. do-icfainn	-ticfainn
3. do-icfed, do-icfad	-ticfed, -ticfad

Plural

3. do-icfitis	-ticf(a)itis

PRETERITE AND PERFECT

Deuterotonic	SINGULAR	*Prototonic*
1. do-ánac		-tánac
2. do-ánac		-tánac
3. do-án(a)ic		-tán(a)ic
Pass.		-tícht

PLURAL

1. do-áncamar		-táncamar
2. do-ánc(a)id		-tánc(a)id
3. do-áncatar		-táncatar

Verbal Noun : **tíchtu.**

ro-ic(c), reaches.

PRESENT INDICATIVE

Deuterotonic	SINGULAR	*Prototonic*
1. ro-ic(c)u, ru-icim		-ricu, -ric(c)im
2.		-ric(c)i
3.		-ric(c)
Pass. ro-ecar		-rec(c)ar

PLURAL

1. ro-ecam		-recam
2.		-ric(c)id
3. ro-ec(c)at		-recat

Imperative : sg. 3 **riced** ; pl. 1 **recam,** 3 **recat.**

Pres. Subj. : sg. 3 **ro-(h)í, -rí,** pass. **-rísar** ; pl. 1 **-rísam,** 3 **-rísat.**

Past Subj. : sg. 3 **ro-ísed, rísed** ; pl. **ro-íst(a)is, ríst(a)is.**

Fut. : sg. 3 **ro-icfea, -ricfea** ; pass. **-ricfider.**

Sec. Fut. : sg. 3 **ricfed, -ricfad** ; pl. 3 **-ricf(a)itis.**

Pret. and Perf. : **ro-án(a)ic, -rán(a)ic** ; pass. **-rícht** ; pl. 3 **ro-áncatar, -ráncatar.**

Verbal Noun : **ríchtu.**

con-ic(c), is able.

SINGULAR

Deuterotonic	*Prototonic*
1. con-icimm	-cumcu, -cumgaim
2. con-ici	-cumci, -cumgai
3. con-ic(c)	-cumaic, -cumaing
Pass. con-ecar	-cumacar, -cumangar

PLURAL

1. con-ecam	-cumcam, -cumgam
2. con-icid	-cumcaid, -cumgaid
3. con-ecat	-cumcat, -cumgat, -cuimcet

IMPERATIVE : pl. 3 **cumgat**

IMPERFECT INDICATIVE

SINGULAR

Deuterotonic	*Prototonic*
3. con-iced (?)	-cumcath, -cumgad

PLURAL

3. con-ictis (?)	-cumcaitis, -cumgaitis

PRESENT SUBJUNCTIVE

SINGULAR

Deuterotonic	*Prototonic*
2. con-ís	
3. con-í	-cumai, -cum

PLURAL

2. con-ísid	
3. con-ísat	-cuimset

Past Subjunctive
SINGULAR

Deuterotonic	*Prototonic*
1. con-ísinn	-cuimsin
3. con-ísed	-cuimsed

PLURAL

3. con-íst(a)is

Future
SINGULAR

Deuterotonic	*Prototonic*
1. con-icub	-cumgub
2. con-icbe	
3. con-icfa	-cumgaba

PLURAL

1. con-icfam	
2. con-icfid	
3.	-cumgubat

Secondary Future
SINGULAR

Deuterotonic	*Prototonic*
3. con-icfed, con-icfad	-cumcaibed, -cumcabad

PLURAL

1. con-icfimmis
3. con-icf(a)itis

Preterite and Perfect
SINGULAR

Deuterotonic	*Prototonic*
1. con-áneccar	-coímnacar
2.	-coímnacar
3. con-ánacuir, con-ánic	-coímnacair, -coímnucuir

PLURAL

Deuterotonic	*Prototonic*
1.	-coímnacmar
2.	-coímnacaid
3. con-áncatar	-coímnactar

do-tuit, later do-fuit, falls.

Pres. Ind. : sg. 3 do-tuit, -tuit ; pass. -tuiter ; pl. 3 do-tuitet, -tuitet.

Ipf. Ind. : sg. 3 do-fuitted ; pl. 3 do-fuititis, -tuititis.

Ipv. : sg. 2 tuit.

Pres. Subj. : sg. 3 do-toth, do-foth, -toth, -tod ; pl. 3 do-todsat, -todsat. Perfective : pl. 1 -torthissem, 3 torthaiset.

Past Subj. : sg. 1 do-todsinn ; pl. 3 -todsitis ; with -ro- ; sg. 3 do-rotsad.

Fut. : sg. 1 do-fóethus, -tóethus, 3 do-tóeth, -toíth ; pl. 3 do-tóethsat, do-fóetsat, -tóetsat.

Sec. Fut. : sg. 3 do-tóethsad, -tóethsad, -tóetsad ; pl. 3 -tóethsitis.

Pret. : sg. 3 do-cer ; pl. 3 do-certar.

PERFECT

SINGULAR

Deuterotonic	*Prototonic*
1. do-rochar	-torchar
2. do-rochar	-torchar
3. do-rochar, do-rochair	-torchar, -torchair

PLURAL

1. do-rochramar	-torchramar
3. do-rochratar	-torchartar, -torchratar

Verbal Noun : tothaim.

OLD IRISH GLOSSES

Present Indicative.

1. Wb. 16ᵈ8. de uobis glorior apud Macedonas .i. *bíuu-sa oc irbáig dar far cenn-si fri Maccidóndu.*

2. Wb. 12ᶜ29. *ní ar formut frib-si as-biur-sa in so.*

3. Wb. 24ᵃ38. et caeteris . . . quorum nomina sunt in libro uitae .i. adiutorum caeterorum ; *ní epur a n-anman sund.*

4. Wb. 14ᵈ26. in persona Christi .i. *is i persin Crīst d-a-gníu-sa sin.*

5. Wb. 12ᶜ9. *ní dēnim gnímu macthi.*

6. Wb. 21ᶜ19. cuius factus sum ego minister .i. *is oc precept soscēli attó.*

7. Wb. 21ᵃ8. ut Deus . . . det uobis spiritum sapientiae .i. *is hed in so no guidimm.*

8. Wb. 14ᶜ18. Et hac confidentia uolui prius uenire ad uos .i. *hōre no-n-dob molor-sa et no-m moídim indib.*

9 Wb. 14ᵃ10. spero enim me aliquantulum temporis manere apud uos .i. *is hed do-moíniur.*

10. Wb. 27ᶜ22. ad loquendum mysterium Christi, propter quod etiam uinctus sum .i. *is airi am cimbid-se hōre no pridchim in rúin sin.*

11. Wb. 20ᶜ25. mihi autem absit gloriari .i. *nīta chumme-se friu-som.*

12. Wb. 9ᵇ4. iam iudicaui ut praesens .i. *amal no-n-da frecṅdircc-sa.*

13. Sg. 159ª2. quia uerba per omnes personas in omni tempore nominatiui casus uim habent, gl. *air in tan no labrither in cētni persin ł in tānaisi do-adbit ainm hi suidiu.*

14. Wb. 6ᵇ22. Tu autem quid iudicas fratrem tuum ? .i. *ni latt ani ara-rethi* et *ní lat in cách forsa mmitter.*

15. Wb. 5ᵇ27. noli gaudere quod illi fracti sunt in per-ditione, *hōre is na n-aicci atai.*

16. Wb. 32ª21. quod et te ipsum mihi debes .i. *at féchem dom.*

17. Ml. 112ᵇ17. te . . . saepto .i. *a no-n-da imbide.*

18. Wb. 6ª13. si autem malum feceris, time ; non enim sine causa gladium portat .i. *is deidbir ha áigthiu, ar is do thabirt díglae berid in claideb sin.*

19. Ml. 129ᶜ8. dum maestitudinem sterilitatis in domina materni prouentus hilaritate commutat .i. *in tan mberes claind, is fáilid iar sin.*

20. Ml. 62ᵇ20. hostium agmina abyssos appellauerat, quae . . . solent diluuium creare .i. *a n-imbed són ind slōig do-lega na ní tēte, fo chosmailius dīlenn.*

21. Wb. 5ᵇ28. quod si gloriaris, non tu radicem portas sed radix te .i. *is inse nduit. ní tú no-d n-ail acht is hé no-t ail.*

22. Ml. 51ᵇ12. cum mentis humilitatis Deo, non sibi, fuerit innexa .i. *ni ind fessin eirbthi ⁊ nāch dō du-aisilbi na nni do-gní acht is do Dīa.*

23. Ml. 51ᶜ9. *isin nūall do-n-gniat hō ru maith for a nāimtea remib.*

24. Sg. 159ª3. sed non possunt participia componi nisi per nominatiuum casum .i. *is airi nī táet comsuidigud fri rangabáil, húare as coibnesta do brēthir, ar is lour comsuidigud fri suidi.*

25. Ml. 102ª15. post solutam maceriam, praetereuntes infestos, exterminatorem aprum . . . in descriptione subiecit

.i. *itius anūas* ┐ *du-s-claid anís* ; *air nī foircᵓea in fíni hithe neich di anūas, amal du-n-gnī int aís sechmaill as-m-beᵓr-som* .i. *aᵓr is cuit adaill ad-n-ellat-sidi in fíni do thabhairt neich doib dia torud.*[1]

26. Sg. 190ᵇ4. natura uerbi et participii communis est trium generum .i. *at-robair cach cenēl.*

27. Wb. 13ᵈ7. nouissimus Adam in spiritum uiuificantem .i. *bēoigidir in spirut in corp in fecht*[2] *so.*

28. Wb. 19ᵇ1. si enim per Legem iustitia .i. *massu recht*[3] *fīriānigedar cách.*

29. Wb. 12ᶜ22. spiritu enim loquitur mysteria .i. *ro-cláine-thar cách in fogur* et *nícon fitir cid as-beir.*

30. Tur. 58ᵃ. confessio et pulcritudo in conspectu eius, gl. *bīid didiu a* confessio *hísin do fóisitin pecthae, bīid dano do molad, bīid dano do atlugud buide; do fóisitin didiu atā-som sunt.*

31. Wb. 3ᶜ2. uita aeterna in Christo Iesu Domino nostro .i. *tri chretim i n-Ísu ꝉ isin beothu i táa Ísu íar n-esséirgu.*

32. Wb. 14ᶜ16. quia gloria uestra sumus .i. *is triun-ni dúib-si ind indocbál no-b tá* in futuro.

33. Wb. 16ᵇ9. ut in nullo detrimentum patiemini ex nobis .i. *nī indráigne dúib cini-n fil lib, ar idib maithi cene.*

34. Wb. 28ᶜ25. *nīpi cían a masse in choirp.*

35. Wb. 26ᵈ19. qualem sollicitudinem habeam pro uobis .i. *is mór in dethiden file dom-sa diib-si.*

36. Wb. 10ᵈ26. Si enim uolens hoc ago, mercedem habeo .i. *massu thol atom-aig dō, manid ar lóg.*

37. Wb. 15ᵇ28. ergo mors in nobis operatur, uita autem in uobis .i. *a mbás tīagme-ni do-áirci bethid dúib-si* .i. *is ar bethid dúib-si tīagmi-ni bás.*

---

[1] *thorud* MS.   [2] *fect* MS.   [3] *rect* MS.

38. Wb. 13ᵇ15. inuenimur autem et falsi testes Dei .i. *is gūforcell do-beram do Dīa amal sodin.*

39. Ml. 117ᵇ9. distamus, gl. *di-taam-ni* .i. *dechrigmir-ni ón.*

40. Ml. 31ᵇ23. quia linguae spectat officium omne quod loquimur, gl. *in bēlrai* .i. *is and atá gním tengad isind huiliu labramar-ni.*

41. Ml. 112ᵇ13. citius oculis quam auribus in adsensum ducimur .i. *is demniu liunn a n-ad-chiam hūa sūlib ol-daas an ro-chluinemmar hūa chlūasaib.*

42. Wb. 17ᵇ5. quales sumus uerbo . . . tales et . . . in facto .i. *ammi tūailnge ar mbrēthre.*

43. Wb. 14ᶜ41. non quia dominamur fidei uestrae .i. *nīdan chumachtig for n-irisse.*

44. Ml. 20ᵇ13. Irascimini et nolite peccare .i. *ní fu¹ indidit atā* irascimini sunt .i. irascimini *fergaigthe-si, acht is fo imcho-marc atā.*

45. Wb. 23ᶜ7. non solum ut in eum credatis, sed etiam ut pro illo patiamini .i. *nī hed a méit non chretid-si acht² fo-daimid fochidi airi.*

46. Wb. 27ᵇ16. induite uos ergo sicut electi Dei . . . et dilecti . . . .i. *gaibid* (ipv.) *immib a n-ētach macc coím sa, amal no-n-dad maicc coíma.*

47. Wb. 11ᵃ4. omnes quidem currunt, sed unus accipit brauium .i. *rethit huili* et *is oínfer gaibes búaid diib inna chomal-nad.*

48. Wb. 20ᶜ21. hi cogunt uos circumcidi, tantum ut crucis Christi persecutionem non patiantur .i. *is dō d-a-gníat³ : maith leu indocbál apstal doib* et *ni fodmat ingreimm ar chroich Crīst.*

49. Wb. 29ᵃ12. qui laborant in uerbo et doctrina .i. *indhí pridchite* et *for-chanat brēthir Dǽ.*

¹ *ni fú* MS.   ² *act* MS.   ³ *dágniat* MS.

50. Sg. 4ᵇ10. x . . . post omnes ponitur literas quibus Latinae dictiones egent, gl. *aidlignigitir*[1] *dano ūadi-si.*

51. Sg. 162ᵃ3. possunt tamen etiam in prima inueniri persona et secunda per poetarum προσωποποιίας .i. *in tan labratar ind filid a persin inna ṅdẹa, do-gniat* primam ┐ secundam in illis.

52. Wb. 19ᶜ20. si autem uos Christi, ergo Abrachae semen estis, secundum promissionem heredes .i. *ma nu-dub fei! i n-ellug coirp Crīst, adib cland Abrache amal sodin,* et *it sib ata chomarpi Abracham.*

53. Wb. 18ᵈ14. ab iis autem qui uidebantur esse aliquid .i. *Petur* et *Iacōb* et *Iohain* .i. *nī airegdu a persan-som ol-daas persan na n-abstal ol-chene, ceto thoísegu i n-iriss.*

54. Wb. 4ᵈ15. offenderunt in lapidem offensionis, gl. *is béss didu ind liacc benir il-bēim friss,* et *inti do-thuit foir con-boing a chnámi, inti fora tuit-som immurgu at-bail-side.*

55. Ml. 25ᶜ5. *foillsigthir as n-īsel in doínacht íar n-aicniud, hūare as in deacht fo-da-raithminedar*[2] ┐ *no-da fortachtaigedar.*

56. Ml. 63ᵈ7. ad omnem infelicitatis commemorationem ut nostrum occurrat exemplum .i. *con-dan samailter fri cech ndodcadchai.*

57. Wb. 22ᶜ10. mulieres uiris suis subditae sint sicut Domino .i. *is bés trā dosom anī-siu cosc inna mban i tossug* et *a tabairt fo chumachte*[3] *a fer*[4] . . . *combi íarum coscitir ind fir* et *do-airbertar fo réir Dǽ.*

Present Subjunctive.

58. Wb. 10ᵈ23. nam si euangelizauero, non est mihi gloria .i. *mad ar lóg pridcha-sa,* .i. *ar m'ētiuth* et *mo thoschith, ní-m bia fochricc dar hési mo precepte.*

---

[1] *aidlignitir* MS. [2] *fodaraithmine* MS. [3] *-cte* MS. [4] *feir* MS.

59. Ml. 92ª17. *cid fáilte ad-cot-sa ⁊ du-n-gnēu, is tussu*[1] *immid-folngi dam, a*² *Dǽ.* *cid indeb dano ad-cot, is tū, a Dǽ, imm-id-folngi dam.*

60. Wb. 14ᵈ17. ut non onerem omnes uos .i. *coní ārim-se peccad lib-si uili* ⊦ *ara tart-sa fortacht dúib-si, arnap trom fuirib for n-oínur.*

61. Wb. 12ᶜ36. si uenero ad uos linguis loquens, quid uobis prodero ? .i. *cotē mo thorbe-se dúib, mad amne labrar?*

62. Wb. 21ᵈ3. quaeso ne deficiatis in tribulationibus meis pro uobis, quae est gloria uestra .i. *nība dimicthe-se lib-si cia beo hi fochidib, ar is* gloria *dúib-si ón.*

63. Ml. 56ᵇ39. noli . . . mirari .i. *ad-n-amraigther* .i. *no n-ētaigther* .i. *ad-cosnae sōn nō no carae.*

64. Ml. 56ᵇ31. aemulatio est effectio, si quod concupiscas alter potiatur, ipse careas .i. *cia thechtid*³ *nach aile nī ad-chobrai-siu ⊓ nī techtai-siu ōn immurgu, ní ētaigther-su imm-anīsin,* .i. *nī ascnae ⊓ ni charae. Is sí indala chīall*⁴ *les isindī as* aemulari *in sin.*

65. Wb. 6ᶜ9. non est regnum Dei in esca et potu .i. *nī hed no-t beir i*⁵ *nem cia ba loingthech.*

66. Acr. 14ª2. nisi forte animum dicis, etiam si moriatur, animum esse, gl. *bés as-bera-su as n-ainm dosom* animus *ci at-bela.*

67. Ml. 114ᵇ18. utrumque secundum defectum personae repugnatricis legendum .i. *nād fil nech con-gnē fris ón acht Dīa.*

68. Wb. 31ª2. non illis reputetur .i. *d-a-rolgea Dīa doib.*

69. Wb. 12ᶜ32. nisi forte ut interpretetur .i. *acht nammáa is samlid is torbe són, co etar-certa a n-as-bera* et *con rucca i n-ǽtarcne cáich.*

70. Ml. 20ᵈ4. sine quibus in totum posse subsistere uita hominum non uidetur .i. *cia ru bé cen ní diib, nī rubai cenaib huli.*

---

¹ *túsu* MS.   ² om. MS.   ³ *techtid* MS.   ⁴ *chall* MS.   ⁵ *i* MS.

71. Wb. 23^b24. dum omni modo Christus . . . adnuntiatur
.i. *ní imned lim, acht*[1] *rop Críst pridches* et *imme-ráda cách.*

72. Ml. 68^b9. docens ut non magno stupore capiantur earum
rerum quae in hac uita gloriosa creduntur .i. *cia beith ar
n-acathar nech inna rétu inducbaidi in betha so, arnách corathar
i mmoth ⁊ machthad dia seirc ⁊ dia n-accubur.*

73. Wb. 31^c11. ut is qui ex aduerso est, reuereatur, nihil
habens dicere malum de nobis, gl. *mad in chrud so bemmi* .i.
co comalnammar a pridchimme et *comman deisimrecht do chách.*

74. Ml. 78^b24. inane est opinari, gl. *du-menammar.*

75. Wb. 25^a10. ut nemo moueatur in tribulationibus istis
.i. *níp imned lib-si mo fochidi-se,* ł *cia chéste ar iriss Críst.*

76. Wb. 7^d10. sitis autem perfecti in eodem sensu et in
eadem sententia .i. *corrop*[2] *inonn cretem bes hi far cridiu* et
a n-as-beraid hó bélib.

77. Wb. 27^c9. non ad oculum seruientes .i. *níbo in tain
no mbeid ar súil* tantum *do-gneith toil far coimded.*

78. Wb. 28^c7. qui enim bene ministrauerint .i. *ma chomalnit
a ngrád.*

79. Wb. 7^d8. obsecro uos, fratres, gl. *do-beir-som ainm bráthre
doib, arná epret is ara miscuis in cúrsachad, acht*[1] *is ara seircc.*

80. Ml. 42^a4. notandum est quam sit in suos moderata
petitio .i. *ní guid dígail du thabairt foraib, acht corru anat
inna arrad.*

81. Wb. 2^c10. non iis tantum qui sunt[3] ex circumcisione
.i. *ní dunaibhí fo-daimet a n-imdibe colnide* tantum, *mani
comolnatar a n-imdibe rúnde* uitiorum.

82. Sg. 207^b11. inueniuntur simplicia apud illos, apud nos
composita, gl. *cit comsuidigthi la Grécu, ní écen dún-ni beta
comsuidigthi linn.*

---

[1] *act* MS.   [2] *ɔrop* MS.   [3] om. MS.

83. Sg. 63ª17. ' oppidum Suthul'. sed melius est figurate
sic esse apposita dicere, ut si dicam ... ' Tiberis flumen ',
quam dicere quod neutri generis in ' ul ' terminantia sint,
gl. *amal nád ṅdéni neutur dindí as* Tiberis *cia do-berthar* flumen
friss, síc *ní dēni neutur dindí as* Suthul *ci ad-comaltar* oppidum
friss.

84. Wb. 34ª4. *is huisse ce ru samaltar fri* Crīst.

85. Wb. 5ᶜ3. donec plenitudo gentium intraret .i. *con
rictar huili genti* ł *drécht caich ceníuil.*

Imperative.

86. Ml 72ᵈ11. iudica me ; ac si dicerct ' pro me ' .i. *du-
m-em-se* ⁊ *deich tarm chenn*[1].

87. Wb. 6ᶜ7. noli cibo tuo illum perdere .i. *léic úait inna
biada milsi* et *tomil innahisiu do-m-meil do chenél.*

88. Ml. 55ª1. noli in tua patientia sustinere .i. *nā dēne
ainmnit.*

89. Ml. 136ª10. audibile Dei per aures indicat .i. *a epert
' cluinte '.*

90. Wb. 29ᵈ19. noli . . . erubescere . . . me uinctum eius
.i. *nába thoirsech cia beo-sa hi carcair.*

91. Wb. 27ª24. nemo ergo uos iudicet in cibo aut in potu
aut in parte diei festi aut neomeniae aut sabbatorum .i. *nāch-
ib mided* .i. *nāch-ib berar i smachtu rechta fetarlicce, inna ndig*
et *a mbiad, inna llithu* et *a ssapati, acht* [2] *bad foirbthe far n-iress.*

92. Wb. 13ª28. omnia . . . secundum ordinem fiant .i. *bíid cach gním inna thēchtu.*

93. Wb. 25ᶜ6. nos autem, qui diei sumus, sobrii simus .i.
hóre ammi maicc laī et *soilse, nā seichem nahisiu.*

[1] *cenn* with ´ over *c* MS.   [2] *act* MS.

94. Wb. 9ª14. imitatores mei estote .i. *bed athramli* [1] .i. *gaibid comarbus for n-athar* et *intamlid a béssu*

95. Ml. 53ᶜ11. affectionis uocabulum miscet .i. *in tan as-m-beir* : ' *taīt á maccu* '.

96. Wb. 22ᵇ26. nolite communicare operibus infructuosis tenebrarum .i. *nā bīth i cobadlus doib, ar atá torad la gnímu soilse.*

97. Ml. 54ᵇ12. conspectum hominum ferre non possint, gl. *nā cumgat* .i. *tīagat for teiched.*

98. Ml. 73ᵈ7. non solito consumantur exitio .i. *nā eiplet hūan bás coitchen hūa n-epil cāch, acht foircniter hūa sain-bás sech cách.*

99. Ml. 56ª23. non . . . conentur .i. *nā aimdetar.*

100. Wb. 9ᶜ12. illos constituite ad iudicandum .i. *bat hé berte bretha lib.*

101. Ml. 56ª22. non subiiciar pedibus superborum .i. *nāch-am indarbanar-sa fo chomthururasib* [2] *inna ndīummassach.*

Imperfect Indicative.

102. Wb. 24ª4. haec arbitratus sum propter Christum detrimenta .i. *no scarinn friu.*

103. Ml. 55ᶜ19. iniquitatem meditatus est in cubili suo .i. *cid in tan no mbíth inna ligiu, ba oc imrādud chloíne no bíth.*

104. Wb. 23ᵈ10. uos desiderabat .i. *no-b carad.*

105. Ml. 30ª3. ita nos alienos a culpa interficere nituntur quasi noctem patiantur inlunem .i. *amal nād n-airigther ⁊ nād fintar a ndu-gnīther hi suidi,* sic *ba in* [3] *fortgidiu ⁊ ba hi temul du-gníth Saūl cona muntair intleda ⁊ erelca fri Dauīd.*

106. Wb. 26ᵇ19. hoc denuntiabamus uobis, gl. *at-beirmis frib.*

---

[1] *adthramli* MS.   [2] *h comtururasib* MS.   [3] *im* MS.

107. Ml. 95ᵃ5. quia in Deum contumeliosi uictoriam prae-
sumebant .i. *is ed as-bertis ba a* [1] *nert fadesin imme-folnged
choscur doib, nību Dīa.*

108. Wb. 15ᵃ18. *do-gnithe a n-as-bered Moysi.*

109. Tur. 110ᶜ. *ba bés leu-som do-bertis da boc leu dochum
Tempuil, ⁊ no lēicthe indala n-aí fon díthrub co pecad in popuil
⁊ do-bertis maldachta foir, ⁊ no oircthe* [2] *didiu and ō popul tar
cenn a pecthae ind aile.*

Past Subjunctive.

110. Wb. 10ᵈ36. ut eos . . . lucrificarem .i. *co no-s berinn
dochum hirisse.*

111. Wb. 14ᶜ23. aut quae cogito, secundum carnem cogito,
ut sit apud me Est et Non ? .i. *co beid* .i. *co mbed a ndēde
sin im labrad-sa* .i. *gáu* et *fír* .i. *combad sain a n-as-berin ō
bélib* et *ani imme-rādin ó chridiu.*

112. Ml. 91ᵇ7. frustra studui, dum ab omni maledicto
abstineo, similis innocentibus inueniri .i. *is dō du-gníinn-se
anīsin, combin cosmail fri encu.*

113. Wb. 29ᵈ8. desiderans te uidere, gl. *ba méite limm nī
scartha friumm.*

114. Wb. 17ᵈ23. ne quis me existimet supra id quod uidet
in me gl. *arnā-m tomnad námmin duine* sed deus.

115. Ml. 109ᵈ5. *ní taīt Dia fo thairṅgere* [3] *con-id chumscaiged.*

116. Wb. 12ᵃ22. num ideo non est de corpore ? .i. *ní nád
ṁbed arse di chorp, acht* [4] *atá de.*

117. Wb. 27ᵈ16. salutatio mea manu Pauli, gl. *combad
notire ro-d scrībad cosse.*

118. Wb. 10ᵇ27. scientia inflat .i. *a fius sin immurgu ba
maith són, act ní bed ūall and.*

<hr>

¹ om. MS.   ² 7 *noircthe* MS.   ³ *tairṅgere* MS.   ⁴ *act* MS.

119. Ml 55ᵈ11. si iustitia Dei reddens singulis pro merito tam magna est, cur contra meritum tu aduersa perpeteris ? .i. *amal du-berad nech hi ceist do Dauíd* : ' *hūare is mōir slēbe* [1] *fírinne Dǽ, cid ara fodmai-siu, á* [2] *Dauíd, didiu a ndu imnedaib* ⁊ *frithoircnib fo-daimi, air it fīriān-su* [3] *?* ' *ícaid-som didiu anīsin, a n-as-m-beir* ' iudicia Domini abyssus multa ' .i. *ataat mesai Dǽ nephchomthetarrachti* [4] *amal abis* ⁊ *amal fudumain. is ed in sin fo-d-era in n-erigim, cid ara fodaim int aís fīriān inna fochaidi,* ⁊ *cid ara mbiat in pecthaig isnaib sōinmechaib.*

120. Wb. 10ᶜ21. numquid non habemus potestatem manducandi et bibendi ? .i. *ba torad saíthir* [5] *dúun in chrud so ce du-melmis cech tūari* et *ce du-gnemmis a ndu-gnīat ar céli.*

121. Ml. 63ᵈ1. tamquam nullae aestimationis digni traditi sumus hostibus .i. *amal nībimmis fíu ní etir.*

122. Wb. 15ᵈ8, 8ᵃ. siue sobrii sumus, uobis .i. *dúib-si.*[6] *is dúib-si* proficit ; *ba coir dúib-si cia do-berthe testas dīn-ni.*

123. Wb. 5ᵇ20. si quomodo ad aemulandum prouocem carnem meam, et saluos faciam aliquos ex illis .i. *trisin intamail sin* .i. *combad ǽt leu buid dom-sa i n-iriss* et *duús in intamlitis.*

124. Sg. 26ᵃ6. uides ergo per se ipsam syllabam deficere praedictorum ratione, nec aliter posse examussim tractari .i. *co n-eperthae cia aiccent* ⁊ *cisī aimser derb thechtas,* reliqua.

125. Wb. 9ᶜ20. quare non magis iniuriam accepistis ? .i. *cid atob-aich cen dílgud cech ancridi do-gnethe frib,* et *nī bethe fria acre ?*

126. Sg. 65ᵃ1. ' abaddir ', deus esse dicitur hoc nomine lapis, gl. *níbu machdath do-rónta dīa dind liac.*

f-Future.

127. Wb. 14ᵃ8. apud uos autem forsitan manebo .i. *níba cuit adill* [7] *cucuib-si, acht ainfa lib, ar nīdad foirbthi-si.*

---

[1] *sleb* MS.   [2] om. MS.   [3] *firianu* MS.   [4] *nephchomtetarrachti* MS.
[5] *sathir* MS.   [6] *dubsi* MS.   [7] *adill* MS.

H

128. Wb. 28ᶜ9. haec tibi scribo, sperans me uenire ad te cito .i. *fo-mentar mo rígtin-se; mos riccub-sa.*

129. Wb. 9ᵃ22. bonum opus, *is hed no molfar.*

130. Ml. 134ᵈ3. ligabis, si quidem est felix malitia .i. *artroídfe-siu* ¹ *inna droch-daíni, a Dǽ, dia n-anduch, air is fechtnach a n-andach mani erthroítar hūa Dīa.*

131. Wb. 13ᵇ19. quod si Christus non resurrexit, uana est fides uestra, adhuc enim estis in peccatis uestris .i. *is súaichnid, manid chretid esséirge Crīst* et mortuorum, *nī-b noíbfea for n-ires in chruth sin* et *ní-b scara fri bar pecthu.*

132. Wb. 23ᵇ7. quia quae circa me sunt, magis ad profectum uenerunt euangelii .i. *hōre am essamin-se precepte asmo chuimriug, is lia de creitfess.*

133. Ml. 14ᵈ8, 10. illis (sc. lecturis) relinquentes occasiones maioris intelligentiae, si uoluerint aliqua addere, gl. *a lléicfimme. is samlid léicfimmi-ni doib-som aisndīs dint sēns ๅ din mōrālus, manip ēcōir frisin stoir ad-fíadam-ni.*

134. Ml. 107ᵃ15. *bid sochaide atrefea indiut-su* ² *ๅ bid* ³ *fāilid nach oín ad-id-trefea.*

135. Wb. 17ᵇ12. *no-n samlafammar frinn fesine.*

136. Ml. 57ᵈ11. ut non ueniant in desperationem salutis .i. *ní derchoínfet a n-íc hō, Dīa.*

137. Ml. 77ᵃ12. *air du-roimnibetar mo popuil-se a rrecht dia n-uilemarbae-siu a nāimtea.*

138. Ml. 14ᵈ3. *cid ēcen aisndís* ⁴ *dɔ neuch as doraid co lēir, ní sechmalfaider cuimre and dano.*

139. Ml. 90ᶜ19. *ní fetar in-dam soírfad Dīa fa nacc.*

140. Ml. 105ᵇ14. ut sententiam bonitatis diuinae impertiendae sibi ratam fore nomine ueritatis exprimeret .i. *no comallaíbthe ๅ ro-m-bad fírién insce Dǽ.*

---

¹ *artroídfeasiu* MS.   ² *indiutsiu* MS.   ³ *bit* MS.   ⁴ *áisndís* MS.

Reduplicated and ē-Future.

141. Ml. 15ᶜ10. futura supplicia, quae quidem non aliter nisi restituti in corpore sustinebunt, .i. *is immalle fo-s-didmat*.

142. Sg. 137ᵇ5. sciendum autem quaedam uerba inueniri defectiua ... et hoc ... uel naturae necessitate fieri uel fortunae casu, gl. *f-a-didmed aicned, acht do-n-d-ecmaiṅg anīsiu*.

143. Wb. 29ᵈ27. ob quam causam etiam haec patior, sed non confundor .i. *ní mebul lemm cia f-a-dam*.

144. Ml. 114ᵇ11. in popul *for-cechnae-siu*.

145. Wb. 7ᵃ2. sed sicut scriptum est .i. *is díim-sa tairrchet ad-cichitis genti* per me.

146 Wb. 19ᵇ6. *ro pridchad dúib céssad Crīst amal ad-cethe*.

147. Wb. 28ᵈ16. te ipsum saluum facies et eos qui te audiunt .i. *cách ro-t-chechladar oc precept*.

148 Ml. 112ᵇ12. *is toīsigiu ad-ciam teilciud in bēla, resīu ro-cloammar a guth-sidi*.

149. Wb. 18ᵃ14. et superimpendar ipse pro animabus uestris .i. *as-ririu-sa mo chumang dar far cenn*.

150. Wb. 25ᵇ6. quoniam uindex est Deus de his omnibus .i. *as-riri Dīa dígail dara n-ési*.[1]

151. Wb. 28ᶜ2. non turpe lucrum sectantes .i. *nī riat na dánu dīadi ara n-indeb domunde*.

152. Wb. 10ᵃ5. *a lliles dind ancretmiuch bid ancretmech*.

153. Ml. 96ᵇ15. medebitur .i. *fris-bia*.

154. Ml. 53ᵇ17. contingetur .i. *ocu-bether*.

155. Ml. 19ᵈ12. mederi . . . adgreditur, gl. *fris-m-bia*.

156. Ml. 65ᵇ7. haerebunt .i. *gíulait*.

---

[1] *darési* MS.

157. Ml. 86ᵇ8. ut non haeream .i. *conī gléu.*

158. Ml. 59ᵇ9. quam uane conturbatur uanis cupiditatibus!
gl. *fo bīthin ara-chīurat.*

159. Ml. 91ᵇ10. *aní as-berinn cosse, is ed as-bǽr beus.*

160. Ml. 97ᵈ10. duplex peccatum, murmurare de inopia,
cum superesset manna, et poscere diffidendo .i. *is peccad diabul
lesom* .i. *fodord doib di dommatu,* ⁊ *du-fūairthed ní leu fora
sāith din main[n],* ⁊ *todlugud inna fēulæ co n-amairis nā-n-da
tibērad Dīa doib.*

161. Ml. 51ᵇ10. *in tan as-m-ber Dauīd* ' intellectum tibi
dabo', *sech is arde*¹ *són do-m-bēra Dia do neuch no-d n-eirbea
ind* ⁊ *gēnas trīit.*

162. Ml. 69ᵃ21. ut . . . appetitu rerum, impetu non iudicio
moueatur .i. *co n-epred* : ' *du-gén a nnoíb sa* ⁊ *ní digen a
n-ǽrgarthe se,*² *cid accubur lium* 3 ' ; *ní eper in sin.*

163. Ml. 56ᵇ15. quoniam plerique mortalium afflictione pro-
borum et impiorum prosperitate turbantur, ut inremuneratas
in hac uita uirtutes deserant et uitia consectentur felicia .i.
*ar chuingid inna sōinmech i mbiat ind ingoir as-berat-som nād
ndignet inna degnīmu, hūare is hi fochaidib bīthir hi suidib,* ⁊
*du-n-gēnat immurgu inna duálchi,*4 *air is sōinmige ad-chotar
tri suidib.*5

164. Sg. 203ᵃ6. ne . . . adiungendum esset ' cum nobis ', gl.
arnā dernimis cum nobis ; *air dia ndēnmis* cum me, *do-gēnmis
dano* cum nobis.

165. Wb. 13ᵇ3. *mad áill dūib cid accaldam neich diib, d-a-
rigénte.*

166. Wb. 22ᵇ23. nemo uos seducat inanibus uerbis .i. *ci
as-bera nech ropia nem cia du-gneid na rétu sa, nīpa fír.*

---

¹ *ardi* MS.   ² *ní digen ǽrgarthae se* MS.   3 *lium* MS.
    4 *dulchi* MS.   5 *suiidib* MS.

167. Wb. 6ᵇ28. itaque unusquisque nostrum pro se rationem reddet Deo .i. *taiccéra cách dara chenn* ¹ *fessin.*

168. Wb. 11ᵃ6. non priuabitur quisque suo labore .i. *niba* unus *gēbas a mbúaid húaib-si.*

s-Future and Subjunctive.

169. Ml. 47ᵈ4, 5. supplicabo etiam pro futuris .i. *gigse-sa* .i. *mo soïrad ar cech gūasacht todochidi.*

170. Ml. 46ᵇ12. frustrata non erit meorum confessio uotorum .i. *niba madae dam m'oísitiu, air na ní no gigius, ebarthi Dīa.*

171. Ml. 53ᶜ3. unumquemque . . . supplicem, gl. *cech oín-gessid* .i. *giges Dīa.*

172. Wb. 14ᶜ2ᵃ. adiuuantibus et uobis in oratione pro nobis .i. *gigeste-si Dīa linn ara fulsam ar fochidi.*

173. Ml. 21ᵇ7, 8. quae alligare compellor .i. *con-da-rīas* .i. *noch is no-n-da ges ōn.*

174. Wb. 30ᵇ4. haec commone, testificans coram Deo .i. *a nno ngeiss cách imma chomalnad.*

175. Ml. 53ᵇ27. utilitatem exortationis inculcat .i. *foilsigidir són* ⁊ *do-adbat nertad coitchen do chách* .i. *ara ngé cách Dīa . . .* ⁊ *ro-n-d-cechladar.*

176. Ml. 39ᵇ3. incipit supplicare, gl. *n̈ges.*

177. Wb. 4ᵃ27. *is and didiu for-téit* spiritus *ar n-énirti-ni, in tain bes n-inunn*² *accobor lenn* .i. *la corp* et *anim* et *la spirut. coir irnigde trā in so, acht* 3 *ní chumcam-ni ón, mani thinib in spirut. is samlid* 4 *trā is lobur ar n-irnigde-ni, mat réte frecndirci gesme,* et *nī-n fortéit-ni in spirut oc suidiu. is hed didiu for-théit in spirut, in tain guidme-ni inducbáil diar corp* et *diar n-animm iar n-esséirgiu.*

¹ *daráchen* MS.   ² *ninun* MS.   ³ *act* MS.   ⁴ *isamlid* MS.

178. Wb. 11ª24. neque tentemus Christum sicut quidam
eorum .i. *nī gessam-ni nii bes chotarsne diar n-icc.*

179. Wb. 17ᵈ27. *anī trā as chotarsne fri hicc nī ētar cia gessir.*

180. Ml. 23ᵈ23. non quod aliquo ⟨loco⟩ loci superioris
erectio faciat altiorem .i. *cia théis hi* ¹ *loc bes ardu, ni ardu de.
ni samlid són dūn-ni, air immi* ² *ardu-ni de tri dul isna lucu arda.*

181. Ml. 126ª4. ne molestius quies segnia ⟨.i. maria⟩ uadet
.i. *arnā té* .i. *féith forsna muire.*

182. Wb. 13ª12. quod si alii reuelatum fuerit sedenti, prior
taceat .i. *ma beid ní di rúnaib do-théi ar menmuin ind fir biis inna
suidiu.*

183. Sg. 26ᵇ7. igitur non aliter possunt a se discerni partes
orationis, gl. *de dliguth trā inna n-iltoimdden sin is de gaibthi*
igitur ; quasi dixisset : ' *ní fail ní nád tai mo dligeth-sa fair i
ndegaid na comroircnech.'*

184. Wb. 15ᶜ23. et ideo contendimus . . . placere illi .i.
hōre ıs cuci rigmi, is ferr dún placere illi.

185. Ml. 118ᵇ6. non simpliciter ' panem ' dixit sed ' panem
meum ' .i. *air mad* panem *nammā du-berad· som* ⁊ *ní taibred*
meum, *robad dund sāsad diant ainm* panis tantum *no regad.*

186. Ml. 117ᵈ3. non contristabar ab secessu eorum, gl. *cia
nu tīastais hūaim ón.*

187. Wb. 29ª28. quorundam hominum (.i. ordinandorum)
peccata manifesta sunt, praecedentia ad iudicium ; quosdam
autem et subsequuntur, gl. *biit al-aili and ro-finnatar a pecthe
resiu* ³ *do-coi grād forru ; al-aili is iarum ro-finnatar : berir dano
fri laa brátha.*

188. Wb. 9ᵈ24. ne tentet uos Satanas propter incontinentiam
uestram .i. *arnā dich cách assa dligud i n-adaltras tri lāthar
demuin.*

---

¹ *thes hí* MS.   ² *airmı* MS.   ³ *rosiu* MS.

189. Ml. 89ᶜ11. *mani ro má*[1] *fora cenn, ní mema forsna bullu.*

190. Ml. 35ᵃ17. de quibus adderet id quod sequitur ? .i. *air cia dunaibhī do-foirmsed?*

191. Ml. 31ᶜ14. exsurgente me, gl. ' *a n-atamm-res-sa²,*' *ol Dīa.*

192. Ml. 67ᶜ5. uindicabit .i. *du-fí* .i. *du-ēma són.*

193. Ml 27ᶜ4. etiamsi tempus pati illos aduersa permittat, non tamen in longum eius ultio protrahetur .i. *connā tīssed etir in dīgal; nība samlid in sin, acht du-fiastar tra cenn-som.*

194. Ml. 32ᶜ20. sed rogat ut sine furore . . . uindicetur .i. *co du-fessar.*

195. Wb. 20ᶜ11. in omnibus bonis .i. *i cach réit ro-hí a less.*

196. Sg. 209ᵇ13. quod nunquam potest hoc pronomen inueniri ... ut non intellegantur actus .i. *iss ed in so nád chumaing ara-n-ísar and coní enggnatar gníma, acht3 asa-gnintar.*

197. Ml. 77ᵃ10. ne occideris, gl. *in n-iírr?*

198. Ml. 15ᵃ10. pestilentiae proprium est . . . inficere multorum corpora, gl. *fris-n-orr.*

199. Wb. 19ᵈ24. oculos uestros . . . dedissetis mihi .i. *cia chon-desin far súli, do-sṁ-bérthe dom.*

200. Ml. 51ᵃ18. in tempore opportuno gl. *in tan imme-romastar són nach noīb, ara cuintea dīlgud Dē isind aimsir sin.*

201. Ml. 73ᵈ1. subportassem .i. *fu-lilsain-se.*

202. Wb. 15ᵃ20. ita ut non possent intendere filii Israhel in faciem Moysi .i. *nī foílsitis4 déicsin a gnúsa.*

203. Ml. 32ᵈ2. ne commotius in se quam modus patitur . . . uindicetur .i. *acht amal fu-n-d-ló.*

204. Ml. 57ᵈ15. ultra mensuram calamitatis .i. *connāch ful.*

. ·. Ml. 59ᶜ12. uideris .i. *atat-chigestar, a Dǽ.*

---

[1] *roim̰.* ᵀS.   [2] *atammresa* MS.   [3] *act* MS.   [4] *foísitis* MS.

206. Ml 50ᵃ5. hoc tantum ad laquei usurpationem referen-
dum, cuius uis ualebit, si latuerit .i. *mani accastar, is samlid
gaibid ní.*

207. Ml. 111ᶜ13. *Is hé ru-fiastar cumachtae inna díglae do-
m-bir-siu* ¹ *húa londas, intí du-écigi is ar thrócairi ⁊ chensi* ²
du-bir-siu forun-ni síu innahí fo-daimem re techt innúnn.

208. Wb. 12ᶜ38. aut scientia .i. *con festar cách.*

209. Ml. 56ᶜ10. examinans, gl. *a mmiastar.*

210. Ml. 30ᶜ9. omnium facta diiudicat, ut cognitione eius
nihil possit elabi .i. *ní digénam-ni nach ngním forná mmestar-som.*

211. Wb. 26ᵃ8. ita ut in templo Dei sedeat, ostendens se
tamquam sit Deus, gl. *seiss i tempul, amal do-n-essid Críst.*
⅃ *do-géntar aidchumtach tempuil less,* et *pridchibid smachtu*³ *rechto
fetarlicce,* et *gēbtit* Iudei *i n-apaid,* et *con-scéra recht*⁴ *nuiednissi.*

Preterite and Perfect.

212. Ml. 91ᶜ1. *no scrūtain-se. in tan no mbīinn isnaib fochaidib,
dús in retarscar cairde ṅDǽ ⁊ a remcaissiu, ⁊ ní tucus-sa in sin,
in ru etarscar fa naic.*

213. Ml. 59ᵇ2. non quem (finem) statui .i. ' *ní a forcenn
ru suidigsiur-sa* ', ol *Dauīd.*

214. Ml. 91ᵇ12. *trén ⁊ mór in chairdine do-rignis* ⁵ *friu hi
tossuch, ⁊ cota-ascrais* ⁶ *īarum.*

215. Ml. 121ᵃ12. intra terminos tuos .i. *ru sudigser-su doib,
a Dǽ.*

216. Ml. 38ᶜ3. non ergo ab apostolo testimonium hoc usur-
patum est .i. *ní hé apstal cita-rogab in testimin* ⁷ *so.* Aliter :
ní fou d-a-uc int apstal fon chēill fūan-d rogab in fāith.

---

¹ *dombiursiu* MS. ² *trocairi ⁊ censi* MS. ³ *smactu* MS. ⁴ *rect* MS.
⁵ *dorigni* MS. ⁶ *cotascrais* MS. ⁷ *testinin* MS.

217. Ml. 38ᵃ13. non sum frustratione deceptus .i. *nī-m thorgaīth mo frescissiu.*

218. Ml. 46ᶜ7. quibus decreuerit, gl. *donahī dian-d rērchoil intí Dīa.*

219. Ml. 126ᵇ16. *im-folṅgi inducbāil dō in molad ro mmolastar Dīa.*

220. Ml. 67ᵇ24. *inna cenél ¹ fo-rrorbris, fo-s-ro-ammamaigestar dia molad ⁊ dia adrad.*

221. Ml. 124ᵇ3. non patrum commemoratione nititur ad-tenuare peccatum, dum se non primum neque solum adserit delinquisse .i. *ní du sēmigud pectha at-ber-som in so* .i. *combad dō f-a-cherred* : ' *ní sní cet-id-deirgni ⁊ nī sní du-d-rigni nammá* ' ; *acht is do chuingid dīlguda do-som, amal du-rolged dia ² aithrib íar n-immarmus.*

222. Lib. Ardm. 77ᵃ1. benedixit, gl. *gabis ailli.*

223. Lib. Ardm. 184ᵇ2. cum ualefecissemus, gl. *lase celebir-simme.*

224. Ml. 24ᵈ24. *ro lēgsat canōin fetarlaici ⁊ nufīadnissi amal ru-n-da lēgsam-ni, acht ro-n-da saībset-som* tantum.

225. Sg. 9ᵃ22. in Latinis tamen dictionibus nos quoque pro *ph* coepimus *f* scribere, gl. *cia for-comam-ni rīagoil sen-Grēc hi scríbunt in dā caractar isnaib consonaib ucut, ro ċruthaigsemmar camaiph immurgu ōencháractar* (.f. *tar hēsi* .p. *co tinfiuth*) *i n-epertaib Latindaib.*

226. Wb. 26ᵇ6. quae praecipimus, et facitis, .i. *ro comalnisid-si an ro pridchissem-ni dúib.*

227. Ml. 67ᵈ14. *amal ru-n-d gab slīab Siōn andes ⁊ antūaid dun chathraig ³ dia dītin,* sic *ru-n-d gabsat ar ṅdā thoīb du dītin ar n-inmedōnach-ni.*

---

¹ *chenel* MS.   ² om. MS.   ³ *duchath* MS.

228. Ml. 91ᵃ21. *is hé forcan du-rat-som forsna mmórchol
du-rigensat a nāmait fris, díltud remdēicsen Dǽ de-som, hūare
nād tarat dīgail forsnahí du-rigēnsat innahísin fris-sium.*

229. Ml. 77ᵃ15. *is dund¹ imchumurc fil isin chanōin fris-gair
les-som a n-imchomarc n-īsiu* .i. ne occideris ? .i. *in n-iírr-siu²?*
.i. non. .i. *nī-s n-ulemairbfe ci as-id-roilliset.*

230. Wb. 31ᶜ7. subditas suis uiris, ut non blasphemetur
uerbum Dei .i. *arnā érbarthar* : ' *ō chretsit, nī-n tá airli ar mban.*'

231. Ml. 124ᵇ6. sed in separatione Aegyptiorum territi .i.
ad-rāigsetar ⁊ robu frithorcun doib a n-etarscarad fri Ǽgeptacdu
.i. *air ad-rāigsetar no-n-da bértais* iterum in captiuitatem.

232. Wb. 2ᶜ4. quia reputata est Abrachae fides ad iustitiam.
quomodo ergo repututa est ?   .i. *cain ro noíbad Abracham
tri hiris?*

233. Sg. 216ᵃ1. ' mane nouum ', ' sponte sua ' .i. *anmman
do-rónta de dobrīathraib.*

234. Wb. 33ᵃ15, 33ᵇ8. uidete, fratres, ne forte sit in aliquo
uestrum cor malum incredulitatis, gl. *fomnid-si, a phopul
nuīednissi, ar ce du-d-rónath ní di maith fri Maccu Israhēl, nī
derlaichtha³ a pecdæ doib, acht du-ratad dígal forru. cenotad
maic-si raith dano, ma im-roimsid, nī dílgibther dūib.*

235. Wb. 18ᵃ10. uos non grauaui .i. *ní tormult far mbíad ł
for n-étach.*

236. Wb. 6ᵈ14. propter gratiam .i. docendi ł praedicandi *ar
is dō ar-roiēit-sa* gratiam *do precept do chách.*

237. Ml. 74ᶜ20. quoniam . . . aduersa nostra secundum tuam
promissionem constant impleta, iustum est iam ut et inimici
nostri subeant ultionem .i. *hūare ro comallada inna imneda ⁊
fo-ruirmed cenn forsnaib cotarsnaib du-rairngirt-su, is fíriēn trā
fūa n-indas sin tabart dīglae foraib-som.*

¹ *dúnn* MS.   ² *inínírrsiu* MS.   ³ *derlaichta* MS.

238. Ml. 56ᵃ18. in ipso lumine .i. *ind roisc du-n-ēcomnacht-su dún, a Dǽ.*

239. Sg. 220ᵃ10. si dicam ' coram Cicerone dixit Catilina '
. . . transitionem . . . facio diuersarum personarum, gl. *atá tairmthechtas persan* híc .i. *is sain indí as-id-rubart ꝯ indí frisa n-érbrath.*

240. Ml. 23ᵇ10. cum enim a Chussi Achitophel fuisset sententia dissoluta, reuersus Achitophel . . . dolorem repudiati consilii sui suspendio publicauit, gl. *hō goistiu* .i. *do-bert goiste imma brāgait fadesin, conid marb, hūare nād ndigni Abisolón a chomairli.*

241. Ml. 144ᵈ3. *nach torbatu coitchenn ro boí indib fri dēnum n-uilc, at-rubalt* ¹ *tar hēsi á pectha.*

242. Ml. 132ᵃ10. aduersa dicta regis te semper orando .i. *ci ar-id-rogart-side* ² *dím-sa do guidi-siu, a Dǽ.*

243. Ml. 49ᶜ9. dissimulauit id quod 'a me peccatum fuerat .i. *con-aicelt ꝯ do-rolaig in peccad ꝯ nī n-ārraim ar chairi dō.*

244. Ml. 59ᶜ3. indulgentiam desiderat, non potentiam .i. *is ed con-aitecht* tantum *dílgud a pecthae ṅdō hō Dīa, ꝯ ní comtacht cumachtae ṅdiglae fora náimtea.*

245. Wb. 13ᵇ12. *masu glé lib trā in precept ro pridchus sa* .i. *as-réracht Críst hó marbaib, cid dia léicid cundubairt for drēcht úaib* de resurrectione hominum ?

246. Ml. 40ᵇ8. sub enumeratione periculorum suorum defensionis diuinae totius loci ipsius contextus amfaticus canitur, ut tali schemate uel potentia diuini adiutorii uel dignitas augeatur .i. *cach la céin aisndís dia thrōgai, in céin n-aili aisndís dind fortacht du-rat Dīa dō ꝯ indas du-n-d-rēι.*

247. Ml. 94ᵇ7. *amal as messe du-da-forsat inna dūli, is mē dano bǣras mes fírián foraib.*

---

¹ *átrubalt* MS.   ² *aridrogatside* MS.

248. Ml. 120ᶜ7. diuersorum elementorum causas effectusque denumerans .i. *cid torbae ara torsata ⁊ cia gním du-gniat inna dūli.*

249. Sg. 55ᵇ5. inueniuntur tamen etiam propria differentiae causa in finem circumflexa, gl. *ar ní ar accuis dechoir aní as-rubartmmar cose.*

250. Wb. 18ᶜ6. miror quod sic tam cito transferimini . . . in aliud euangelium .i. *is machthad limm a threte do-rérachtid mdam fírinne* et *soscéli* .i. *is sūaignid ¹ nírubtar gaítha for comairli; is dian do-rrērachtid² maâm ind soscéli.*

251. Ml. 20ᵇ2. iterum propter susceptae adsertionis causam sanctum se appellare non timuit .i. *is airi d-a-rogart-som noīb ar frithtuidecht ³ innaní as-rubartatar nād robae remdēicsiu nā lāthar nDǽ dia dūlib.*

252. Wb. 5ᵇ11. numquid sic offenderunt ut caderent ? .i. *cair, in sí a mēit fris-comartatar con dodsitis⁴ huili* a fide Christi ?

253. Ml. 44ᶜ17. consecratus sum .i. *atam-roipred.*

254. Wb. 33ᵇ3. sed non profuit illis sermo auditus .i. *nī-s rabœ a ndu-rairngred ⁵ doib.*

255. Ml. 32ᶜ15. nos, quibus pro uenia accepta nullus sponsor accessit .i. *amal as-robrad fri Dauīd do-rolgida a pecthi dō, ní eperr immurgu frin-ni, in tain du-luigter dūn ar pecthi.*

256. Ml. 127ᵈ6. quid Deus Abrachae in procinctu belli dixerit .i. *in tan ro mmemaid re n-Abracham forsna cōic rīga bertar Loth a Sodaim.*

257. Ml. 54ᵈ7. numquam a me promouit oratio mea, adhaesit mihi .i. *ro lil⁶ dím m'ernigde ⁊ nī dechuid hūaim.*

258. Ml. 96ᶜ13. turbati sunt Aegyptiorum currus, rotae axibus adhaeserunt .i. *ro leldar dīb són, connāch-a glūaistis in charbait.*

---

¹ *ısuaıgnid* MS.   ² *dorreractid* MS.   ³ *frithuidecht* MS.   ⁴ *dositis* MS.
⁵ *nduraingred* MS.   ⁶ *lin* MS.

259. Wb. 4ᵈ8. praedixit Essaias .i. *tairchechuin resiu for-cuimsed.*

260. Ml. 17ᵈ1. institui .i. *for-roīchan-sa.*

261. Ml. 22ᶜ3. ualde nos decretui auxilio commonuisti, gl. *dond érchoīliud* .i. *for-tan-roīchan-ni hō fortacht dund ērchoīliud as-rochoīlsem.*

262. Ml. 64ᵃ13. tamquam simile, non tamquam proprium .i. *ní fris ru chét·a* propheta.

263. Wb. 20ᵃ4. qui sub lege uultis esse .i. *masu ed do-roīgaid.*

264. Ml. 124ᶜ13. ac si diceret : in hoc ministerium . . . delectum, gl. *do-rogad.*

265. Ml. 47ᵃ8. quoniam misericordia tua ante meos oculos est. .i. *is airi fris-racacha-sa,* quoniam misericordia, reliqua.

266. Ml. 44ᶜ9. haec irrisio aemulorum testimonium est sancto Dauid omnibus eum retro temporibus spem suam in Deo repositam habuisse, gl. *inna n-ascad* .i. *inna nāmat són, as-berat bid cobuir dō in Dīa dia*[1] *forgēni ⁊ hi ru frescachae. hiróin són immurgu.*

267. Wb. 12ᶜ13. nunc cognosco ex parte .i. *is rann*[2] *din deacht ad-gén-sa* ɫ *is rann*[3] *indium-sa ad-géuin in deacht* .i. anima tantum *ad-id-géuin.*

268. Wb. 32ᵈ10. nusquam enim angelos apprehendit, sed semen Abrachae apprehendit .i. *is ūaidib ar-roít colinn* et *it hé do-rraidchíuir.*

269. Ml. 125ᵇ9. a redemptis et per hoc obnoxiis .i. opus redemptionis .i. *is follus romtar bibdaid-som isindí do-rathchratha.*

270. Ml. 50ᵈ7. ideo ergo audisti quia desperatissime conflictabar in eo .i. *hūare is hi foscud menman ru rādus-sa inna brīathra as-ruburt, is airi in sin ro-cūala-su guth m'ernaigde-se.*

271. Ml. 53ᵇ26. *as-rubart-som ro ngāid Dīa ⁊ ro-n-d-cūalae.*

---

[1] om. MS.   [2] *rán* MS.   [3] *ran* MS.

272. Wb. 18ᵈ3. eram autem ignotus facie ecclesiis Iudaeae
.i. *immu-n-cūalammar, nīmu-n-accamar.*

273. Wb. 22ᵃ23. si tamen illum audistis .i. *sech r-a-cūalid*
a me.

274. Wb. 25ᵈ14. in flamma ignis dantis uindıctam iis qui
non nouerunt Deum, et qui non oboediunt euangelio Domini
nostri Iesu Christi .i. *do-sn-aidlibea uili; nī ain nechtar n-aíi,
indí nāch-id chūalatar* et *tremi-tíagat.*

275. Wb. 23ᶜ11. *is hed in so sís ro-chlos* et *ad-chess inna
bésaib* et *a gnímaib.*

276. Sg. 144ᵇ3. *feib fo-n-d-úair-som la auctoru, is samlid
d-a-árbuid.*

277. Ml. 65ᵈ16. non ergo uilescat . . . ob contumeliam
passionis .i. *air ní tárbas a chumachtae hi suidiu nach mór.*

278. Sg. 32ᵇ6. Acrisioneis Danae fundasse colonis .i. *hūanaib*[1]
*aitrebthidib Acrisiōndaib. a mmuntar-sidi ad-rothreb-si lee, it
hē con-rótgatar in cathraig.*

279. Ml. 48ᵈ27. psalmus laudis renouationis domus Dauid
.i. *combad de no gabthe*[2] *in salm so di chossecrad inna cathrach
con-rōtacht la Dauīd hi Siόn fri Ebustu* .i. *íarna n-indarbu á
Hirusalem, arnāch-a toirsitis aithirriuch.*

280. Wb. 33ᵈ10. Abrachae namque promittens Deus, quoniam neminem habuit per quem iuraret maiorem, iurauit per
semet ipsum, gl. *in tan du-rairngert Dīa du Abracham a maith
sin, du-cuitig tarais fadeissin, ar nī robe nech bad hūaisliu, tara
tōissed.*

281. Wb. 27ᵈ19. sicut rogaui te ut remaneres Ephesi .i.
precor multifarie sicut rogaui .i. *is lērithir in so no nguidim-se
Dīa n-erut-su, amal ro-t gád-sa im anad i n-Ephis, sech ropo
léir són.*

---

[1] *hunaib* MS.   [2] *gagthe* MS.

282. Sg. 29ᵃ8. alia incorporalia in appellatiuis, ut ' uirtus ' dea et ' pudicitia ' Penelope .i. *do-rochair i ndílsi dī, conid ainm dī* pudicitia.

283. Tur. 131. hic adest Eliseus cum ligno ad quaerendam securem .i. *do-cer in biāil dia samthig issa mmuir, ⁊ fo-caird* Eliseus *a samthig inna diad, ⁊ do-luid in biāil arithissi ar chenn inna samthige, co mboí impe.*

284. Ml. 123ᵇ10. neque . . . perimendo .i. *ní lasse etir-rudib.*

285. Wb. 30ᵈ11. ego enim iam delibor, gl. Pelagius : mortem suam sacrificium Deo futurum dixit.i.*tánicc aimser mo idbarte-se.*

286. 18ᵈ9. *is Tīamthe imme-ruidbed* et *nī ro imdibed Tit.*

287. Ml. 123ᵈ4. omnium dictorum finem ad principia reuocauit .i. *aní ad-chuaid hi tosuch int sailm, is ed ad-fēt* iterum híc.

288. Wb. 24ᶜ17. ipsi enim de uobis adnuntiant qualem introitum habuerimus ad uos .i. *is cucci a lére ro pridchissid ¹ doib-som, co n-éicdid doib cruth ro pridchissem* et *do-n-dechommar cucuib-si i tossogod.*

289. Wb. 18ᵈ6. post annos xiiii iterum ascendi Hierosolymam cum Barnaba, adsumpto et Tito .i. *de Iudéib do Barnaip, di geintib do Thit. ro-fitir in dias sin nī do lēgund and do-coad-sa.*

290. Sg. 199ᵇ1. sed etiam cum ipsa agit et sic alia in ipsam, id est cum retransit quae dicitur .i. *gním do neuch for-rochongart, cēsad do neuch for-rorcongrad; gním iarum dondí do-dechuid, cēs.ˑd dondí cosa tuidches.*

291. Ml. 58ᶜ4. ut Semei, qui, ut lapides in eum, ita etiam mala dicta iaculatus est .i. *dia luid Dauīd for longais tri glenn Iosofád, d-a-mbidc Semei di chlochaib oca thecht,² ⁊ do-bert maldachta foir dano di mulluch int slēbe.*

292. Ml. 127ᵈ3. Abrachae serui .i. *mug luide hūa Abracham do thochmurc Rebicae do Isác.*

---

¹ *pridchissi* MS.　　　² *techt* MS.

293. Ml. 130ᵈ4. mente ac ratione cum ita excedissem ut supra humana me attollerem .i. *as-ringbus* .i. *toimtin armbenn duine, acht du-rumēnar romsa dīa.*

294. Wb. 26ᵇ21. *con-ammadar-sa a ndígail forru.*

295. Wb. 4ᵇ22. aestimati sumus .i. *ro-n mess-ni.*

296. Acr. 7ᵃ1. quos esse posse necessarios iam dedisti .i. *it hē-sidi ad-rodamar-su.*

297. Ml. 105ᵇ9. metu similia . . . patiendi .i. *amal fo-n-d-rodamnatar riam.*

298. Wb. 14ᶜ40. quod parcens uobis non ueni ultra Corinthum .i. *is ar airchissecht dúib-si nī dechud-sa cucuib* statim *do thabirt dígle* et *do aidbiur foirib, sech cot-āneccar-sa són.*

299. Wb. 8ᵃ14. *aní nād comnactar doíni tria n-ecne, cot-ánic-som tria chroich.*

300. Sg. 31ᵃ6. ' Euripides ', non Euripi filius, sed ab Euripo sic nominatus est .i. *di airisin do-ratad foir a n-ainm sin, ar iss ed laithe in sin ro ngénair-som, ní airindī ro ṅgenad-som isind luc sin.*

301. Ml. 90ᵇ12. regina Austri, quae beatos appellat regi sapientissimo seruientes .i. ' *mad-gēnatar á thimthirthidi* ', ol *sī.*

302. Wb. 17ᵈ17. si gloriari oportet, non expedit quidem mihi .i. *ci ad-cobrinn moídim do dénum, nī boí adbar* hic.

Participle Passive.

303. Ml. 47ᵃ5. adhibita examinatione, gl. *a n-as tedbarthe in mes.*

304. Sg. 208ᵇ13. egomet ipse, gl. ego *a n-as tórmachte* ipse ɫ met *fris.*

305. Ml. 83ᵇ4. inimicis attritis .i. *a n-ata tūartai.*

306. Ml. 45ᵈ6. nulla . . . formidine perculsus, gl. *annárobsa bíthe.*

307. Ml. 18ᶜ14. inuaso imperio .i. *a mba n-indrisse.*

308. Sg. 6ᵃ13. nulla alia causa . . . inducti, gl. *anámtar tuidchissi-sidi¹ ó nach fochunn² ailiu.*

309. Bcr. 32ᵇ5. cantato ipso mense .i. *a mbas cēte* .i. *acht as-robarthar in mí.*

Verbal of Necessity.

310. Ml. 62ᶜ5. *du-árbaid³ Dīa in déni as comallaidi a forgaire* .i. *in déni as mbuidigthi dō ind fortacht imme-trēnaigedar ⁊ du-m-beir.*

311. Wb. 1ᶜ12. scimus enim quoniam iudicium Dei est secundum ueritatem .i. *níbo chomitesti⁴ dó, acht ba léicthi* iudici iusto.

312. Ml. 82ᵃ7. *ní dēnti dūib-si anīsin, air atā nech dubar ńdēicsin* .i. *Dīa.*

313. Ml. 23ᶜ16. ea quae merito prima sunt in relationis ordine secunda ponuntur .i. *innahí batar buthi ar thuus, du-s-rale fo diad.*

314. Ml. 107ᵈ8. *is ed á eret is gessi Dīa, cēne mbether* in hac uita.

315. Ml. 22ᵃ4. *in loc diambu thabarthi ermitiu fēid ⁊ imbu choir frecur céil Dǽ, at-léntais-som⁵ adi ⁊ do-gnītis cech ndochrud and.*

Variations in Prepositions.

ess-

316. Sg. 148ᵇ7. itaque omnis modus finitus potest per hunc modum interpretari .i. *is tríit as-toascther intsliucht cach muid.*

317. Ml. 24ᵈ9. ideo superscriptum esse illum (psalmum) ' pro torcularibus ', gl. *arnaib damdabchaib* .i. *hūare is sí aimser sin i ndēntae estōsc inna fīne i ndamdabchaib.*

---

¹ *duidchisidi* MS. ² *fochun* MS. ³ *duairbaid* MS.
⁴ *comitesti* MS. ⁵ *atléntaisom* MS.

318. Ml. 96ᵃ4. et uentilabam in mente spiritum meum .i.
fu-sscannainn .i. *as-gleinninn*.¹

319. Ml. 120ᵈ2. amal *du-n-eclannar* ² ētach ṅderscaigthe hi tig
cennaigi do buith immin ríg, is samlaid du-érglas ind soilse
sainriud asnaib dūlib do imthimchiull in Choimded.

320. Wb. 10ᵈ5. an et lex haec non dicit ? *cani epir? náte !*
at-beir.

321. Wb. 20ᵃ10. Ego Paulus dico uobis .i. *nī nach aile*
ass-id-beir.

322. Ml. 14ᵈ13. in praesenti (psalmo) tamen uidetur facere
distinctionem .i. *conid sain inthí dia n-aiperr* impius et peccator
hic.

323. Sg. 197ᵇ16. is est qui uicit Turnum .i. *intí ad-rubartmar.*

ad-

324. Ml. 27ᵇ15. aliqua quae motum eius desiderant .i.
inna ancride inna fochaide do-bertar forsin n-aís noīb, ad-
cobrat-sidi cumscugud fercæ Dé do thabairt díglae tara n-ési.

325. Wb. 6ᵃ10. uis ? .i. *in accobri?*

326. Wb. 10ᵇ8. ita oportet fieri .i. *amal as-in-chobra ind*
ingen.

327. Wb. 31ᶜ23. omnem mansuetudinem ostendentes ad
omnes homines, gl. *ci at-roillet cini ārillet.*

328. Ml. 61ᵇ17. Congregauerunt iniquitatem sibi. optimi de
se meriti obtarent interitum .i. *du-árchomraicset cloīni ndoib*
fesin ; meriti .i. *ind áirilti* .i. *indí ass-id-roilisset ;* optimi .i.
*ind foircimim*³ *;* de se *díb ;* .i. *indí ad-id-roillisset co mmór in*
*cloīni n-ísin du tháirciud*⁴ *doib ;* optarent .i. *indí assa-gūiset,*
amal bid qui optarent *no beth dnd* .i. *du-áirci cloīni ṅdó fadesin*
intī asa-gūsi etarthothaim á charat.

---

¹ *asgleinn* MS.   ² *duneclan* MS.   ³ *foircimi* (?) MS.   ⁴ *tairciud* MS.

329. Ml. 2ᵇ4. xxxii (psalmi) non sunt suprascripti .i. *ní feil titlu remib ci as-id-chiam-ni*[1] *titlu re cech oīnsalm.*

330. Ml. 93ᵈ14. *is ed as-berat-som, is gāu dún-ni innahī ad-fīadam*[2] *di Chrīsst, hūare nād n-acat hi frecndairc gnimu cosmaili du dēnum du Chrīst indas as-n-da-fīadam-ni du-ṅ-da-rigni.*

331. Wb. 15ᵈ20. eum qui non nouerat peccatum, pro nobis peccatum fecit .i. *idbart, ar ba ainm leu-som* peccatum *dund idbairt ad-oparthe dar cenn* peccati. *dar cenn* peccati *didiu síl Ādim ad-ropred-som, combo uisse ci as-berthe* peccatum *dī.*

332. Ml. 66ᵇ4. datorem diligit Deus .i. *ad-idn-opair fessin du Dīa co ndegnīmaib.*

aith-

333. Wb. 22ᶜ2. omne enim quod manifestatur, lumen est .i. *intí ad-eirrig tre precept dō, is preceptóir-side iar n-aithirgi.*

334. Wb. 9ᵃ23. *aithirgid bésu.*

air-

335. Wb. 4ᶜ19, 20. igitur non uolentis neque currentis sed miserentis est Dei .i. *ar-cessi do neoch bes meldach less* [in marg.] .i. *nī torbe do neuch a n-accobor, mani thobrea Dīa dō a n-accobor;* similiter ' neque currentis '; *intí dia n-airchissi Dīa, is dō is torbe.*

336. Ml. 17ᶜ7. *is ed as-berat*[3] *ind heretic as laigiu deacht Maicc in-daas deacht Athar, air is hō Athir ar-roét Macc cumachtae. is laigiu didiu intí ara-foīm indaas intí hō n-eroīmer.*

337. Wb. 10ᶜ1. nondum cognouit quemadmodum oporteat eum scire .i. *is samlid*[3] *ba coir dō fiuss inna n-idol, ac[h]t ní arbarat biuth inna túari ad-opartar dond idol.*

---

[1] *ciasidciamni* MS.   [2] *adfidam* MS.   [3] *berat* MS.   [4] *isamlid* MS.

338. Ml. 136ᵃ8. *in moltai do-ngniin-se tri bindius* ⁊ *chlais, ara-ruichīuir mo guth occaib.*

339. Ml. 57ᵃ10. uice fumi omnis eorum elatio euanescit et deperit, gl. *amal ar-in-d-chrin dǽ* ⁊ *as-in-d-bail.*

com-

340. Wb. 29ᵈ29. certus sum quia potens est depositum meum seruare in illum diem .i. *rodbo Dīa ad-roni* et *con-oí a rrad file and-som* ɫ *is hésom ad-roni do Dīa in fochricc file dō i nnim,* et *is Dīa cota-óei-ade trea gnímo-som.*

341. Wb. 27ᵃ3. sicut ergo accepistis Iesum Christum, in ipso ambulate, gl. *amal ro pridchad dúib, comid.*

342. Ml. 59ᶜ10. tuae (.i. plagae) etenim sunt per patientiam .i. *hūare con-da-airleci són.*

343. Ml. 56ᵈ6. destituet .i. *sech is con-scēra Dīa són.*

344. Wb. 2ᵇ20. destruimus?   .i. *in coscram-ni?*

345. Wb. 14ᶜ11. *con-degar lóg ar sodin* et *indocbál.*

346. Wb. 14ᶜ12. *ro-fitis mo bésgne-se frib* .i. *nád cuintgim lóg ar mo precept.*

347. Sg. 65ᵇ9. in multis enim uidemus commutatione terminationis genera quoque esse conuersa, gl. *con-osciget chenēl, ma chon-osciget tairmorcenn.*

348. Sg. 65ᵇ8. eadem seruant . . . genera . . . si eandam seruant terminationem, gl. *mani cumsciget tairmorcenn, nī cumsciget cenēl.*

dí-

349. Sg. 40ᵃ17. non tamen ad totum genus fieri comparationem, gl. *ní derscaigi dind huiliu chenēul, ıs di hilib immurgu a chenīuil feissin di-rōscai ca-lléic.*

350. Ml. 84ᵇ1. niue dealbabuntur .i. subaudi ' ipsi regis '
.i. *du-rōscibet-sidi hūa etrachtai cumachtai sech cech rīga.*

351. Wb. 9ᵈ2. is bésad inna *flatho, do-em* et *do-fich.*

352. Ml. 24ᵇ17. qui quamuis per patientiam peccata dissimu-
let .i. *ní-s ndíg fo chétóir* ¹.

353. Sg. 221ᵇ1. ' e ' in compositione uel priuatiuum est,
ut ' eneruus ', gl. *do-opir sēns in dīuit.*

354. Sg. 28ᵇ21. priuatam substantiam, gl. *díuparthe.*

355. Sg. 12ᵃ3. ut . . . ' χορεία chorea ' e paenultima modo
producta modo correpta .i. *in tan do-fūarat ind* .e. *timmorte
iar foxul* .i. *as.*

356. Ml. 56ᵈ2. ita delebitur ut memoriae eius nulla signa
remanere uideas .i. *nícon diūair ni do foraithmiut etir.*

to-

357. Sg. 191ᵃ2. diuellimur inde | Iphitus et Pelias mecum
.i. *do-cuirethar cétna persan sin persana aili chucae.*

358. Ml. 22ᶜ1. Domine, ut scuto bonae uoluntatis tuae
coronasti nos, gl. *trop trā du-n-adbat-som isindísiu* .i. *intamail
in so fri nech tarsa tochuirther scīath, airnāch rī olc.*

359. Sg. 6ᵃ5. sed hoc potestatem literae mutare non debuit,
gl. *nī cumscaichthi cumachtae n-airi, ce do-inscanna-sí ó guttai.*

360. Tur. 49. *amal for-cantar cathchomnidi hō sacardd hi
tosuch* ² ⁊ *mbaithsetar* ⊓ *amal n-oingter īarum hō epscop,* síc
dano in-tindarscan Iohain forcital inna ndoīne ⊓ *a mbaithsed
hi tosuch* ⊓ *ro oingthea īarum hō Chrīst.*

361. Sg. 71ᵇ6. aduerbium uero, quamuis saepe demonstret
numerum .i. *do-fōirṅde árim fo chosmailius do-fóirndet* nomina
numeri.

¹ *cetoir* MS.   ² *tosch* MS.

362. Sg. 25ᵇ12. monosyllabae dictiones quodammodo esse
et syllabae .i. *ūalailiu mud fri sillaba nád tóirndet folad.*

363. Wb. 1ᵇ5. hic ut ministerii sui apud Deum habeat
fructum .i. *ar do-fórmaich fochricc dosom sochude do chreittim* [1]
tria precept.

364. Ml. 105ᵈ4. adde ad augmentum benignitatis tuae ut
ab errore nos conuertas .i. *tórmaig la cach maith du-bir dún-ni
ar nglanad hūa duálchib ⁊ chomroircnib.*

365. Wb. 4ᶜ7. sed in Isaac uocabitur tibi semen .i. *is hō
Isaác do-fuisémthar a síl n-airegde,* non *i n-Ismaíl.*

366. Ml. 74ª11. nec ad mediam, qua uiuere poterant compositione corporis, aetatem . . . peruenient .i. *a n-aīs*[2] *ru delbad
doib oc tuistin a coirp, nī roisset á leth-adi.*

fo-

367. Bcr. 18ᵇ. deponunt .i. *fo-ácbat.*

368. Lib. Ardm. 17ª2. *fácab Pātricc a daltæ n-and.*

369. Wb. 2ª17. non est intelligens .i. *buith cen æccne fo fora
ainfirinni.*

370. Wb. 27ᵈ24. quaestiones praestant magis quam aedifi-
cationem Dei .i. *nī foíret cumtach n-irisse.*

371. Wb. 16ᵈ7. *is ind almsan ara-fócair anúas, acht* [3] *is for
oís tūaithe ar-fócarar; ar chuit ind oíssa gráid* et *ind aísa foirbthi
ní écen a irócre.*

frith-

372. Wb. 10ᶜ12. in Christo peccatis .i. *is amal bid fri Crīst
fris-orthe.*

373. Ml. 114ª9. *nā frithorcaid don popul.*[4]

---

[1] *creittim* MS.   [2] *áanais* MS.   [3] *act* MS.   [4] *pul* MS.

374. Ml. 33ᵃ1. donec tu auertis faciem tuam a me, gl. *cēine no soīfe-siu* .i. *is ed a erat frittam-iurat inna huli remi-ǣrbart-mar cēine no soīfe-siu* ¹ *húaim.*

375. Ml. 39ᵃ20. laedentibus, gl. *donaibhí friss-idn-oirctis.*

imb-, imm-

376. Wb. 5ᵃ5. quam speciosi pedes euangelizantium pacem .i. *is hécen sainēcoscc leo-som for accrannaib innaní predchite*² pacem et *imme-churetar cōri hō rígaib, ara n-epert[h]ar is do immarchor chóre do-tíagat ind fir so.*

377. Sg. 59ᵃ13. ' uitabundus ' similis uitanti, gl. *ní fírimm-gabāil; is cosmailius*³ *indí imma-imgaib.*

íar-, íarm-

378. Ml. 70ᶜ6. it hé in so inna edbarta *íarmi·foig-som.*

379. Wb. 2ᵃ18. non est intelligens, non est requirens Deum i. *hūaire nād ríarfacht*⁴, *fu-ruar buid cen engne* et *cen fírinni.*

ind-

380. Wb. 9ᵃ15. Timotheum, qui est filius meus carissimus .i. *in-samlathar-side mo bésu-sa.*

381. Wb. 5ᵃ13. ego in aemulationem uos adducam, gl. *do intamil* .i. *ata-samlibid-si i n-airitiu* ⁵ *hirisse.*

oc-

382. Ml. 54ᵃ12. *ní aisndet Dauīd airmdis hé* iusti *indí nād ocmanatar hō thrōgaib,* acht it hé iusti les, *indí ocu-bendar hō thrōgaib inna n-ingramman ⁊ inna fochaide.*

rem-

383. Sg. ɩ97ᵇ5. quod facit in genere primae et secundae personae . . . praesentia utriusque, gl. *derbaid cenél dano i suidib aní remi· ta-tét.*

---

¹ *soisu* MS. ² *prechite* MS. ³ *cosmail* MS. ⁴ *riarfact* MS. ⁵ *áiritiu* MS.

384. Wb. 5ᵃ30. si autem iam non ex operibus alioquin gratia .i. *massu rath-som, ní remdechutar gníma.*

sech-

385. Sg. 196ᵇ2. communia . . . deficiunt in participiis, gl. *sechmo-ella coitchen hō rangabáil sechmadachti in tan aram-berar gnīm eissi,* ⁊ *hō rangabáil frecndairc in tain ara-m-berar cēsad essi.*

trem-

386. Ml. 21ᶜ3. indicatur autem laetitia hoc nomine (sc. mane), ob hoc quia cum diei tempus in quo curarum fluctus et sollicitudines experimur, noctis uicissitudo exceperit, relaxatis otio corporibus et obliuione in locum angoris admissa ita mane securi laetique consurgimus, quasi omnis praeterita sollicitudo fuerit cum nocte finita .i. *in tan téte* [1] *a laithe di chiunn cosnaib gnīmaib* ⁊ *cosnaib imnedaib gnīter and, do-tét īarum imthánud* [2] *aidche tara* [3] *hǣsi, co ndermanammar-ni inna imned sin i mbiam isind laithiu tri chumsanad inna aidche do-d-īarmōrat,* ⁊ *is dind fáilti bīs isin matin i ndiad* [4] *inna aidche sin is* nomen mane .i. *hūare as fáilith in menmae isin matin oc ǣrgiu īar foscaigiu inna aithche, trimi-berar dind aimsir matindi* [5] *sin anī as* mane, *co n-eperr dind fáilti bīs indi* .i. mane *fáilid, īarsindí ba* mane *moch riam.*

387. Ml. 21ᵈ4. neque permanebunt iniusti ante oculos tuos .i. *is faittech ro-n-d boī-som nant* neque manebunt *as-rubart, air ataat al-aili* [6] *feidligte hō aimsir, ní tremfeidliget immurgu issa suthin; air is tremfeidligud suthin in-chosig* permaneo, non sic maneo.

[1] *tét* MS.	[2] *imthanu* MS.	[3] *tar* MS.
[4] *dad* MS.	[5] *matíndi* MS.	[6] *alai* MS.

NOTES

[', e.g. **fòrcenna,** denotes the accented syllable.]

Present Indicative. 1-57.

2. **ní.** The 3 sg. of the negative form of the copula is **ní,** which includes both the negative and the copula. In Mid. Ir. a trace of the copula form, which has become fused with the negative, is seen in the **h** which follows when the predicate begins with a vowel.

formut=formut ; see 51.

4. **d-a-gníu.** The infixed pron. anticipates the object : cf. 177, 221, 247, 335.

7. **no guidimm.** In 1 and 2 sg. and 2 pl. of the pres. ind., pres. subj., and fut. of simple verbs, when they are used relatively, the particle **no** is prefixed. With regard to relative usage, it should be noted that when part of a sentence is brought forward emphatically with the copula, the main verb is put in a relative form if the part so brought forward is the subject or the object : cf. 21, 47, 52, 71, etc. ; but not if some other part of the sentence is so brought forward : cf. 4, 15, 18, 22, 24, 37, 40, 141, etc. ; unless it be some word which requires to be followed by relative **-n-** : cf. 25, 250, 281.

8. **no-n-dob molor.** Here **no-** serves to infix the pronouns ; **-n-** is inserted after **hóre ;** **-dob** is the infixed pron. of the 2 pl., Class C. It may be noted that in the first and second persons the specially relative forms of the infixed pronoun are not always used : cf. 21, 147 ; in such a case relative **-n-** is not inserted, even when otherwise it would be required.

10. **am cimbid-se :** for the position of **-se** see Paradigms, p. 25. **no pridchim** (*p=b*), fr. **no n-pridchim,** with relative **-n-** after **hóre.**

11, 12. **níta, no-n-da :** see **Copula** (Paradigms).

13. **no labrither,** fr. no n-labrither.

14. **ara-rethi.** In verbal composition **ara-** appears for **ar-** in relative use. The second **a** is a rel. pron., which also appears after **imm** (**imm-a-** or **imm-e-**) ; after other prepositions it disappears, leaving behind lenition of the following consonant : cf. 41, 49, 71, 107, 111, 336, 376, 377.

forsa mmitter, *on whom thou passest judgement* ; see **midithir.** The relative particle after leniting preps. is **-a n°**, but regularly **-sa n°** after those which originally ended in a consonant. Hence : **ara** 119, 248 ; **hua n-** 98, **hó n-** 336 (from **ó-a n-**) ; **dia n-** (=both **do-a n-** and **di a n-**) 322, 335 ; **frisa** 239 ; **cosa** 290 ; **tarsa** 358 (but **tara** 280 ; cf. **fora** 54). The rel. particle is not used after **i n°** : **i táa** 31 ; **i mbiam** 386. It is also omitted with neg. : **forná** *on which not* 210.

15. **is. hóre** is regularly followed by a relative form of the verb, but in the copula the non-relative form **is** also appears, particularly in periphrasis as here.

na n-aicci=**inna n-aicci.**

20. **ind slōig**=**int ṡlóig,** etymological spelling ; cf. 185, 250, 319.

na ní : see **nach** and **nech.**

téte : see **téit.**

21. **inse**=**anse** ; cf. Early Mod. **innsa, ionnsa** beside **annsa.**

ṅduit. n is the transposed **n** after the neuter **inse.**

22. **eirbthi,** fr. **erbith-i :** with a simple verb, instead of a pronoun infixed by means of **no-,** a suffixed pronoun is sometimes used. See **Suffixed Pronoun** (Paradigms).

nách. The change from the direct **ní** to the dependent **nách** is peculiar. Cf. perhaps Mod. Ir. **agus nách,** *since it is not.*

na nní=**na ní.**

23. **ru maith** (=**maid**) : see **maidid** and **ro.** In subordinate clauses of sentences of a general type the pres. ind. with **ro** has the force of a perfect.

24. **ní táet,** lit. *does not come* (see **do-tét**), i.e. *does not take place.*

as coibnesta (*c=g*), fr. **as n-coibnesta,** with relative n after **húare.** When not followed by **n-, as** lenites a following consonant. **coibnesta** is a later form of **coibnestae.**

25. **itius,** fr. **ithith-us** *he eats it* (fem.) : see **Suffixed Pronoun** (Paradigms). **-foircnea,** fr. **-fòrcenna.**

ad-n-ellat-sidi in fíni, (*by*) *which the latter visit the vine.* For the **-n-** cf. 219.

26. **at-robair,** fr. **ess-d-rò-beir :** see **as-beir** and **ro.** For **at-** (*t=d*) fr. **ess-** with infixed pronouns of Class B see Paradigms p. 26 and note on 316-23. Here **ro-** signifies possibility : **at-robair,** *can say it.*

28. **fíriánigedar.** In the third persons of the pres. ind., pres. subj., and fut. of simple verbs, the relative forms of the deponent and passive are the same as the conjunct. Similarly in 1 pl. of deponent, 40.

29. **-fitir :** see **ro-fitir.**

30. This sentence illustrates well the difference between **atá** and **bíid ; atá,** *is,* asserts existence, **bíid,** *is wont to be,* implies use and wont.

31. **i táa** (*t=d*), *in which is.* The relative is not expressed after the prep. **i n-.** Cf. 14 note.

32. Note that the predicate of the copula is here a prepositional phrase : cf. 288.

33. **ní-n fil.** In O. Ir. **fil** is impersonal ; if the logical subject is a noun, it is expressed by a following accusative ; if a pronoun, by an infixed pronoun. See Paradigms, p. 69.

34. **nípi,** consuetudinal present negative of the copula. The possessive **a** anticipates the following genitive.

36. **atom-aig** ($t=d$), fr. **ad-dom-aig** (Class B) : see **ad-aig** and **Infixed Pronoun** (Paradigms).

37. Note the distinction between the absolute **tíagmi** and the relative **tíagme** : cf. 73, 133, 177, 223.

bás, an extension of the cognate accusative.

40. **and,** *therein,* anticipates the following **isind huiliu.**

41. **a n-** *that,* **ad-chiam** *which we see* ; cf. note on **ararethi,** 14. The non-rel. form is **ad-ciam,** for in absolute construction there is no lenition after a pretonic preposition. But when the stress falls on the first element of compound vbs., lenition follows preps. originally ending in a vowel : **aith-, air-, di-, fo-, imb-, ind-, to-, ro-** ; see 316 ff. ; hence **ar-cessi** : **-airchissi,** etc.

a n- is used as antecedent before a rel. vb. It is not itself a rel. pron., but a demonstrative, identical with the neut. art. nom. and acc. Here it is the subject of the copula **is** ; in 105 it is nom. to **-airigther** and **-fintar** ; cf. 108, 254. In 73 it is acc. after **comalnammar.** After a prep. it requires the particle **-í** (see **intí**), which may also appear in nom. and acc., see 14, 111 (both **a n-** and **aní**), etc. Similarly in the gen. one expects **indí** : **cen chomalnad indí no pridchim,** lit. *without the fulfilment of that which I preach* Wb 11ª15 (**nebchretem a n-ad-íadar** (=**a n-ad-fíadar**) 27ª10 is exceptional). It is sometimes separated from the rel. clause, 119. It is never followed by rel. **n** (2. **n°** (a)); contrast **a n-as-m-beir** *when he says* 119.

In the later language the construction changes : **a n-** is follcwed by dependent forms, conjunct in simple and prototonic in compound vbs. ; **a mbíis** Wb. 24ᵇ17 becomes **a mbí** (now **a mbíonn**) ; **a ndu-gniat** 120 becomes **a ndénat.** This may be due to the analogy (1) of **a fil,** for **fil** is both rel. and dependent, cf. **ní fil** ; (2) of certain deponent and passive forms, e.g. **labrathar, labramar, labratar, berar,**

bertar. etc., where the rel. and conjunct are indistinguishable ;
(3) of comp. vbs. beginning with **to-**+vowel, in which the
prototonic is commonly used for the deuterotonic, and may
be used as rel., **a tuc-side** *what he has brough*[4] Wb. 24^{b}25,
a tairchet *what has been prophesied* 15^{a}34, etc. The analogy
of the nasalizing rel. particle after preps. (**forsa mmitter,**
14 note) may also have played a part.

42. **túailnge,** predicative genitive, lit. *we are of the ability
of our word ;* i.e. *we are able to maintain our word.*

45. **no-n chretid,** fr. **no-n-d chretid,** with loss of infixed
neut. pron. **d** between **n** and **ch** ; cf. 326.

46. **sa** goes with **a n-, étach macc coím** being treated as a
connected phrase.

coíma, for **coím,** is the only instance of such a form of the
masc. attributive adj. in O. Ir. Probably it is an error for **coím.**

47. **inna chomalnad,** *for completing it.*

48. **-fodmat** fr. **-fòdaimet.** For **dó** see note on 112.

51. **filid. f** (and **s**) to express lenited **f** (and **s**) first appear
regularly in Sg. In Wb.[1] and Ml. lenited **f** is either expressed
by **f,** as in 2, or it is left unwritten, as in 170.

52. **ma nu-dub feil** *if ye are* : see **Substantive Verb**
(Paradigms). See also note on 131, Add.

it sib. One would expect **is sib.**

ata. If the predicate is in the first or second person, the
verb of the rel. clause is in the third person. If the predicate
is 1 or 2 pl., then except in the copula, the verb of the rel.
clause is in the 3 sg. : cf. 221, further **combad sissi do-
berad teist dim-sa,** Wb. 18^{a}3.

54. **is béss . . . benir,** lit. *it is a custom . . . it is struck ;* i.e.
it is customary that it is struck. **Is béss** is idiomatically used with
a verb following without any connecting particle : cf. 109, 351.

---

[1] Except perhaps **fir** 33^{c}9.

il-béim, usually translated *many blows.* But **béim** is not likely to be a collective, ar ∴ one would expect the plural **il-béimmen.** Meyer, Contt. 38, connects **ilbéim** with the later **ailbéim** (mod. **oilbhéim**) *stumbling ; lapis offensionis* might be rendered **lie (a)ilbéimme,** and **benir . . . friss** would mean *it is stumbled against.*

intí. The nom. is here used out of construction to bring into prominence the logical subject of the sentence.

at-bail ($t=d$), fr. **ess-d-bail,** with infixed neut. **-d-.** The verb is in origin transitive, and has developed an intransitive force along with the infixed pronoun. The **-d-** is manifest after an infixed relative **-n- :** cf. **as-in-d-bail,** 339.

55. **as n-ísel.** In O. Ir. indirect speech is formally expressed by the relative form of the verb along with relative **-n- :** cf. 66, 140, 163. But the form of direct speech may be kept : cf. 79.

fo-da-raithminedar. Here the compound **for-aith-minedar** is treated as though the first element were **fo + r,** and thus the pron. **da,** 3 sg. f. Class C, is inserted in the prep. **for.** Similarly the particle **ro** in **fo-ro-r-bart** beside **for-rubart,** *has grown,* pf. of **for-beir :** cf. **fo-rrorbris,** fr. **fo-n-ro-r-briss,** 220, and **fo-da-ro-r-cenn** *who has put an end to them* Wb. 11ᵃ27, pf. of **for-cenna.**

56. **con-dan samailter.** In consecutive clauses **co n-** is followed by the indicative. Cf. 288.

57. **tabairt,** for **tabart.** In the verbal noun there is a strong tendency for the form of the dat. and acc. sg. to spread to the nom.

Present Subjunctive. 58-85.

In O. Ir. there are two types of subjunctive : the $\bar{a}$-sub-junctive, e.g. **as-ber, as-berae, as-bera** (like Lat. *feram, feras, ferat*) ; and the *s*-subjunctive, which will be illustrated later. Some verbs have the one and some have the other ; but both forms are not found in the same part of the same verb. Except in the singular of the active, the 1 sg. deponent, and certain passive forms,[1] the forms of the *ā*-subjunctive have for the most part fallen together with those of the indicative, and can be distinguished only syntactically. In a number of verbs, however, the subjunctive stem can be distinguished throughout. Such are :—ind. **bíid, -bí** : subj. **beid, -bé ; gníid** : **gneid ; ad-cí** : 3 sg. impf. ind. **ad-cíd** : past subj. **ad-ced ; -cuirethar** : **-corathar** : **daimid, -daim** : **damaid, -dama ; gaibid, -gaib** : **gabaid, -gaba ; at-bail** : **at-bela ; gainithir, -gainethar** : **genaithir, -genathar ; -moinethar** : **-menathar.** So, further, some verbs which have **n** in the indicative, but not in the subjunctive :—**benaid, -ben** : **-bia, -be ; crenaid, -cren** : **-cria ; ara-chrin** : ***ara-chria ; glenaid, -glen** : **-glia** (pl. 3 rel. **glete**) ; **as-gnin** : **as-gné ; lenaid** : **-*lia ; renaid, -ren** : **-ria ; ro-cluinethar** : **ro-cloathar ; marnaid** : **meraid, -mera.** Such subjunctive stems are further exemplified, 146-57.

58. **ní-m bia,** *there will not be to me, I shall not have.*

59. **ad-cot** (*c*=*g*), fr. **ad-n-cot.** Note that in such periphrasis with the copula, if the copula is in the subjunctive or the imperative, the main verb is in the subjunctive : cf. 71, 77, 100.

60. **árim,** 1 sg. pres. subj of **ad-rími.**

-**tart** : see **do-beir** (Paradigms).

62. **ní ba dímicthe-se lib-si,** *ye should not despise me ,* jussive subjunctive : cf. 64, 75, 77, 178.

63. **ad-n-amraigther, no n-étaigther, ad-cosnae** (*c*=*g*) (fr. **ad-n-cosnae**), **no carae** (*c*=*g*) (fr. **no n-carae**). The relative form of the subjunctive with relative **n** is common

---

[1] e.g. ind. **berair, -berar** : subj. **berthair, -berthar.**

in dependent clauses : cf. 74, 82 (**beta** fr. **beta n-**), 155, 173, 176, 196, 198.

64. **cia thechtid . . . ꝝ nī techtai-siu :** when two parallel conditions are thus combined, the second is put in the indicative.

-ascnae, fr. **-àdcosnae.**

ní charae. In O. Ir., lenition after **ní** always implies an infixed neut. pron. : cf. 177, 335.

isindí as aemulari, lit. *in that which is* aemulari, i.e. *in (the word)* aemulari : cf. 83, 386.

66. **bés as-bera-su,** *perchance thou mayest say.* **as-bera-su** =**as-berae-su.**

67. **nád fil nech con-gné,** *that there is no one to help.*

68. **d-a-rolgea,** fr. **de-a-ro-loga :** see **do-luigi.** Subjunctive of wish.

69. **as-bera.** For the subjunctive in the relative clause, cf. 76, 77, 195, 200, 203.

con rucca=**co rrucca :** see **berid.**

70. **-rubai,** fr. **-rò-bí :** see **ro-.**

71. **acht rop,** *provided it be.*

imme-ráda. imme- is the relative form of **imm- :** see note on 14 and 376.

72. **ar n-acathar,** fr. **ara n-àdcethar :** see **ad-cí,** Paradigms.

arnách corathar ; see **fo-ceird.** In O. Ir. **nách** before a verb always implies an infixed personal pronoun, and **nách** is the regular dependent negative before an infixed pronoun. The only exceptions which I have noted are **arna-m tomnad,** 114 see note, and **nadid chreti,** Wb. 15^{b}14, if the text be sound.

73. **comman,** fr. **com-ban :** see **Copula** (Paradigms).

79. **-epret,** fr. **-èss-berat :** see **as-beir** (Paradigms).

80. **foraib.** The older construction would be **forru,** as 234 ;

but in the pronoun confusion of the dat. and acc. pl. had already begun. In 237 there is an O. Ir. instance of similar confusion in the noun.

corru, fr. con-ro.

82. beta 3 pl. pres. subj. of the copula. The initial of the following word is nasalized by rel. n- (c=g).

85. con ríctar=co rríctar fr. con ro-íctar : see ícaid.

Imperative. 86-101.

In those verbs in which the indicative and subjunctive are formed from different stems (p. 143), the imperative goes with the indicative, not with the subjunctive, e.g. deich 86, cluinte 89, -mided 91, gaibid 94, -cumgat, tíagat 97, indarbanar 101.

86. du-m-em (=-eim). The rule that the stress falls on the first syllable of the ipv. is crossed by the rule that the stress must follow the infixed pron., Paradigms p. 39.

deich, fr. dè-fich : see 1. do-fich.

88. déne, 2 sg. ipv. of do-gní.

89. cluinte, 2 sg. ipv. of ro-cluinethar. In a epert, lit. *its saying*, or *the saying of it* (*namely*) ' hear,' i.e. *the use of the word* ' hear,' a is proleptic, as in Mod. Ir. a rádh, a fhios, etc. Not *his saying*, which would be epert dó.

93. seichem, 1 pl. ipv. of sechithir.

94. intamlid : see in-samlathar.

96. taít : see do-tét, (Paradigms).

97. cumgat : see con-icc (Paradigms).

98. eiplet, -epil : see at-bail.

foircniter, fr. fòrcennatar.

99. aimdetar, fr. àdmidetar. In the ipv. of the deponent, the 3 pl. has a specially deponent form, but not the 3 sg. : cf. 91.

Imperfect Indicative. 102-9.

The imperfect indicative denotes repeated or customary action in past time.

103. **ba.** The copula has no forms for the imperfect indicative as distinct from the preterite.

105. **-fintar :** see **ro-fitir.**

107. **choscur.** In Wb. lenition of the object is found only when the object is **cách ;** in Ml. and Sg. such lenition extends to other words. Cf. 347, 362.

109. **do-bertis,** 3 pl. impf. ind. pass. The dual subject takes a plural verb. Cf. 227.

no oircthe : see **orcaid.**

Past Subjunctive. 110-26.

There are the same differences between the stem of the past subj. and impf. ind. as between the stem of the pres. subj. and the pres. ind. In the normal *ā*-subj. of radical verbs, the ind. and subj. are partly distinguishable in form in the 3 sg. act., e.g. ind. **as-bered,** subj. **as-berad.** But the prototonic form of both is **-epred.**

111. **co beid .i. co mbed.** The former is 3 sg. pres. subj. with **co ;** the latter is 3 sg. past subj. with **co n-.** **co** is followed by an absolute or deuterotonic form of the verb, **co n-** by a conjunct or prototonic form. The negative of **co** is **coní,** of **co n-, conná.**

112. **dó,** *for this (purpose),* anticipates the following final clause.

113. **ba méite limm,** an idiomatic phrase meaning probably *I should think it likely* : see *Ériu* x. 190-3. **méite** is apparently gen. sg. of **méit.** The indic. **ba,** neg. **níbu,** has here, as often, a modal sense : cf. 118, 120, 126. In **ní scartha,** subordination

is not formally expressed : *I should think it likely (that) thou wouldst not part from me ;* cf. 125.

114. **arnā-m tomnad :** read **arná tomnad** or **arnáchim thomnad,** and see **do-moinethar.**

námmin, fr. **ná-m-bin :** see **Copula** (Paradigms). The subjunctive marks the rejected thought : cf. 293.

116. **nád mbed,** *that it is not.* Past subjunctive of rejected fact or reason : cf. 300.

117. **combad :** copula with **co n-.** Subjunctive of suggestion or conjecture, *it would have been.*

ro scríbad. Here **ro** gives to the past subjunctive the sense of a pluperfect : cf. 126, 300.

118. **a fius** (= **fius**) **sin,** *the knowledge of that.* Distinguish : **in fius sin,** *that knowledge.*

act ní bed, an exception to the general rule that **acht,** *provided that,* is followed by a **ro-** form or its equivalent.

119. **amal,** *as though,* takes the past subjunctive.

móir, *as great as,* equative of **mór.** Such comparatives are followed by the acc.

-fodmai, fr. **-fòdaimi.**

a ndu, etc. The usual order would have been **a fo-daimi du** (=**di**) **imnedaib,** etc.

ataat . . . nephchomthetarrachti, *the judgements of God are incomprehensible.* The substantive verb with predicative adjective is rare in O. Ir. It is occasionally found, however, with participles (e.g. **amal no mbemmis érchcílti,** *as though we were destined,* Wb. 9ᵃ3 ; **biid ersoilcthi,** *be ye opened,* Ml. 46ᵃ7 ; **ó ro bátar ind liss dúntai,** *when the courts were closed,* Im. Br. § 1) and **nephchomthetarrachte** is a compound of the part. pass. of **con-tetarrat,** *comprehends.*

fo-d-era, with infixed **d** (= **fo-d-fera**), serves as a relative form to **fo-fera.**

124. **cía aiccent ⁊ cisí aimser :** cf. 248. Note the various forms of the pronoun, m. **cía,** f. **ci-sí, ce-sí,** n. **ced, cid** (fr. **ce ed**).

thechtas. Lenition of the initial consonant of a relative form is not found in Wb., but it appears in later O. Ir.

125. **cid atob-aich cen dílgud,** lit. *what impels you without forgiving ?* an idiomatic expression for *what impels you not to forgive ?* **atob-aich, ad-dob-aich :** see **ad-aig.**

126. **do-rōnta** (=**do-róntae**), fr. **de-n-rò-gnethe :** see **do-gní** (Paradigms). For the construction, cf. **nibu machdad bed** (fr. **bed n-**) **coitchenn,** Sg. 68ᵃ3.

liac, a scribal error for **lieic.**

f-Future. 127-40.

127. **ainfa.** From **anaid** ***anfa** might have been expected, but there is a very strong tendency for verbs of this class to have their future like that of **léicid :** cf. 131, 134.

128. **fo-mentar,** fr. **fo-mènātheɪ,** 2 sg. present subjunctive of **fo-moinethar.**

rígtin=**ríchtin.**

130. **daíni**=**doíni,** acc. pl. of **duine.**

131. **maⱮi-d.** For **ceni, mani,** followed by an indicative, **cenid, manid** are regularly substituted, unless there be an infixed pronoun. In the simple verb the same is true of **cía** and **ma,** for which we find **ce no-d, ma no-d** (where **no-** serves to infix the **d**), **cía ru-d, ce ru-d, ma ru-d ;** in compound verbs the usage is less fixed : cf. 234, 242, 329.

134. **atrefea**=**atrebfea :** see **atreba.**

ad-id-trefea, lit. *who shall dwell it* ; i.e. *who shall dwell such a dwelling, who shall so dwell.* The infixed neut. pron. has somewhat of the force of a cognate accusative.

136. **-derchoínfet :** see **do-rochoíni.**

137. **-uile-marbae,** *slay utterly.* A compound of **marbaid,** with **uile :** cf. 229.

138. **co léir. co,** *to,* which afterwards is the common vehicle for the formation of adverbs, is rarely so used in O. Ir. : cf. **co mmór,** 328.

140. **no comallaibthe** (*c=g*), fr. **no n-comallaibthe.** The **-n-** marks indirect speech : see 2. **n°** (c). Similarly **ro-m-bad,** 3 sg. sec. fut. of copula, *that it would be* : see **ro.**

Reduplicated and ē-Future. 141-68.

The reduplicated future is like a reduplicated form of an *ā*-subjunctive, the reduplication vowel being *i.* Thus, e.g., 3 pl. past subj. **ad-cetis :** 3 pl. sec. fut. **ad-cichitis ;** 3 sg. pres. subj. **-ria :** 3 sg. fut **asriri ;** 3 sg. pres. subj. **-*lia :** 3 sg. fut. ind. ***lili ;** 3 sg. pres. subj. **fo-dama ;** 3 sg. fut. **fo-didma** (fr. ***fo-didama**) ; 3 sg. pres. subj. **canaid :** 3 sg. fut. ind. **cechnaid** (fr. ***cicanaid**) ; 3 sg. pres. subj. **ro-cloathar :** 3 sg. fut. ind. **ro-cechladar ;** 3 pl. pres. subj. **ara-chriat :** 3 pl. fut. ind. **ara-chíurat** (fr. **-*cicriat**). Side by side with the futures are given examples of the corresponding subjunctives. The *ē*-future is in origin only a particular kind of reduplicated future. It arose regularly in one or two verbs, e.g. **-céla** (fr. ***-cechla**), to **celid,** ' conceals,' **do-gén, do-génae, do-géna** (fr. ***-gigna . . .**) to **do-gní,** and thence spread more and more as a convenient type.

142. **f-a-didmed :** see **fo-daim.**

acht do-n-d-ecmaing, *save that it so happens.* **acht** followed by relative **n** has the force of *save that* : cf. 224. **-d-** is the object in impersonal construction.

144. **for-cechnae :** see **for-cain.**

145. **tairrchet :** see **do-airchain.**

ad-cichitis : see **ad-cí** (Paradigms).

146. **ad-cethe**, 3 sg. past subj. pass. of **ad-cí**.

147. **ro-t-chechladar** : see **ro-cluinethar**.

149. **as-ririu** : see **as-ren**.

151. **-riat** : see **renaid**.

152. **liles** : see **lenaid**.

153. **fris-bia** : see **fris-ben**.

154. **ocu-bether** : see **ocu-ben**.

156-7. **gíulait, gléu** : see **glenaid**.

158. **ara-chíurat** : see **ara-chrin**. This verb is in itself transitive, and has become apparently intransitive through the infixed neut. pron. **-a-** : cf. 338; **ara-chrinim** gl. *defetiscor*. Sg. 145[b]1. In relative construction **-d-** would be substituted for **-a-** : cf. **ar-in-d-chrin** 339. As **fo bíthin** is followed by relative **n**, **ar-in-d-chíurat** might have been expected here ; there is the same irregularity in **is dénithir sin ara-chrin**, *even so quickly does it perish*, Ml. 57[c]12. In Mid. Ir. the relative **n** is gradually lost, and already in later O. Ir. it is sometimes omitted. In this way the present irregularity may be explained.

160. **lesom**=**less-som**.

⁊ **du-fúairthed ní**, lit. *and something used to remain over*, i.e. *though something used to remain over ;* see **do-fúarat**. **fora sáith**, *after they were satisfied*.

161. **-eirbea**, fut. of **erbaid**.

génas : see **gníid**.

162. **du-gén, -digen** : see **do-gní**, Paradigms.

164. **-dernmis**, fr. **-dè-ro-gnemmis**.

165. **áill** : see **áil**. Here *l* is doubled before the initial *d* of the following closely-connected **dúib**, as it is in the interior of a word.

d-a-ri-génte, *ye could have done it*. Here **-ri-** appears where **-ro-** would have been regular, just as it appears in the perf. **do-ri-géni** with assimilation of the vocalism to forms without **ro**, **do-rigénte** after **-digénte**, and **do-rigéni** after **-digéni**.

166. **ropia=ro-b bia**. With all parts of the substantive verb from the stem **bi-, ro-**, not **no-**, is used to infix a personal pronoun.

167. **taiccéra :** see **do-accair**.

168. **gébas :** see **gaibid**.

húaib-si goes with **unus**, *not* (*merely*) *one of you*.

Sigmatic Future and Subjunctive. 169-211.

A sigmatic future and a sigmatic subjunctive regularly go together.[1] The future is a reduplicated form of the subjunctive ; the reduplication vowel is -i-. Thus, e.g. 1 sg. subj. -gess, fr. *gessu, *getsō : 1 sg. fut. -gigius,[2] fr. *gigessu, *gigetsō. In verbs beginning with **f** or **s** the reduplication is obscured by the loss of intervocalic **f** or **s**, e.g. **do-fí,** fr. **de-fífe, do-fiastar,** fr. **de-fìfestar : do-fich.** If the root begins with a vowel, **i** is lost before **a**, e.g. **-ain: aingid ;** it contracts with **e** or **i** to **í** e.g. **ístir :** subj. **estir** (**ithid**) **;** before **o** it remains. In compound verbs the reduplication is often obscured by loss of the unaccented vowel. A few roots show no trace of reduplication.

169-79. for **gigse** (=**gigsea**) etc. see **guidid**, and Paradigms, p. 59.

170. **oísitiu=foísitiu**. The lenited **f** was mute, and it is not infrequently omitted in writing; see 51.

ebarthi, fr. **ebraith-i,** *will give it :* cf. **ebarthir,** *will be given*, Wb. 32ª27. See **ernaid**.

---

[1] -icc (in **do-icc,** *comes;* **ro-icc,** *reaches,* etc.) is an exception ; it has an s-subjunctive and an f-future. Another exception is **téit,** *goes,* which has an s-subjunctive, while **regaid** is used as the future.

[1] It will be seen that in -**gess,** where the accent stands on the radical syllable, no effect of the following lost vowel is apparent ; in -**gigius,** where the accent does not stand on the radical syllable, the vowel is modified : cf. **mess,** *judgement,* fr. *messus ,but **frithmius**.

172. -fulsam, fr. -fòlōsam : see fo-loing.

173. con-da-rías (=con-n-da-rias ; cf. con-da-airleci, 342) *that I bind them* : see con-rig, and note on 63. It is a literal translation of *alligare*, an error for *allegare*.

177. chumcam : see con-ic.

-thinib : see do-infet.

179. -étar : see ad-cota.

180-1. théis, té : see téit.

arda. In attributive use arda, the form of the fem. and neut., has here replaced the old masc. ardu.

182, 183. do-théi, -taí : see do-tét (Paradigms).

183. toimdden=toimten.

gaibthi, fr. gaibith-i, *he says it.* The suffixed pron. anticipates igitur.

ní fail . . . fair, lit. *there is nothing that my law does not touch upon it* ; i.e. *there is nothing on which my law does not touch.* The more usual form of expression in O. Ir. would be ní fil ní forná taí mo dliged-sa. But cf. nech suidigther loc daingen dó, *one to whom is established a strong place*, Ml. 87ᵈ15. For do-tét for, *touches upon*, cf. Wb. 2ᵃ3.

184. rigmi : see téit (Paradigms).

187. bíit . . . pecthe, lit *there are some, their sins are found out*, i.e. *there are some whose sins are found out* ; a device for expressing the genitive relation of the relative, for which there is no formal means of expression in O. Ir. : cf. 195.

do-coí : see téit (Paradigms).

189. ro má : perfective pres. subj. of maidid. The MS. reading roima is a scribal error, for -roíma could only be the prot. form of *ro-mema. But ma is not used with the future, and mani would become manid with ind. ; see 131.

190. cia dunaibhí, lit. *who of them ?* i.e. *of whom ?* see intí. This is an artificial construction used only in glossing the Lat. interrog. governed by a prep. ; cf. cia isnaib-hí

gl. **in quibus** ? Ml. 49ᶜ13 ; **cia du forcunn** gl. *quem ad finem ?* 33ᵃ9. In idiomatic Irish we should expect to find the intcrrog. at the head of the sentence, as predicative nom., followed by a rel. clause : **citné doíni dia tóirmsed,** *who are the people of whom he would add ?*

   do-foirmsed, fr. **to-fòr-mässed :** see **do-formaig.**

   191. **atamm-res,** fr. **ess-dam-res,** lit. *when 1 shall raise myself,* i.e. *when I shall arise ;* see **at-reig.** This verb shows no trace of reduplication in the future.

   192. **du-fí :** see 1. **do-fich. du-éma :** see **do-eim.**

   193. **tíssed :** see **do-ic** (Paradigms).

   tra=tar a.

   195. **ro-hí :** see **ro-icc** (Paradigms).

   196. **nád chumaing ara-n-ísar,** *which cannot be found* : see **con-ic** and **ar-ic.**

   -enggnatar, fr. **-èn-gninatar,** seems to supply the prototonic form to **asa-gnintar :** cf. the verbal noun **engne,** *understanding,* by the side of **ecne** (fr. **ess-gne**), *wisdom.*

   197. **íirr :** cf. 229 ; see **orcaid.**

   198. **fris-n-orr :** see **fris-oirg.**

   199. **chon-desin :** see **con-dieig.**

   200. **imme-romastar :** see **im-roimdethar.**

   -cuintea, fr. **-còm-di-sā :** se **con-dieig.**

   201. **fu-lilsain :** see **fo-loing.**

   205. **atat-chigestar,** fr. **ad-dat-chigestar :** see **ad-cí.** (Paradigms).

   206. **-accastar,** fr. **-àd-cestar :** see **ad-cí.**

   207. **ru-fiastar :** see **ro-fitir.**

   du-écigi : see **do-écci.**

   208. **con festar=co festar.**

   209. **miastar** cannot be explained from ***mimastar** with regular reduplication ; it is due to the analogy of **fiastar :—miastar : mestar=fiastar : festar.** See **midithir.**

211. **seiss, do-essid :** see **saidid.**

gébtit, etc., *they will take him as lord.* **gébtit** is peculiar. **gébait,** with the affixed pron. **-i,** would give **gébti.** Under the influence of the ending of **gébait,** **gébti** was transformed into **gébtit.**

Preterite and Perfect. 212-302.

In the active these tenses are made up of three forms, of different origin, but of the same syntactic value, (1) the *s*-preterite or perfect, 212-34 ; (2) the *t*-preterite or perfect, 235-55 ; (3) the suffixless preterite or perfect, generally reduplicated, 256-302. In the passive there is only one formation ; examples of the passive are given along with the corresponding active forms.

The perfect is commonly distinguished from the preterite by the addition of **ro-,** e.g. **as-bert,** *he said* ; **as-rubart,** *he has said.* Other particles are also found. **ad-** (in verbs compounded with **com-**) :—e.g. **con-celt,** *concealed* : **con-aicelt ; con-scar,** *destroyed* : **con-ascar ; con-diacht** (**con-dieig**), *sought* : **con-aitecht. com-** :—e.g. **do-indnacht,** *gave* : **do-écom-nacht** (fr. **to-en-com-anacht**) ; **fris-ort,** *offended* : **fris-comort. ess-** :—**ass-ib,** *has drunk*, to **ibid,** *drinks.* A double preposition appears in **do-cuitig,** *has sworn*, to **tongid,** *swears*, and **do-essid,** perf. of **saidid,** *sits*, which has for its preterite **síassair.** Sometimes preterite and perfect come from different roots : see **berid, do-beir, do-cuiredar, fo-ceird, téit** in the Vocabulary. A few verbs have no distinction between preterite and perfect, e.g. **ro-cluinethar, ro-fitir, do-icc, ro-icc, ar-icc, fo-gaib.**

The preterite is the narrative tense. Further, it is used in indirect speech to represent a present of direct speech ; it is used in a modal sense, e.g. **ní boí,** *there were not*, 302 ; further, after **mad-,** *well*, 301, and after **ó,** *since*, 230.

Of the perfect it may be said that it marks the occurrence of an action in past time from the point of view of the present. Such action may fall within the recent experience of the speaker (or the person spoken to), or within his more remote experience, or it may fall in an indefinite past. In subordinate clauses, the perfect may denote action prior to the action of the main verb.

212. **-retarscar** comes from **-rò-etarscar ; ru etarscar** implies an accentuation **ru ètarscar.** After **in n-** the accent should stand on the following syllable ; but already in O. Ir. there is a strong tendency for the accent to pass from **ro** to the next syllable.

214. **cota-ascrais,** fr. **com-ta-ad-scarais:** see **con-scara.**

216. **d-a-uc.** Note the infixed neut. pron., though **testimin** is masc. : see note on 267.

217. **-thorgaíth :** see **do-gaítha.**

218. **donahí=donaib-hí :** see **intí.**

-rérchoíl, fr. **-rò-ess-ro-choíl ;** see **as-rochoíli.** As a general rule, if the verb is a compound containing **ro-, ro-** is not added again in the perfect. But, in prototonic position **ro-** is occasionally inserted at the beginning : cf. **níru derchoín,** Ml. 44ª1.

219. **in molad ro mmolastar,** *the praise wherewith he praised* : cf. 25.

220. **fo-rrorbris,** fr. **fo-n-ro-r-briss :** see note on 55.

221. **f-a-cherred :** see **fo-ceird.**

cet-id-deirgni : see **ceta-déni.**

du-rolged : see **do-luigi.**

224. *tantum*=**nammá.**

225. **ro cruthaigsemmar.** If the dot over *c* in the MS. is intended to denote lenition, the lenition is irregular.

226. **an ro,** regularly **a rro.**

227. **ru-n-d gab, ru-n-d gabsat. ro-n-d gabus,** or, with loss of the neut. **-d-, ro-n gabus,** is used in the sense of *I am,*

after conjunctions that take **n** with relative form of the verb, and in indirect speech. After Lat. *sic*=Ir. **is samlaid,** the relative form is irregular : see note on 7.

228. **forcan=forcenn.**

229. **as-id-roilliset :** see note on 326 and 327.

230. **-érbarthar :** see **as-beir** (Paradigms).

231. **ad-ráigsetar :** see **ad-ágathar.**

no-n-da bértais. Here the verb of fearing is followed by the construction of indirect speech.

233. **do-rónta :** see **do-gní** (Paradigms). Contrast 126.

234. **fomnid :** see **fo-moinethar.**

a phopul : nom. for voc., as often in collective nouns ; cf. Mod. Ir. **a phobal.** See *Ériu* ix. 89, 93, 94.

du-d-rónath : see **do-gní** (Paradigms), and note on 131.

-derlaichtha, -dílgibther : see **do-luigi.**

cenotad : see **Copula** (Paradigms).

235. **-tormult,** fr. **-tò-ro-miult :** see **do-meil.**

236. **ar-roiēit :** see **ar-foím.**

237. **fo-ruirmed :** see **fo-rumi.**

du-rairngirt : see **do-airngir.**

238. **du-écomnacht,** fr. **to-èn-com-anacht :** see **do-indnaich.** Note that before the perfective **com-, en-,** a shorter form of **ind-,** is used.

239. **as-id-rubart :** see **as-beir** and note on 316-23.

-érbrath, fr. **-èss-ro-breth.**

240. **conid marb,** fr. **con-(d)id n-marb,** *so that he killed himself* : see **marbaid** and **Infixed Pronoun** (Paradigms).

-digni : see **do-gní** (Paradigms).

241. **at-rubalt :** see **at-bail.**

243. **con-aicelt :** see **con-ceil.**

-árraim, fr. **-àd-ro-rìm.**

244. **con-àitecht, -còmtacht :** see **con-dieig.**

245. **as-réracht,** fr. **ess-rò-ess-recht :** see **as-érig.**

246. **du-rat :** see **do-beir** (Paradigms).

du-n-d-rét : see **do-eim.**

247. **du-da-forsat :** see **do-fuissim.** The infixed pronoun anticipates the object.

250. **a threte,** lit. *the speediness of it.* For this idiomatic use of the neut. poss. pron. cf. 252, 288, 314, 374.

do-rérachtid, do-r-réractid, fr. **di-n-rò-ess-rechtid :** see **do-érig.**

251. **d-a-rogart-som,** *he has called himself :* see **do-gair.**

252. **fris-comartatar,** fr. **fris-n-com-ortatar :** see **fris-oirg.**

in sí a méit, *is this the extent of it,* with proleptic **a** referring to **-n-,** *how they have offended,* i.e. *have they offended so greatly ?*

con dodsitis, fr. **co n-todsitis :** see **do-tuit.** In O. Ir. an initial tenuis was subject to nasalization as in Mod. Ir. ; but such nasalization was rarely expressed in writing. For **con dodsitis, co dodsitis** would be the correct orthography, for the nasalizing **n** disappeared in the process.

253. **atam-roipred,** fr. **ad-dam-rò-oss-breth :** see **ad-opair.**

254. **du-rairngred :** see **do-airngir.**

256. **ro mmemaid,** fr. **ro n-memaid :** see **maidid.**

257. **ro lil :** see **lenaid.** **-dechuid :** see **téit** (Paradigms).

259. **tairchechuin :** see **do-airchain.**

for-cuimsed : see **for-comnacuir.**

260. **for-roíchain :** see **for-cain.**

262. **ru chét :** see **canaid.** The lenition is irregular as the verb is not properly relative. See note on 7.

263. **do-roígaid :** see **do-goa.**

265. **fris-racacha,** fr. **fris-rò-ad-cecha.** The corresponding prototonic form is **ru frescacha,** fr. **ro frìs-ad-cecha.** See **fris-acci.** Observe that in the prototonic form of this compound **ro** shifts backward to the beginning, similarly **imme-**

ruidbed, ro imdibed, 286. In other compounds, again, such as **-dèirgni** the prototonic form of **do-rìgēni, ro-** maintains its position. The latter represents the older, the former the later, principle.

266. **-forgéni :** see **fo-gní.**

267. **ad-id-géuin.** According to Pedersen,[1] *which knows the aforementioned knowledge* (i.e. *which has such knowledge*) : cf. note on 134. This is possible ; but, on the other hand, it can hardly be denied that an infixed pronoun of the neut. sg. is found referring loosely to a preceding noun of another gender or number : cf. Wb. 9^a23, 26^a22, Ml. 46^c7, 84^c13 ; further **d-a-beir,** Thesaurus Palaeohibernicus, ii. 241, 3, referring back to **manchi** and **andoóit.** With Ml. 84^c13, cf. Ml. 116^d3, **in dígal do-m-beir-som is ed in-chosaig a frecńdarcus.**

268. **ar-róit :** see **ar-foím.**

do-rraidchíuir, fr. **do-n-raìdchíuir :** see **do-aidchren.**

269. **romtar,** fr. **ro-m-batar,** 3 pl. perf. of the copula, with rel. **n.**

270. **ro-cúala :** see **ro-cluinethar.**

274. **-ain :** see **aingid.**

tremi-tíagat, fr. **tremi-d-tíagat,** as the absence of lenition shows.

276, 277. **fo-n-d-úair :** see **fo-gaib.**

do-árbuid, -tárbas : see **do-adbat.**

277. **nach mór,** *to any great extent,* dat. sg. of **na mmór,** *any great thing ;* see **nach.**

278. **ad-rothreb. atreba,** *inhabits,* is often used in Sg. to express Lat. possidet, *possesses.*

278, 279. **con-rógatar, con-rótacht :** see **con-utaing.**

279. **-toirsitis :** generally taken as perfective past subj.

[1] KZ. xxxv. 403.

of 2. **do-fich.** But it may be prot. past subj. of **do-roich** (fr. **to-ro-sag-**), *that they might not come to it again.* Cf. **doig leo ní thoirsitís do-ridisi** LL 13ª33.

280. **du-cuitig, -tōissed :** see **tongid.**

282-3. **do-rochair, do-cer :** see **do-tuit** (Paradigms)

283. **do-luid :** see **do-tét** (Paradigms).

fo-caird : see **fo-ceird.**

arithissi (= a **frithissi**), *again,* lit. *its return course* ; **frithissi** acc. of **frithiss,** *return course,* fr. **frith + éis,** *track.*

284. **etir-rudib :** see **etir-diben.**

286. **imme-ruidbed :** see **im-diben.**

287, 288. **ad-chuaid, -éicdid :** see **ad-fét.**

do-n-decnommar : see **do-tét** (Paradigms).

289. **di Iudéib do Barnaip,** lit. *of the Jews to Barnabas,* i.e. *Barnabas was of the Jews.* This is the regular form of expression in O. Ir. when the subject of the copula is a pronoun and the predicate is not a noun or an adjective : cf. **is ónd athir dó,** *it is from the Father,* Wb. 21ᵈ4, with **is úadib Críst,** *Christ is from them,* Wb. 4ᶜ2.

do-coad : see **téit** (Paradigms).

290. **for-rorcongrad :** see **for-congair. for-rò-r-con-grad** is probably a contamination of **fo-rò-r-congrad** (see note on 55) and **for-rò-chongrad.**

291. **oca thecht,** *as he so went.* The poss. pron. with the verb. noun has the same force as an infixed neut. pron. with the verb : cf. **d-a-chotar,** *they so went,* Ml. 38ᵇ2, and note on 134.

293. **armbenn,** *that I was,* past subj. sg. 1 of copula with **ara n-.**

du-rumēnar : see **do-moinethar.**

romsa (= **ro-m-b-sa**), *that I was,* past ind. sg. 1 of copula with rel. **-n-.**

294. **con-ammadar,** fr. **con-àd-mídar :** see **con-mide-thar.**

295. **ro mess** : see **midithir.**

296. **ad-rodamar** : see **ataim.**

297. **fo-n-d-ro-damnatar** : see **fo-daim.**

298-9. **cot-áneccar, -comnactar, cot-ánic** : see **con-icc,** and **Infixed Pronoun,** Paradigms, p. 26.

300. **ro ngénair, ro ṅgenad** : see **gainithir.**

301. **mad-génatar,** lit. *happily born were,* an idiom for *blessed are.*

302. **ní boí,** in a modal sense, *there were not, there would not be* : see note on 113.

Participle Passive. 303-9.

303. **tedbarthe** : see **do-edbair.**

304. **tórmachte** : see **do-fórmaig.**

305. **túartai** : see **do-fúɜirc.**

306. **an-ná-robsa,** *when I was not* : see **Copula** (Paradigms). **bíthe** : see **benaid.**

307. **indrisse** : see **in-reith.**

308. **anámtar = an-ná-m-batar,** *when they were not* : see **Copula** (Paradigms). **tuidchissi** : see **do-dichet.**

309. **céte** : see **canaid.**

Verbal of Necessity. 310-15.

310. **comallaidi,** later O. Ir. assimilation of **comalnaidi.**

311. **comitesti,** an irregular formation from **con-étet, -cometig ;** as the root ends in a guttural, ***comitechti** might have been expected.

312. **dénti** : see **do-gní** (Paradigms).

313. **buthi** : see **Substantive Verb** (Paradigms).

du-s-rale : see do-cuirethar.

314. gessi : see guidid.

315. at-léntais : see as-léna.

Variations in Prepositions. 316-87.

316-23. ess-.

(a) Under the accent ess-, liable to various changes before consonants :—ess-b- to ep-, ess-g- to ec-, ess-l- to él-, ess-r- to ér-.

(b) Before the accent as-, e.g. as-beir.[1] Before an infixed personal pronoun not distinguished from ad-, e.g. at-beir, *he says it* (but ass-id-beir, *who says it*). Hence in later O. Ir. ad- appears for ess- under the accent, e.g. -àiperr for -èperr,

316. intśliucht : properly intliucht, fr. Lat. *intellectus*, but wrongly supposed to be a compound of ind and sliucht.

319. du-eclannar, du-érglas (fr. to-èss-ro-glēss) : see do-eclainn.

323. ad-rubartmar : ad- probably for at-, with unmeaning neut. infix, as regularly in Mid. Ir. at-beir for as-beir, later ateir, adeir.

324-32. ad-.

(a) Under the accent ad- ; before uss : ed-, id-, aud- ; liable to various changes before consonants, e.g. adc- to acc-, ac-,[2] ad-g- to ac-, acc-,[3] ad-b- to ap-, ad-m- to amm-, ad-r- to ár-, ad-s- to as-.

(b) Before the accent ad-.

(c) But before the 3 sg. infixed pron. -idn-, -id- in relative construction, e.g. as-id-indissed, Ml. 42ᵇ18 ; before -id- after

---

[1] In rel. construction usually as-, but asa-gúsi, 328 (also ad-gúsi, Sg. 148ᵃ4, and non-rel. sg. 1 ad-gúisiu, Thesaurus Palaeohibernicus ii. 293); cf. non-rel. asa-gnintar, 196.
[2] =Mod. Ir. ac-.   [3] =Mod. Ir. ag-.

cia, e.g. ci as-id-chiam, and before relative n, e.g. indas as-ṅ-da-fíadam, there is a strong tendency to substitute as- for ad-.[1]

327. at-roillet : see ad-roilli. In later O. Ir. as- tends to spread beyond its proper sphere in this verb, giving as-roilli for ad-roilli.

328. du-árchomraicset : see do-erchomraici.

áirilti, properly *the deserved* (*ones*), is used artificially to translate the Latin deponent. So ind foircimim is an artificial rendering of the Latin *optimi*. The whole gloss is a forced explanation of an incomplete text. The original was probably *cum optime de se meriti optarent interitum*.

330. as-ṅ-da-fíadam. The infixed pronoun anticipates the object of the dependent clause.

333-4. aith-.

(*a*) Under the accent aith-.

(*b*) Before the accent ad-.

335-9. air-.

(*a*) Under the accent : air-, aur-, er-, ir-, ur-. àir+ro- becomes àr-.

(*b*) Before the accent : (α) ar- ; (β) in the relative sense, ara-.

335. -thobrea : usually thaibrea : see do-beir.

337. -arbarat, fr. -àir-ro-berat.

túari. The acc. is governed by the phrase arbarat biuth.

338. ara-ruichíuir : see note on 158.

339. as-in-d-bail : see note on 54.

340-8. com-.

(*a*) Under the accent com-, liable to various changes, e.g. com-c- to coc-, com-t- to cot-, com-g- to cong-, com-d- to cond-, con-s- to cos-. For com-, cum- is found, par-

---

[1] But adind-rími, Wb. 13ᵈ17 ; adid-roillifet, Ml. 61ª20, adid-roillisset, 61ᵇ17 ; adid-trefea, Ml. 107ª15 ; adid-chotatsat, Sg. 50ª3 ; adind-chomlat, Sg. 212ᵇ7.

ticularly where *u* has been lost in the following syllable, e.g.
-cumsciget, fr. -còm-uss-scoichi. Analogically com- may
be restored before a consonant before which *m* is regularly lost,
e.g. comthinól, comsuidigthe.

(*b*) Before the accent con-, for which cot- is substituted
before an infixed personal pronoun. See Paradigms, p. 24.

345. con-degar, fr. con-dè-segar : see con-dieig.

346. ro-fitis, a peculiar 2 pl. fr. ro-fitir.

-cuintgim, fr. -còm-de-saigim : cf. -cuintea, 200.

349-56. di-.

(*a*) Under the accent dí-, di-, de-.

(*b*) Before the accent do-, du- (earlier di-).

349. di-róscai, -derscaigi. The syllable most weakly accented is that which follows the chief accent. Hence di-rò-oss-
scoichi gives diróscai ; but -dè-ro-oss-scoichi gives -der-
scaigi.

350. cech, for older cecha, cf. Sg. 43ª5.

351. do-em=do-eim.

355-6. do-fúarat, fr. di-òss-reth. -diúair, fr. -dì-oss-ré.
In the deuterotonic form the *f* is noteworthy : cf. do-fuisémthar 365, by tuistin 366, from the compound to-uss-sem-.
The *f* is analogical. In many compounds an original *f* is lost
in the prototonic form, e.g. do-fòr-maig, but -tórmaig.
The influence of such pairs led to the introduction of *f* in the
deuterotonic forms of verbs in which the *f* is not etymologically
justified.

357-66. to-.

(*a*) Under the accent to-. tò-fo- to tō-, tò-for- to tōr-,
tò-air- to tair-, tò-ess- to tess-, tò-ind- to tind-, etc.

(*b*) Before the accent do-, du- (earlier to-).

357. sin, *here*.

chucae. The lenition of adverbial expressions begins in
later O. Ir.

358. **airnách rí olc,** *that evil may not reach him.* see **ro-ic** and 72 note.

359. **cumscaichthi :** see **con-oscaigi.**

360. **in-tindarscan,** fr. **ind-tò-ind-ro-scann.**

361, 363. **do-fóirndet, do-fórmaich.** The long vowel has spread analogically from the contracted forms **-tóirndet, -tórmaich.** So 367, in **fo-ácbat** the long *a* has come from **fácbat.**

362. **úalailiu**=**úa al-ailiu.**

366. **roisset :** see **ro-saig.**

367-71. **fo-.**

(*a*) Under the accent **fo-, fu-. fo-a-** to **fā-, fo-e-, fo-i-** to **foí-, fo-o-** to **fō-.**

(*b*) Before the accent **fo-, fu-.**

370. **-foíret,** fr. **-fòferat.**

372-5. **frith-.**

(*a*) Under the accent **frith-, frith-b-** to **frep-, frith-g-** to **frec-, frith-t-** to **fritt-.**[1]

(*b*) Before the accent **fris(s)-.** But before an infixed personal pronoun **frit-** (but before relative **-id(n)- friss-,** e.g. **friss-idn-oirctis**).

376-7. **imm-.**

(*a*) Under the accent : **imm-.**

(*b*) Before the accent : (α) **imm-** ; (β) in relative sense, **imma-, imme-.**

377. **imma-imgaib :** in this verb (fr. **imm-oss-gaib**) the stress always remains on the same syllable ; when a deuterotonic form is required, the prep. **imm-** is repeated at the beginning.

378. **íarmi-foig.** For **íarm-, íar-, íarmi-** or **íarmu-** appears before the accent.

---

[1] Also etymologically **frithbeir, frithgnom,** etc.

381. **intamil.** **ind-s-** becomes **int-.**

ata-samlibid. For **ind-** before an infixed pronoun, see Paradigms, p. 26.

382-7. **ocu-, remi-, sechmo-, tremi-.**

(a) Under the accent : **oc-, rem- sechm-, trem-.**

(b) Before the accent : **ocu-, remi-, sechmo-, tremi-.**

382. **airmdis** past subj. pl. 3 of copula with **ara n-.**

386. **-dermanammar** may be ind., *so that we forget*, or subj. *that we may forget*, see **do-roimnethar.**

foscaigiu : this looks like the dat. of a noun **foscaige**, *departure*. But the verb. noun of **fo-scoichi**, *departs* is **foscugud.** Pedersen, VG ii. 617, suggests that it is a scribal error for **foscaigiud.** Cf. **dánaigiud**, *bestowing, giving*, Ml. 96ª8, verb. noun of **dánaigidir**, for the usual **dánugud.**

aithche=aidche.

387. **ro-n-d boí.** The infixed neut. **-d-** is peculiar : cf. Ml. 136ᵇ7. It does not affect the meaning.

VOCABULARY

For words beginning with æ, see e; for words beginning with h, see the following vowel. ', e.g. a', indicates that the word lenites a following consonant. °, e.g. a n°-, indicates that the word nasalizes a following consonant which is capable of nasalization. - before a verb, e.g. -écid, signifies a prototonic or conjunct form of the verb. (-n-), e.g. óre (-n-), denotes that the word is followed by relative -n-.

1. a', (á',) *O*; particle of address, 95, 130.
2. a', (á'), *his, its* ; 18, 301 ; anticipating a following gen. 34, a following clause, 45, 89, 252, 288, 314.
3. a, *her,* 278.
4. -a-. See **Infixed Pronoun** (Paradigms).
5. a, prep. with dat. ; before proclitics **as(s)**, with art. **asnaib**, 319 ; with poss. pron. sg. 1 **asmo**, 132, sg. 3 **assa**, 188, *out of,* 256 ; **a persin,** *in the person,* 51.
6. a n°-, *their* 3 ; á, 241.
7. a n°-, *that (which), what.* See note on 41.
8. a n°- (-n-), *when* ; a **no-n-da,** *when thou art,* 17 ; a **n-as-m-beir,** *when he says,* 119.
abis, *abyss,* 119.
Abisolón, *Absalom,* 240.
Abracham, g. id. and **Abrache** (Lat.) 52, 232, etc.
abstal : see **apstal.**
accaldam, f. *addressing,* 165 ; verb. noun of **ad-gládathar.**
accobor (accubur), g. **accobuir,** n. *desire,* 72, 177 ; verb. noun of **ad-cobra.**
accrann, *shoe,* 376.
accuis, g. **aicsen,** f. *cause.* **ar accuis,** gl. Lat. causā, *for the sake of,* 249.
acht, conj., *but,* 21 ; **acht** (-n-), *save that,* 142, 224 ; **acht** with subj., *provided that,* 71, 309, 337 ; see note on 118.
acre (ad-gare), n. *act of suing, bringing an action against* 125 ; verb. noun of **ad-gair.**
Acrisióndae, *Acrisionian,* 278.
ad-ágathar, -ágathar, *fears* ; perf. pl. 3 **ad-ráigsetar,** 231.
adaig, g. **aidche, aithche,** f. *night,* 386.

ad-aig, *drives, impels,* 36 ; **cid atob-aich ?** 125.

adall, g. **ad(a)ill,** *visit,* 25, 127 ; verb. noun of **ad-ella**

adaltras, m. *adultery,* 188.

Ádam, g. **Ádim,** *Adam,* 331.

ad-amraigedar, *wonders, admires,* 63.

adbur, adbar, n. *material, cause,* 302.

ad-cí, -acci, *sees,* 41, 205-6, 275, etc. See Paradigms.

ad-cobra, -accobra, *desires,* 64, 302, 324-5.

ad-comla, *joins* ; subj. pres. pass. sg. 3 **ad-comaltar,** 83.

ad-cosnai (ad-com-sní-), **-ascnai,** *strives after,* 63-4; verb. noun **ascnam.**

ad-cota, -éta, *obtains,* 59 ; pass. sg. 3 **ad-cotar, -étar,** 163, 179.

ade, adi : see **suide.**

ad-eir-rig (aith-air-reg-), *reforms, brings to repentance,* ipv. pl. 2 **aithirgid,** 334.

ad-ella, -aidlea, *visits,* 25.

ad-fét, *tells,* pl. 1 **ad-fíadam ;** perf. sg. 3 **ad-cuaid, -écid,** 133, 330, 287.

ad-gnin, (aith-gnin-) *knows* ; perf., with pres. sense, sg. 1 **ad-gén,** sg. 3 **ad-géuin,** 267.

ad-gúsi (ess-gús-), *wishes* ; rel. sg. 3 **asa-gúsi,** 328.

adib, 52, see **Copula** (Paradigms).

ad-midethar, *attempts* ; ipv. pl. 3 **aimdetar,** 99 ; verb. noun **ammus.**

ad-noí (aith-no-), *entrusts* ; perf. sg. 3, **ad-roni,** 340 ; verb. noun **aithne.**

ad-opair (ad-oss-ber-), *offers,* 332, 337 ; perf. pass. sg. 3. **ad-roipred,** 253 ; verb. noun **idbart,** 331, **edbart,** 378.

adrad, g. **adartha,** m. *worship,* 220.

ad-rími, -áirmi, *reckons* ; pres. subj. sg. 1 **-árim,** 60 ; perf. sg. 3, **-árraim,** 243 ; verb. noun. **áram.**

ad-roilli (ad-ro-slí-), **-áirilli,** *deserves,* 229, 327-8.

ad-roni, see **ad-noí**).

aí (**áii**), stressed gen. sg. and pl. of 3rd pers pron. ; see **indala** and **nechtar.**

aicce, f. *fosterage* ; **na n-aicci,** *fostered with them,* 15.

aiccent, aiccend, g. **aiccind,** m. *accent,* 124.

aicned, g. **aicnid,** n. *nature,* 55, 142.

aid-ber, aith-ber, g. **aithbir,** d. **aidbiur,** *reproach,* 298.
aid-chumtach, g. **aidchumtaig,** n. *rebuilding,* 211.
aidlignigidir (ó), *needs,* 50.
áigthiu, g. **áigthen,** f. *fear,* 18 ; verb. noun of **ad-ágathar.**
áil, *fitting, desirable* ; is **áil dom,** *I desire,* 165.
aile, *other,* 64, **indala n-aí**—**ind aile,** 109, *the one—the other.*
ailid, -ail, *nourishes, supports,* 21.
aille, f. *blessing,* 222.
aimser, g. **aimsire,** f. *time,* 124, 200 ; **hó aimsir,** *for a while,*
   387.
ain-fírinne, f. *unrighteousness,* 369.
aingid, -anich, *protects* : fut. sg. 3 **-ain,** 274 ; verb. noun
   anacul.
ainm, g. **anmae,** n. *name,* 3, 79 ; *noun,* 13, 233.
ainmne, g. **ainmnet,** f. *patience,* 88.
air, ar, conj. *for,* 25, etc.
airchissecht, g. **airchissechtae,** f. *compassion,* 298 ; verb.
   noun of **ar-cessi.**
airegde, *noble, eminent,* 365 ; compar. **airegdu,** 53.
airigidir, *perceives* ; pass. sg. 3 **-airigther,** 105.
airindí (-n-), conj., *because,* 300 ; see **intí.**
airisiu, g. **airissen,** f. *story, history,* 300.
airitiu, g. **airiten,** f. *receiving, assuming,* 381 ; verb. noun of
   ar-foim.
airli, *management* (?) ; 230.
1. **aís,** g. **aís,** n. *age,* 366.
2. **aís, (áes, oís, óes),** g. **aísso, aísa,** etc., m. *folk.* **aís sech-**
   maill, *passers-by,* 25 ; **oís gráid,** *clergy* ; **oís túaithe,**
   laity, 371 ; **aís noíb,** *saints,* 324.
aisndís, g. **aisndísen,** f. *exposition,* 133, 138 ; verb. noun
   of **as-indet.**
aithirge, f. *repentance,* 333 ; verb, noun of **ad-eirrig,**
aithirrech, *repetition* ; dat. sg. **aithirriuch,** *again,* 279.
aitrebthid, g. **aitrebthedo,** m. *inhabitant,* 278.
al-aile, *other, the other,* **al-aili**—**al-aili,** *some—others,* 187.
   Before a noun *certain* (quidam) ; **úalailiu mud fri,** *in*
   certain way (quodammodo) *other than,* i.e. *in a different*
   way from, 362.
almsan, g. **almsine,** f. *alms,* 371.

am : see **Copula** (Paradigms).

am-aires, g. **amirisse,** f. *disbelief,* 160.

1. **amal, amal (-n-)** conj. *as,* 25, 281, 360 ; with past. subj. *as if,* 372.   See note on 119.

2. **amal',** prep. with acc., *like.* **amal sodin,** *in that case,* 38, 52.

amne, (stressed on second syllable) *thus,* 61.

anad, m. *remaining,* 281 ; verb. noun of **anaid.**

anaid, *remains* ; fut. sg. 1, **ainfa,** 127 ; pres. subj. pl. 3 **-anat,** 80.

an-cretmech, *unbelieving,* 152.

an-cride, n. *injury, hurt,* 125, 324.

and : see **i n°-.**

andach, g. **andaig,** n. *iniquity,* 130.

andess, *from the south* ; **andes do,** *on the south of,* 227.

aní : see **intí.**

anim(m), g. **anme,** f. *soul,* 177.

anís, *from below,* 25.

antúaid, *from the north.* **antúaid do,** *on the north of,* 227.

anúas, *from above,* 25 ; *above,* 371.

ap, abb, g. **apad,** *abbot, lord,* 211.

apstal, g. **apstail,** m. *apostle,* 216 ; pl. gen. **apstal,** 48, **abstal,** 53.

ar : see **air.**

ar', prep. with dat. and acc. ; with art., **arnaib,** 317 ; **ara n°-,** 151 ; with poss. pron. **ara n°-,** 79 ; with rel. **ara n°-,** 119, *before* : **ar súil,** 77 ; **dothéi ar menmuin,** *comes to the mind,* 182. *at* : **ar thuus,** *at the beginning,* 313. *for* : **arnaib damdabchaib,** 317 ; **ní n-árraim ar chairi,** *he has not reckoned it as a reproach,* 243. (*deliver, take*) *from* : **soírad ar,** 169 ; *on account of* : **ar formut,** 2 ; **ara n-indeb,** 151, etc. **airi,** *on account of this, therefore,* 10, 24.

ar n°-, *our,* 42, 364.

ara-chrin, *perishes* ; fut. pl. 3 **ara-chíurat,** 158 ; perf. sg. 3 **ara-ruichíuir,** 338.

áram (ad-rím), g. **áirme,** f. *number,* 361 ; verb. noun of **ad-rími.**

ara n°, conj., *in order that,* 60, 79 ; explicative, *that,* 72, 382 ; neg. **arná,** 79, with infixed pron, **ɹrnách,** 72, **airnách,** 358 ; with copula subj. pres. sg. 3, **arnap,** 60.

ar-beir, *brings out, expresses,* 385 ; **ar-beir biuth,** *partakes of,* 337.

ar-cessi, -airchissi, *has compassion on* (**di**), 335.

ard, *high* ; compar. **ardu,** 180.

arde, n. *sign, token,* 161.

ar-foím (air-fo-em-), *receives, assumes,* 336 ; perf. sg. 1 **ar-roiéit,** 236, sg. 3 **ar-roít, ar-roét,** 268, 336; pres. pass. sg. 3 **-eroímer,** 336.

ar-fócair (air-fo-oss-gair-), *commands, enjoins* (**for**), 371 ; verb. noun **irócre.**

ar-gair (**di**), *forbids* ; perf. sg. 3 **ar-rogart,** 242.

ar-icc, *finds* ; pres. subj. sg. 3 pass. **ar-ísar,** 196.

árim : see **áram** and **ad-rími.**

arithissi (a frithissi), *again,* 283.

ar n-, arná : see **ara n°-.**

arrad. i n-arrad, with poss. pron. or gen., *beside, with,* 80.

ar-reith, *assails* ; pres. indic. sg. 2 rel. **ara-rethi,** 14.

ar-se, *on account of this, therefore,* 116.

ar-troítha, *checks, restrains* ; fut. sg. 2 **ar-troídfe** ; pass. subj. sg. 3 **-erthroítar,** 130.

asa-gnin (ess-gnin-) *knows* ; pass. pres. pl. 3 **asa-gnintar,** but **-enggnatar** (en-gnin-) 196.

as-beir, -epir, later **-aipir** (ess-ber-), *says.* See Paradigms.

ascae, g. **ascad,** m. *rival,* 266.

*****as-érig** (ess-ess-reg-), *arises* ; perf. sg. 3 **as-réracht,** 245.

as-gleinn, -eclainn, *searches out, scrutinizes,* 318.

as-indet (ess-ind-fiad), **-aisndet,** *declares,* 382.

as-in-gaib (ess-ind-gab-), *exceeds* ; perf. sg. 1 **as-ringbus,** 293.

as-léna, *pollutes,* 315.

as-ren, *pays, gives out, expends* ; fut. sg. 1 **as-ririu,** 149, 3 **as-riri,** 150.

as-ro-choíli, -érchoíli, *determines,* 218, 261.

as-to-asci (ess-to-fāsc-), *presses out, expresses,* 316.

ata, 52, see **Copula** (Paradigms).

ataim (ad-dam-), *concedes* ; perf. sg. 2 **ad-rodamar,** 296.

at-bail, -epil (ess-ball-), *dies*, 54, 98 ; pres. subj. sg. 3 **at-bela,** 66 ; perf. sg. 3 **at-rubalt,** 241 ; ipv. pl. 3 **eiplet,** 98.

athir, g. **athar,** m. *father*, 94, 336.

athramail, *fatherlike*, 94.

atlugud buide, *giving thanks*, 30 ; verb. noun of **atluchethar buidi.**

atreba (ad-treb-), *dwells, possesses* ; fut. sg. 3 **atrefea,** 134 ; pf. sg. 3 **ad-rothreb,** 278.

at-reig (ess-reg-), *arises* ; fut. sg. 1 **atamm-res,** 191. The verb is in origin transitive, *raises*, and hence has an infixed pron., e.g. **atom-riug,** *I arise* ; **at-reig,** *he arises* ; **ata-reig,** *she arises*, etc.

attá : see **Substantive Verb** (Paradigms).

auctor, m. *author* (Lat. auctor), 276.

-b- : see **Infixed Pronoun** (Paradigms).

baithsed, *baptism*, 360 ; verb. noun of **baithsid.**

baithsid, baitsid, *baptizes*, 360.

ball, g. **baill,** m. *limb, member*, 189.

bar n°- : see **for n°-.**

Barnaip, *Barnabas*, 289.

bás, g. **báis,** n. *death*, 37, 98.

béim, g. **béime,** n. *blow* ; verb. noun of **benaid.** See note on 54.

bél, g. **béoil,** m. *lip*, pl. *mouth*, 76.

béla : see **biáil.**

bélrae, n. *speech*, 40.

ben, g. **mná,** f. *woman*, 57, 230.

benaid, *strikes*, 54 ; part. pass. **bíthe,** 306.

béoigidir, *vivifies*, 27.

beothu : see **bethu.**

berid, *brings, carries, bears* (*children*) 18, 19, 91, etc. See Paradigms. Subj. corresponding to perf., sg. 3 **rucca,** 69. **berid breith, mess (for),** *passes judgement on*, 247 ; **berir fri,** *reference is made to*, 187.

1. **bés,** with subj., *perchance*, 66.

2. **bés(s),** g. **béso, bésa,** m. *custom*, 54, 57 ; acc. pl. **bés(s)u,** *manners, morals*, 94, 380.

bésad, *custom,* 351.

bésgne, n. *custom, usage,* 346.

beta, 82, see **Copula** (Paradigms).

bethu, beothu, g. **bethad,** m. *life,* 31, 37.

beus (disyllabic) *still, always,* 159.

biad, g. **biid,** n. *food,* 87, 91.

biáil, g. **béla,** m. *axe,* 148, 283.

bibdu, g. **bibdat,** *guilty* (gl. reus, obnoxius), n. pl. **bibdaid,** 269.

bindius, g. **bindiusa,** m. *melody,* 338.

bíid : see **Substantive Verb** (Paradigms).

bith, g. **betha,** m. *world,* 72.

bíthe, see **benaid.**

bíthin, in **fo bíthin,** *because,* 158.

boc, g. **buic,** m. *he-goat,* 109.

bráge, g. **brágat,** m. *neck,* 240.

bráth, g. **brátho, brátha,** m. *doom,* 187.

bráthir, g. **bráthar,** m. *brother,* 79.

breth, g. **brethe,** f. *judgement,* 100.

bríathar, g. **bréthre,** f. *word, verb,* 24, 42, 270.

búaid, g. **búado, búada,** n. *victory,* 47, 168.

buide, f. *thanks,* 30.

buidigidir, *gives thanks* ; verb. necess. **buidigthi,** 310.

buith, buid, g. **buithe,** f. *being* ; verb. noun of **attá,** 123, 319.

cach, cech, *every,* 56, 315 ; **cech óin-salm** 329. **sech cech ríga,** *beyond all kings,* 350.

cách, g. **cáich,** *every one,* 28, 69. Also with art., **in cách,** 14.

cain : see **cani.**

cair, *query,* introducing a direct question, 252.

cairde, n. *compact, covenant,* 212.

cairdine, f. *covenant,* 214.

cairc, f. *fault,* 243.

ca-lléic, *still, however,* 349.

camaiph, *still, yet,* 225.

canaid, *sings* ; pf. pass. **ro cét,** 262 ; part. pass. **céte,** 309.

cani, cain, an interrogative (=nonne ?) expecting an affirmative answer, 232, 320.

canóin, g. **canóne,** f. *canon, Scripture-text,* 224, 229.

carachtar, g. **carachtair,** n. *character, letter,* 225.

caraid, *loves,* 63, 64, 104.

carcar, g. **carcre,** f. *prison,* 90.

carae, g. **carat,** m. *friend,* 328.

carpat, g. **carpait,** **carbait,** m. *chariot,* 258.

cathchomnid, m. *catechumen,* 360.

cathir, g. **cathrach,** f. *city,* 227, 278-9.

ce : see 2. **cía.**

cech : see **cach.**

ceist, g. **cesto,** f. *question, difficulty,* 119.

céle, m. *fellow,* 120.

celebraid (do), *bids farewell ;* pret. pl. 1 rel. **celebirsimme,** 223.

cen', prep. with acc., *without,* 70 ; with suff. pron. sg. 3 n. **cene,** *without that, already,* 33 ; with verb. noun, as neg., 125.

céne (-n-), gen. of **cían** f., *as long as, while,* 314 ; **céine,** 374. Cf. **óre.**

cenél, g. **cenéoil,** **cenéuil,** **ceníuil,** n. *race, people, kind,* 85, 87, 220 ; *gender,* 26, 383.

cenn, g. **cinn,** n. *head, end,* **fo-ruirmed cenn for,** *an end has been put to,* 237. **ar chenn,** *to meet,* 283 ; **di chiunn,** *away,* 386. **tar (dar) cenn,** with poss. pron. or gen., *instead of, on behalf of, for,* 1, 86, 109.

cennaige, m. *merchant,* 319.

cenotad, *though ye are,* 234. See **Copula** (Paradigms).

cens(a)e, f. *mildness, gentleness,* 207.

cés(s)ad, g. **césto,** **césta,** m. *suffering, passion,* 146, 290, 385 ; verb. noun of **céssaid.**

céssaid, *suffers ;* pres. subj. pl. 2 **céste,** 75.

ceta-déni, *does first,* 221.

cétnae, **cétna,** preceding its noun, *first,* 13, 357 ; after its noun, *same.*

ceto', *though they are,* 53 ; see **Copula** (Paradigms).

cét-óir, in **fo chétóir,** *at once,* 352.

ci : see 2. **cía.**

1. **cía,** n. **cid,** *who ? what (is it) ?* 29 ; pl. **cit n-é ;** before a noun, m. **cía (cía hé, cé hé),** f. **ce-sí, ce-ssí, ci-sí,** 124,

n. ced' (fr. ce ed), cid', pl. cit n-é. cid ara n°-, lit. *what (is it) on account of which ?* i.e. *why ?* 119. cid dia n°-, *what (is it) from which ? why ?* 245.

2. cía', ce', ci', conj. *although* ; also *that*, e.g. 65, 83, 84, 122, 331. ciní *though not*, 33 ; ci . . . cini, *whether . . . or not*, 327.

cíall, g. céille, f. *sense*, 64, 216.

cían, *long, lasting*, 34.

cían, g. céne, f. *a while*. cach la céin (<cach ala céin)—in céin n-aili, *at one time—at another*, 246.

1. cid : see 1. cía.

2. cid, *though it be*, 59 : see Copula (Paradigms). As particle, *even*, 103, 165.

cimbid, g. cimbedo, m. *captive, prisoner*, 10.

cisí, see 1. cía.

cit, *though they be*, 82 : see Copula (Paradigms).

cita-gaib, *first utters* ; perf. sg. 3 cita-rogab, 216.

claideb, g. claidib, m. *sword*, 18.

cland, g. clainde, f. *offspring*, 19, 52.

class, g. claisse, f. *choir*, 338.

cloch f. *stone*, 291.

cloíne, f. *iniquity*, 103, 328.

closs, see ro-cluinethar.

clúas, g. clúaise, f. *ear*, 41.

cnáim, g. cnámo, cnáma, m. *bone*, 54.

1. co, prep. with acc., *to*, 184 ; cucci, *up to this*, i.e. *so great*, 288 ; with rel., cosa n°-, 290.

2. co', conj., final and explicative, *so that, that*, 110, 69, 194 ; with neg. coní, 60, 196.

1. co n°-, prep. with dat., *with*, 160, 332; with art. cosnaib, 386 ; with poss. pron. sg. 3 cona, 105.

2. co n°-, conj. (1) with ind. *so that*, 56, 57, *until*, 85 ; (2) with subj. *(in order) that*, 112, 123 ; (3) explicative, *that*, 69, 73 ; with neg. conná, 204.

cobadlus, m. *fellowship*, 96.

cobuir, g. cobrad, *help*, 266.

coibnesta(e), *akin*, 24 ; fr. coibnius, m. *affinity*.

cóic', *five*, 256.

coím, *dear*, 46.

coimdiu, g. **coimded,** m. *lord, master,* 77, 319.

1. **coir,** *right, fitting,* 122, 315.

2. **coir,** *right course,* 177.

coitchen(n), *common,* 98, 175, 241.

col, g. **cuil,** n. acc. pl. **col,** n. *sin,* 228.

colinn, g. **colno,** f. *flesh,* 268.

colnide, *carnal,* 81.

com-airle, f. *counsel,* 240, 250.

comalnad, m. *fulfilment,* 47, 174 ; verb. noun of **comal-naithir.**

comalnaithir, *fulfils* ; pass. sec. fut. sg. 3 **no comallaibthe,** 140 ; pres. subj. pl. 1. **-comalnammar,** 73, 3 **comalnit,** 78, **-comolnatar,** 81 ; perf. ind. pl. 2 **ro comalnisid,** 226 ; pass. pl. 3 **ro comallada,** 237 ; verb. necess. **comallaidi,** 310.

comarbus, m. *inheritance,* 94.

comarpe (com+orbe, *inheritance*), m. *heir,* 52.

comrorcon (com-air-org-), g. **comroircne,** f. *error,* 364.

comroircnech, *erroneous,* 183.

com-śuidigud, g. **comśuidigtheo,** m. *composition,* 24.

com-śuidigthe, *compounded,* 82.

comthururus (com-to-air-fo-reth-), *incursion,* 101.

con-air-leci, *permits,* 342.

con-boing, *breaks,* 54.

con-ceil, *hides* ; perf. sg. 3 **con-aicelt,** 243.

con-dieig (com-di-sag-), **-cuintig,** *seeks, asks,* 345, 346 ; pres. subj. sg. 3 **-cuintea,** 200 ; past subj. sg. 1 **con-desin,** 199 ; perf. sg. 3 **con-aitecht,** **-comtacht,** 244.

con-étet (com-en-tēt-), *is indulgent to* (**do**) ; verb. neces. **comitesti,** 311.

con-gní, *works with, helps* (with **fri**) ; pres. subj. sg. 3 **con-gné,** 67.

coní : see 2. **co.**

con-icc, **-cumaing,** *is able,* 177, 196, 298. See Paradigms.

conid, *so that it is,* 282, 322 : see **Copula** (Paradigms).

con-midethar, *settles, determines* ; perf. sg. 1 **con-ammadar,** 294.

con-oí, con-oéi, -comai, *guards, preserves,* 340 ; ipv. pl. 2 **comid,** 341.

con-oscaigi (com-uss-scoch-), **-cumscaigi**, *removes, alters* ;
pl. 3 **con-osciget, -cumsciget,** 347, 348 ; past subj. sg. 3
-cumscaiged, 115 ; verb. necess. **cumscaichthi,** 359.
con-rig, *binds* ; pres. subj. sg. 1 **con-rías,** 173.
con-scara, -coscra, *destroys,* 344 ; fut. sg. 3 **con-scéra,** 211,
343 ; perf. sg. 2 **con-ascrais,** 214.
conson, g. **consine,** f. *consonant,* 225.
con-utaing (com-uss-ding-), *builds, upbuilds* ; perf. pl. 3 **con-
rótgatar,** 278, pass. **con-rótacht,** 279.
corathar : see **fo-ceird.**
córe, f. *peace,* 376.
corp, g. **coirp,** m. *body,* 27, 34.
cosc, g. **coisc,** n. *reprimand, correction,* 57.
coscid, *reprimands, corrects* ; pres. ind. pass pl. **coscitir,** 57.
coscur, g. **coscair,** m. *victory,* 107.
cosmail (fri), *like,* 112, 330.
cosmailius, g. **cosmailseo,** m. *likeness,* 377. **fo chosmailius,**
after the manner of, 20 ; followed by rel. **-n-,** *as,* 361.
co-sse, co-se, *up to this, hitherto,* 117, 249.
cossecrad, m. *consecration,* 279.
cotarsne, *contrary, opposed* (**do,** 178, **fri,** 179) ; neut. pl.
adversities, 237.
coté ? *what is ?* 61.
cretem, g. **creitme,** f. *belief, faith,* 31, 76 ; *act of believing,*
363 ; verb. noun of **cretid.**
cretid, *believes,* 45, 131, 230 ; fut. sg. 3 rel. **creitfess,** 132.
cride, n. *heart,* 76.
Críst, *Christ,* 4, 48.
croch, g. **cruche,** f. *cross* ; acc. **croich,** 48, 299.
cruth, g. **crotha,** m. *form, manner.* **in chruth (chrud) so,**
in this way, 73, 120. **in chruth sin,** *in that way,* 131. **cruth
ro pridchissem,** *the manner in which we have preached,* 288.
cruthaigidir, *forms,* 225.
cucci : see 1. **co.**
cuimre, f. *brevity,* 138.
cuimrech, g. **cuimrig,** n. *bond, fetter,* 132 ; verb. noun of
con-rig.
cuingid, *seeking,* 163 ; verb. noun of **con-dieig.**

cuit, g. **cota,** f. *share, portion.* **cuit adaill,** *a mere passing visit,* 25, 127. **ar chuit,** *as to,* 371.

cumacht(a)e, n. *power,* 57, 207.

cumachtach, *powerful*; with gen. *potent over,* 43.

cumang, *power,* 149.

cumme (fri), *like,* 11.

cumsanad, g. **cumsanto,** m. *rest,* 386 ; verb. noun of **con-osna** (com-uss-an-).

cumscugud, m. *change, motion, stirring,* 324 ; verb. noun of **con-oscaigi.**

cumtach, g. **cumtaig,** n. *building, upbuilding,* 370 ; verb. noun of **con-utaing.**

cundubart, f. *doubt,* 245.

cúrsachad, g. **cúrsaigtheo,** m. *reprimand,* 79.

1. **-d-** : see **Infixed Pronoun** (Paradigms).
2. **-d-,** particle with ind. after **cia** and **ma** : see note on 131.
3. **-d-,** rel. particle, 119.

-da- : see **Infixed Pronoun** (Paradigms).

da, *two,* 109 : see Paradigms.

daltae, m. *fosterling, pupil,* 368.

-dam- : see **Infixed Pronoun** (Paradigms).

dam-dabach, f. *tub,* 317.

-dan- : see **Infixed Pronoun** (Paradigms).

dán, g. **dáno, dána,** m. *gift, endowment, craft,* 151.

dano, *moreover,* 30, 50.

dar : see **tar.**

de : see **di.**

dé, g. **diad,** f. *smoke* ; **dǽ,** 339.

dea, *a pagan divinity,* 51.

deacht, g. **deachte,** f. *divinity,* 55, 267.

dechrigidir, *differs*; pl. 1 **dechrigmir,** 39.

dechur, g. **dechoir,** n. *difference, distinction,* 249.

déde, n. *two things,* 111.

deg-, dag-, in composition, *good* ; **deg-gním,** *good deed, well-doing* ; pl. acc. **degnímu,** 163 ; dat. **degnímaib,** 332.

degaid, in phr. **i ndegaid,** *after,* 183.

déicsiu, g. **déicsen,** f. *beholding, looking at,* 202, 312; verb. noun of **do-écci.**

deidbir, deithbir, *proper,* 18.

deisimrecht, g. **dessimrechta,** n. *example,* 73.

delbaid, *forms*; perf. pass. **ru delbad,** 366.

demin, *certain*; compar, **demniu,** 41.

demon, g. **demuin,** m. *the devil,* 188.

déne, f. *swiftness, speed,* 310.

dénum, g. **dénmo, dénma,** m. *doing, making,* 330; verb. noun of **do-gní.**

derb, *certain,* 124.

derbaid, *certifies,* 383.

derscaigthe, *distinguished, of surpassing excellence,* 319; part. pass. of **do-róscai.**

dethiden, g. **dethidne,** f. *care,* 35.

deug, g. **dige,** f. *drink,* 91.

di', de', do', du', prep. with dat.; with rel. **dia n°**; with poss. **dia',** etc. *from*: **di mulluch,** 291, **dia samthig,** 283, **dia n-anduch,** 130, **de dobríathraib,** 233. **dind liac,** *of the stone,* 126. **di chorp,** *of the body,* 116. **di chlochaib,** *with stones,* 291. **dethiden di,** *care for,* 35. *of* (partitive): **oínfer diib,** *one of them,* 47, cf. 70, 165, 182, etc. *of, concerning*: **aisndís dint sens,** 133, cf. 160, etc. **de,** lit. *of it,* after the compar. corresponds in sense to Eng. *the* before the compar.: **lia de,** *the more,* 132; **ardu de,** *the higher,* 180.

Día, g. **Dé, Dǽ,** m. *God,* 38, 57, *a god,* 293.

dia n°-, conj., with subj. *if,* 137, 164; with ind. pret. *when,* 291.

diabul, *twofold,* 160.

diad, n. *end.* **fo diad,** *at the end, last,* 313; **i ndiad,** *after,* 283, 386.

díade, *divine,* 151.

dían, *swift,* 250.

diant, *to whom is, to which is,* 185: see **Copula** (Paradigms)

dias, g. **desse,** f. *pair, two men,* 289.

didiu (fr. di ṡuidiu), *hence, therefore,* 30, 54.

dígal (dī-gal), g. **dígl(a)e,** f. *punishment, vengeance,* 18, 80, 193, 298; serves as verb. noun to 1. **do-fich.**

díle, g. **dílenn,** f. *flood,* 20.

dílgud, g. **dílguda,** m. *forgiveness,* 125, 221, 200 ; verb. noun of **do-luigi.**

dílse, f. *propriety, state of being a proper noun,* 282.

díltud, m. *denial,* 228 ; verb. noun of **do-sluindi.**

dímicthe, *contemptible,* 62 ; part. pass. of **do-meiccethar,** *despises.*

di-róscai : see **do-róscai.**

di-taa, *stands apart* (distat), *differs,* 39.

díthrub (dī-treb), g. **díthruib,** m. *desert,* 109.

dítiu, g. **díten,** f. *protection,* 227 ; verb. noun of **do-eim.**

diuit, *simple,* 353.

díummassach, *proud,* fr. **díummus** (di-uss-mess), *pride,* 101.

dliged, dligeth, g. **dligid,** n. *law, rule, duty,* 183, 188.

-dn- : see **Infixed Pronoun** (Paradigms).

1. **do',** *thy,* 87.

2. **do', du',** prep. with dat., *to, for* ; with art. **dund',** 185, **dun',** 227 ; with poss. pron. sg. 3 m. **dia',** 220, f. **dia,** 227 ; pl. 1 **diar** n°-, 177, 178, 2 **dubar** n°-, 312 ; with rel. **dia** n°- 218, 322. **ní samlid són dún-ni,** *it is not so with us,* 180 ; cf. note on 289. **dó,** proleptic, *for this,* 48, 112. **dia n-aiperr,** *for whom is said,* i.e. *who is called,* 322. Before verb. noun (1) it expresses purpose : **do thabirt díglae,** *to inflict punishment,* 18 ; cf. 25, 221, 227, etc. (2) it is used idiomatically to attach the verb. noun to another noun which is in case relation to what goes before : **do-fórmaich fochricc dosom sochude** (nom.) **do chreittim,** *that a multitude should believe* (lit. *a multitude for believing) increases reward for him,* 363 ; **ci ad-cobrinn moídim** (acc.) **do dénum,** *though I desired to boast,* lit. *boast for making,* 302 ; cf. 330. It expresses the agent after verb. noun : **fodord doib,** *murmuring by them,* 160, cf. 123, 330, and after the verbal of necessity : **ní dénti dúib-si anísin,** *ye must not do that,* 312.

do-accair (to-ad-gar-), **-taccair,** *pleads*; fut. sg. 3 **taiccéra,** 167.

do-adbat, -tadbat, *shows*; sg. 2 **do-adbit,** 13 ; perf. sg. 3 **do-árbuid,** 276, **du-árbaid,** 310, pass. **-tárbas,** 277.

do-aid-chren, -taidchren, *ransoms, redeems* ; perf. sg. 3 **do-raidchíuir,** 268, pass. pl. **do-rathchratha,** 269.

do-aidlea (to-ad-ella), *visits* ; fut. sg. 3 **do-aidlibea,** 274.

do-airbir, -tairbir, *bows down, reduces* ; pass. pl. 3 **do-airbertar,** 57.

do-airchain, -tairchain (to-air-fo-can-), *prophesies* ; perf. sg. 3 **tairchechuin,** 259, pass. **tairrchet,** 145.

do-áirci, *effects, causes,* 37.

do-airngir, -tairngir (to-air-in-gar-), *promises*; perf. sg. 2 **du-rairngirt,** 237, sg. 3 **du-rairngert,** 280, pass. **du-rairngred,** 254.

do-ais(s)ilbi (to-ad-selb-), *assigns,* 22.

-dob- : see **Infixed Pronoun** (Paradigms).

do-beir, -tabair, (1) *gives* ; (2) *brings forward, puts, carries off.* See Paradigms. **do-beir dígail for,** *punishes.* **do-beir maldachta for,** *curses,* 109.

do-bidci, *pelts,* 291.

do-bríathar, g. **dobréthre,** f. *adverb,* 233 ; an artificial translation of Lat. aduerbium.

do-chrud, *unseemly,* 315.

dochum nᵒ-, *to,* with poss. pron. or gen., 109, 110.

do-claid, -tochlaid, *roots up,* 25.

do-cuirethar, -tochuirethar ; (1) *places, puts,* 358 ; impers. perf. sg. 3 **du-rale.** 313. (2) *takes to himself, adopts, invites,* 357.

dodcadchae, f. *misfortune,* 56.

do-dichet, *leads* ; part. pass. **tuidchisse,** 308.

do-écci (di-en-cī-), **-décci,** *sees* ; fut. sg. 3 **du-écigi,** 207.

do-eclainn (to-ess-glenn-), *searches out* ; pass. pres. **du-eclannar,** perf. **du-érglas,** 319.

do-ecmaing, *happens,* 142.

do-edbair (to-ad-uss-ber-), *applies* (adhibet) ; part. pass. **tedbarthe,** 303.

do-eim (di-em-), *covers, protects,* 86 ; fut. sg. 3 **du-éma,** 192 ; perf. sg. 3 **du-rét,** 246 ; verb. noun **dítiu.**

do-erchomraici, -terchomraici, *collects,* 328.

do-érig (di-ess-reg-), **-dérig,** *deserts* ; perf. pl. 2 **do-rérachtid,** 250 ; verb. noun **dérge** n.

1. **do-fich** (di-fich-), **-díg,** *punishes, avenges* ; ipv. sg. 2 **deich,** 86 ; pres. subj. pass. **du-fessar,** 194 ; fut. sg. 3 **du-fí,** 192 ; pass. **du-fiastar,** 193 ; verb. noun **dígal.**

2. **do-fich** (to-fich-), *attacks, destroys*; past subj. pl. 3 **-toirsitis** (but see note on 279); verb. noun **togal**, f.

do-fóirnde (to-fo-rind-), **-tóirnde**, *signifies*, 361, 362.

do-fórmaig, **-tórmaig**, *adds, increases*; **do-fórmaich**, 363; ipv. sg. 2 **tórmaig**, 364; sec. fut. sg. 3 **do-foirmsed**, 190; part. pass. **tórmachte**, 304.

do-fúairc (to-org- and to-fo-org-), **-túairc**, *wears away, grinds (corn)*; part. pass. **túartae**, 305; verb. noun **túarcon**, f.

do-fúarat (di-oss-reth-), **-díurat**, *remains over*, 355; impf. sg. 3 **do-fúairthed**, 160; fut. sg. 3 **-diúair**, 356;

do-fuisim (to-uss-sem-), *generates, creates*; fut. pass. sg. 3 **do-fuisémthar**, 365; perf. sg. 3 **du-forsat**, 247, pass. pl. **-torsata**, 248.

do-gair (to-gar-), *calls*; perf. sg. 3 **do-rogart**, 251.

do-gaítha, **-togaítha**, *deceives*; perf. sg. 3 **-torgaíth**, 217.

do-gní, **-déni**, *does, makes*, 4, 5, 22, etc. See Paradigms.

do-goa (to-gus-), *chooses*; perf. pl. 2 **do-roígaid**, 263; pass. **do-rogad**, 264; verb. noun **togu.**

do-íarmórat (to-iarm-fo-reth-), *follows*, 386.

do-icc, **-tic**, *comes*, 193, 285. See Paradigms.

doínacht, g. **doínachte**, f. *humanity*, 55.

do-indnaig, **-tindnaig** (to-ind-aneg-), *bestows, gives*; perf. sg. 2 **do-écomnacht**, 238.

do-infet, *inspires*; pres. subj. sg. 3 **-tinib**, 177.

do-inscanna, **-tinscanna**, *begins*, 359.

do-lega (di-leg-), *destroys*, 20.

do-luigi, **-dílgai**, *forgives*; pl. 3 pass. **du-luigter**, 255; perf. sg. 3 **do-rolaig**, 243; pass. sg. **do-rolged**, 221; pl. **do-rolgida**, 255, **-derlaichtha**; fut. pass. sg. **-dílgibther**, 234.

do-meil, **-tomil**, *consumes, partakes of, enjoys*; ipv. sg. 2 **tomil**, 87; past subj. pl. 1 **du-melmis**, 120; perf. sg. 1 **-tormult**, 235.

dommatu, g. **dommatad**, m. *want, poverty*, 160.

do-moinethar (to-muin-), *thinks*, 9; pres. subj. pl. 1 **du-menammar**, 74; past subj. sg. 3 **-tomnad**, 114; perf. sg. 1 **do-ruménar**, 293.

domunde, *worldly*, 151.

-don- : see **Infixed Pronoun** (Paradigms).

do-opir (di-oss-ber-), *deprives, takes away*, 353 ; part. pass.
  díuparthe, 354.
doraid, *difficult*, 138.
do-ro-choíni, -derchoíni, despairs, 136.
do-roich (to-ro-sag-), *reaches* ; see note on 279.
do-roimnethar (di-ro-muin-), *forgets* ; pres. ind. or subj. pl.
  1 **-dermanammar,** 386; fut. pl. 3 **du-roimnibetar,** 137.
do-róscai, di-róscai (di-ro-oss-scoch-), **-derscaigi,** *surpasses*,
  349 ; fut. pl. 3 **du-róscibet,** 350.
dos(s)om, 57 : see Paradigms, p. 29 note.
do-tét, *comes*, 115, 283, etc. See Paradigms.
do-tuit (to-to-tud-), **-tuit** (to-tud-), *falls*, 54, 282-3. In the
  deuterotonic forms **to-** is put twice, in the prototonic once.
  See Paradigms.
do-ucci, tucci, *understands*, 212.
drécht, *portion*, 85, 245.
droch-, *bad*, in composition with a following noun, 130.
du- : see **do-.**
du' ; see **do'.**
du-álaig, f. *vice*, 163, 364.
dubar n°- : see 2. **do'.**
dúil, g. **dúlo, dúla,** f. *element, creature*, 247, 248.
duine, *man*, 114 ; pl. **doíni,** 299, gen. **doíne,** 360.
dul, *going* ; serves as verb. noun to **tét,** 180.
dús, duús (do fiuss) **in** n°-, *to see if, if perchance*, 123, 212.

Ebustae, m. *Jebusite*, 279.
écen, f. *necessity.* **is écen,** *it is necessary*, 82, 138, 371.
ecne, (ess-gne), n. *knowledge*, 299, 369 ; cf. **asa-gnin.**
écóir (an-coir), *unfitting, improper* ; **écóir fri,** *at variance with*,
  133.
écoscc (en-cosc), n. *distinguishing mark, appearance*, 376.
edbart, see **idbart.**
Égeptacde, *Egyptian*, 231.
éiss, f. *track.* **tar (dar) ési,** with poss. pron. or gen. *in place
  of, for*, 58, 150, 225.
ellach, n. *conjunction, union*, 52.
engne, n. *understanding, cognition*, 379.

énirte, f. *weakness, infirmity,* 177 ; fr. **énirt** (ess-nert), *weak.*

ennac, *innocent* ; acc. pl. m. **encu,** 112.

epert, g. **eperte,** f. *saying, word,* 89, 225 ; verb. noun of **as-beir.**

Ephis, *Ephesus,* 281.

epscop, g. **epscuip,** *bishop,* 360.

erbaid, *entrusts,* with infixed or suffixed pron. **no-m erpimm, no-t erpi, eirbthi,** etc., *trusts in* (**i n-** with acc.), 22, 161.

érchoíliud, m. *determination,* 261, verb. noun of **as-rochoíli.**

eregem, g. **ereigme,** f. *complaint,* 119 ; verb. noun of **ar-égi.**

erelc : pl. **erelca,** glosses Lat. insidiae, *ambush,* 105.

eret, erat, n. *space of time,* 314, 374.

eretec, g. **eritic,** m. *heretic,* 336.

ergarthe, *forbidden,* 162 ; part. pass. of **ar-gair.**

érge, n. *rising,* 386 ; verb. noun of **at-reig.**

ermitiu, g. **ermiten,** f. *honour.* **ermitiu féid,** *reverence,* 315 ; verb. noun of **ar-muinethar féid.**

ernaid, *grants, gives*; pres. subj. sg. 3 **-era;** fut. **ebraid,** 170.

ernigde : see **irnigde.**

essamin (ess-omun), *fearless, bold, confident,* 132.

esséirge, n. *resurrection,* 31, 131 ; verb. noun of ***as-érig.**

estósc, g. **estóisc,** *pressing out,* 317 ; verb. noun of **as-toasci.**

ét, g. **éoit, éuit,** m. *emulation, jealousy,* 123.

étach, g. **étaig,** n. *garment, raiment,* 46, 235, 319.

étaigidir, *is emulous, jealous,* 63, 64.

-étar : see **ad-cota.**

etar-certa, *interprets, explains,* 69.

etarcne, n. *knowledge, understanding,* 69 ; verb. noun of **etir-gnin.**

etar-scara, *departs,* 212.

etarscarad, m. *parting with, separation,* 231 ; verb. noun of **etar-scara.**

etarthothaim (etar+tothaim, verb. noun of **do-tuit**), n. *perishing, destruction,* 328.

etir, *at all,* 121, 193, 356.

etir-di-ben, *destroys*; perf. sg. 3 **etir-rudib,** 284.

étiuth, *raiment,* 58.

etrachtae, f. *brightness, splendour,* 350.

VOCABULARY 185

fa nacc (naic) : see **in** n°-.
fadeissin, 280 : see **féin** (Paradigms).
fáilid, fáilith, *joyous,* 19, 134, 386.
fáilte, f. *joy,* 59, 386.
fáith, g. **fátho, fátha,** m. *prophet,* 216.
faittech, *cautious,* 387.
far n°- : see **for** n°-.
féchem, g. **fécheman,** m. *debtor,* 16.
fecht, g. **fechte,** f. *turn, time* ; acc. **in fecht so,** *now,* 27.
fechtnach, *prosperous,* 130.
feib (-n-), *as,* 276.
féid, see **ermitiu.**
feidligidir, *endures,* 387.
féith, *a calm,* 181.
féuil, féoil, f. *flesh* ; pl. gen. **féulæ,** 160
fer, g. **fir,** m. *man, husband,* 47, 57.
ferc, ferg, g. **fercae,** f., *anger,* 324.
fercaigidir, *is angry,* 44.
ferr, *better,* 184 ; compar. of **maith.**
fesine, fessin : see **féin** (Paradigms).
fetarlicc, g. **fetarlicce,** f. (g. also **fetarlicci** [1]), *Old Testament,* 91, 211.
fil : see **Substantive Verb** (Paradigms).
fili, g. **filed,** m. *poet,* 51.
fíne, f. *vine, grape,* 25, 317.
fír, *true,* 166 ; in composition, **fír-immgabáil,** 377 ; as substantive, *truth,* 111.
fírián, fírién, *just, righteous,* 119, 140, 237, 247.
fíriánigidir, *justifies,* 28.
fírinne, f. *righteousness,* 119, 250, 379.
fiss, fius(s), g. **fesso, fiss,** *knowledge,* 118, 337.
fíu, *worth, worthy* ; with acc. 121.
flaith, g. **flatho, flatha,** f. *sovereignty, prince,* 351.
fo', fu', prep. with dat. and acc., *under*; with art., **fon',** 216, **fua** n°-, 237 ; with rel. **fua** n°-, 216. **ní taít fo thairngere,** *he comes not under a promise, does not subject himself to a promise,* 115. **fon díthrub,** *into the desert,* 109. **fo imcho-**

1 Through the influence of the neut. **núfíadnisse,** *New Testament.*

marc, *in interrogation*, 44. **fon chéill,** *according to the sense*, 216. **fo chosmailius,** *after the fashion of, like,* 20. **fua n-indas sin,** *in that way,* 237.

fo-ácaib, fácaib (fo-ad-gab-), *leaves,* 367 ; pret. sg. 3 **fácab,** 368.

fo-ammamaigedar (fo-ad-mām-), *subjugates,* 220.

fo-ceird, *throws, puts* ; past subj. sg. 3 **fo-cerred,** 221 ; fut. sg. 3 **fo-cicherr, -foícherr** ; pret. sg. 3 **fo-caird,** 283. Except in the fut. the prototonic forms are supplied by -**cuirethar** ; pres. subj. sg. 3 -**corathar,** 72 ; pret. -**coras-tar** ; perf. sg. 3 **ro lá, -ralae.**

fochaid, g. **fochado, fochada,** f. *tribulation,* pl. nom. and acc. **foch(a)idi,** gen. **fochaide,** 382, etc. ; verb. noun of **fo-saig,** *assails.*

fochunn, g. **fochuinn,** m. *cause,* 308.

fochricc, g. **fochricce,** f. *reward,* 58, 340, 363.

fo-daim, -fodaim, *suffers,* 45, 48, 81, 119 ; pres. subj. sg. 1 **fo-dam,** 143 ; fut. pl. 3 **fo-didmat,** 141 ; sec. fut. sg. 3 **fo-didmed,** 142 ; perf. pl. 3 **fo-rodamnatar.**

fo-dord, g. **foduird,** n. *murmuring,* 160.

fo-fera, -foírea, *causes,* 119, 369, 370 ; perf. sg. 3 **fu-ruar,** 379.

fo-fúair : see **fo-gaib.**

fo-gaib, *finds* ; perf. sg. 3 **fo-fúair, -fúair,** 276.

fo-gní, *serves* ; perf. sg. 3 **fo-ruigéni, -forgéni,** 266.

fogur, g. **foguir,** m. *sound,* 29.

foillsigidir, *makes clear, manifests,* 55, 175.

foirbthe, *perfect,* 91, 127 ; part. pass. of **for-fen,** *completes.*

foircimem, glosses Lat. optimus, *best,* 328. -**imem** is a double superlative suffix found in Ml. Cf. **forgu,** *choice.*

foísitiu, g. **foísiten,** f. *confession,* 30, 170.

folad, g. **folaid,** n. *substance,* 362.

follus, *clear, manifest,* 269.

fo-loing, *supports, sustains* ; pres. subj. sg. 3 **fo-ló, -ful,** 203-4 ; pl. 1 -**fulsam,** 172 ; sec. fut. sg. 1 **fu-lilsain,** 201, pl. 3 -**foílsitis,** 202.

fo-moinethar, *attends to, is on his guard against* ; ipv. pl. 2 **fomnid,** 234 ; pres. subj. sg. 2 **fo-mentar,** 128.

for, prep. with dat. and acc., *on, upon* ; with art. **forsnaib,** 237, **forsna,** 181, 189, 256 ; with poss. pron. sg. 3 m. **fora',** 244, pl. **fora n°-,** 23, 160 ; with rel. **forsa n°-,** 14, **fora n°-** 54, neg. **forná,** 210. **for teiched,** *in flight,* 97. **for n°-,** *your,* 43, 235, 250, **far n°-,** 1, 76, 77, **bar n°-,** 131.

foraithmet, g. **foraithmit,** n. *recollection, commemoration,* 356.

for-aith-minedar, *calls to mind, commemorates,* 55.

for-brissi, *routs,* 220.

for-cain, *teaches,* 49, 360 ; fut. sg. 2 **for-cechnae,** 144 ; perf. sg. 1, 2, **for-roíchan,** 260, 261.

forcenn, g. **forcinn,** m. n. *end,* 213 ; **forcan,** 228.

for-cenna, -foircnea, *ends, exterminates,* 25, 98.

forcital, g. **forcitil,** n. *teaching,* 360 ; verb. noun of **for-cain.**

for-comai, *preserves,* 225.

for-comnacuir (for-com-icc-), *has come about* ; past subj. sg. 3 **for-cuimsed,** 259.

for-con-gair, *orders* ; perf. sg. 3 **for-rochongart,** 290, pass. **for-rorcongrad,** 290.

format, n. *envy,* 2 ; verb. noun of **for-moinethar.**

forṅgaire, forgaire (for-com-gare), ·n. *a command,* 310 ; verb. noun of **for-con-gair.**

fortacht (for-techt), g. **fortachtae, fortachtan,** f. *help,* 60, 246, 261 ; verb. noun of **for-tét.**

fortachtaigidir, *helps,* 55.

for-tét, for-téit, *helps,* 177.

fortgide, *covered, hidden* ; in **fortgidiu,** *covertly,* 105 ; part. pass. of **for-tuigethar,** *covers.*

fo-rumi, -fuirmi, *places, puts* ; perf. pass. **fo-ruirmed,** 237.

foscad (fo-scáth), d. **foscud,** *darkness,* 270.

foscaigiu : see note on 386.

fo-scanna, *tosses* ; impf. sg. 1 **fu-sscannainn,** 318.

foxul, *taking away,* 355 ; verb. noun of **fo-coislea,** *carries off, takes away.*

frecur (frith-cor) **céil(l),** *cultivation, cult, worship,* 315 ; verb. noun of **fris-cuirethar céill,** *cultivates.*

frecṅd(a)ircc (frith-com-derc-), *present,* 12, 177. **hi frecṅdairc,** *at present,* 330.

frescissiu, frescsiu, g. **frescsen,** f. *expectation, hope,* 217 ; verb. nouh of **fris-acci.**

fri, prep. with acc. ; with art. **frisin** n°-, 133 ; with rel. **frisa n**°-, 239. *towards* : 125, 234 ; **do-rignis friu,** *which thou hast made with them,* 214. *says* (*to*) : 106, 239. (*adds*) *to* : 83. **comsuidigud fri,** *composition with,* 24. *against* : 54, 105, 279. With words of likeness, unlikeness, comparison, etc., **cumme fri** 11, **cosmail fri,** 112, **écóir fri,** 133, **cotarsne fri,** 179, **samlaidir fri,** 56, 84, **intamil fri,** 358. **con-gní fri,** *helps,* 67. (*parts*) *with* : 102. *with reference to* : 262. **fri dénum n-uilc,** *for doing evil,* 241. **ní bethe fria acre,** *ye should not be about to complain of it,* 125.

fris-acci (fris-ad-cí), **-frescai,** *expects, hopes* ; perf. sg. 1 **fris-racacha,** 265, sg. 3 **ru frescachae,** 266. In this verb **fris-** extends likewise to prototonic forms.

fris-ben, *heals* ; pres. subj. sg. 3 **fris-bia,** 155 ; fut. sg. 3 **fris-bia,** 153.

fris-gair, *answers,* 229.

fris-oirg, *hurts, offends,* ipv. pl. 2 **frithorcaid (do),** 373 ; ipf. pl. 3 **friss-oirctis,** 375 ; pres. subj. sg. 3 **fris-orr,** 198 ; past subj. pl. 2 **fris-orthe (fri),** 372 ; fut. pl. 3 **fris-iurat,** 374 ; perf. pl. 3 **fris-comartatar,** 252.

frithorcun, g. **frithoircne,** f. *offence, hurt,* 119, 231 ; verb. noun of **fris-oirg.**

frithtuidecht, g. **frithtuidechtae,** f. *opposition,* 251 ; verb. noun of **fris-taít** (frith-to-tét), *opposes.*

fu' : see **fo'.**

fu- : for compounds beginning with **fu-** see **fo-.**

fudumain, *deep* ; neut. *depth,* 119.

-gád, 271, 281. See Paradigms, p. 66.

gaibid, *takes, utters, sings, says,* 47, 183, 206 ; fut. sg. 3 rel. **gébas,** 168. **gaibid imm,** *puts on,* 46. **ro-n-d gab, ro-n gab,** *is* : see note on 227.

gainithir, *is born* ; past subj. 3 **-genad ;** perf. ind. sg. 3 **ro génair,** 300.

gaíth, *wise,* 250.

gáu, gó, g. **gue,** f. *falsehood.* **is gáu dún-ni,** lit. *it is a lie for us,* i.e. *we lie when we say,* 330.

genti, pl. m. *the Gentiles,* 85, 145, 289.

gessid, g. **gessedo,** m. *suppliant,* 171.
glanad, m. *cleansing,* 364 ; verb. noun of **glanaid.**
glé, *clear,* 245.
glenaid, *sticks fast* ; pres. subj. sg. 1 **-gléu,** 157 ; fut. pl. 3
  gíulait, 156.
glenn, g. **glinne,** n. *valley,* 291.
glúaisid, *sets in motion, moves,* 258.
gníid, *does, works,* 386 ; fut. sg. 3 rel. **génas,** 161.
gním, g. **gnímo, gníma,** m. *deed, action,* 5, 40, 96, etc. ; verb.
  noun of **gníid.**
gnúis, g. **gnúso, gnúsa,** f. *countenance,* 202.
goiste, d. **goistiu,** *halter,* 240.
grád, g. **gráid,** n. *grade, order, (ecclesiastical) orders,* 78, 187,
  371.
Gréc, g. **Gréic,** m. *a Greek,* 82, 225.
gúasacht, g. **gúassachtae,** f. *danger,* 169.
gú-forcell, n. *false testimony,* 38.
guide, f. *praying, prayer,* 242 ; verb. noun of **guidid.**
guidid, *prays,* 7, 80, 169-179, 281. See Paradigms, p. 49-51,
  59, 66 ; verb. necess. **gessi,** 314.
guth, g. **gotho, gotha,** m. *voice, sound,* 148, 270, 338.
guttae, f. *vowel,* 359.

-i : see **Suffixed Pronoun** (Paradigms).
i n°-, prep. with dat. and acc., *in, into* ; with art. **isind',**
  40, 300, **isin',** 23, 31, **issa,** 387, **isnaib,** 119, 212, **isna,**
  180 ; with poss. pron. sg. 1 **ím,** 111, 3 m. **inna',** 80, 92,
  pl. 2, **hi far n°-** 76, 3 **inna n°-,** 91, **na n°-,** 15. *and, in
  it, there, then,* 40, 118, 177 ; **i táa,** *in which is,* 31.
Iacób, *James,* 53.
íar n°-, prep. with dat., *after, along, according to* ; with poss.
  pron. **íarna n-,** 279. **íar sin,** *after that, then,* 19.
íarmi-foig (íarmi-fo-sag-), *seeks,* 378 ; perf. sg. 3 **-ríarfacht,**
  379.
íarsindí (-n-), conj. *after,* 386. See **intí.**
íarum, *afterwards, then,* 57, 187, 360.
íc(c), g. **ícce,** f. *healing, salvation,* 136, 178 ; verb. noun of
  íccaid.

íc(c)aid, *heals, saves* (saluat), 85 ; *solves*, 119.

idbart, edbart, g. idbarte, f. *offering*, 285, 331, 378 ; verb. noun of ad-opair.

ídol, g. ídil, m. *idol*, 337.

il, *many*, 349 ; in composition, 183. See also 54, note.

imbed, g. imbid, n. *abundance*, 20.

imbide (imb-fithe), *hedged in*, 17 ; part. pass. of im-fen ; verb.noun imbe.

imchomarc, g. imchomairc, d. imchumurc, n. *question, interrogation*, 44, 229 ; verb. noun of im-comairc, *asks*.

im-curethar, *conveys*, 376.

imdibe, n. *circumcision*, 81 ; verb. noun of im-di-ben.

im-di-ben, *circumcises* ; perf. pass. im-ruidbed, ro imdibed, 286.

im-folngi (imb-fo-long-), *causes, effects*, 59, 107, 219.

imgabál, g. imgabále, f. *avoiding*, 377 ; verb. noun of imm-im-gaib.

im(m)´, prep. with acc., *about, around* ; with art. immin ríg, 319 ; with poss. pron. sg. 3 m. and n. imma´ 174, 240, guidid imm, 174, 281. étaigidir imm, 64. Unstressed before verbs in the sense of *mutually* ; with inf. pron. immu- (Paradigms, p. 26), contracted with ní to nímu-, 272.

immalle (stressed on final syllable) *together*, 141.

immarchor, *errand*, 376 ; verb. noun of im-curethar.

immarmus (imb-ro-mess), g. immarmussa, m. *transgression*, 221 ; verb. noun of im-roimdethar.

imm-im-gaib, -imgaib (imm-oss-gaib), *avoids*, 377.

immurgu, *however*, 54, 118, 163.

immu-s-cluinetar, *they hear one another* ; perf. pl. 1 immu-n-cúalammar, 272.

immu-sn-aiccet, *they see one another* ; perf. pl. 1 immu-n-accamar, 272.

imned, g. imnid, n. *trouble*, 71, 75 ; pl. imneda, 237, imned, 386.

im-rádi, *meditates*, 71, 111.

imrádud, g. imráto, m. *meditating*, 103 ; verb. noun of im-rádi.

im-roimdethar (imb-ro-mid-), *transgresses, sins* ; pres. subj. sg. 3 **im-romastar,** 200, pl. 2 **im-roimsid,** 234.

imthánud, m. *alternation,* 386.

imthimchell, *surrounding,* 319 ; verb. noun of **im-timchella** (imb-to-imb-cell-), *surrounds.*

im-trénigedar, *assures,* 310.

in, f. **ind',** n. **a n°-,** *the.* See Paradigms.

in-cosig (ind-com-sech-), *signifies,* 387.

in n°-, interrogative particle, 123. **in n°—fa nacc** (naic), *whether—or not,* 139, 212.

in-daas, sg. 3, *than,* 336 ; the latter part of the word is verbal and is inflected like **ol-daas.**

indala, *second, one of two,* 64. **indala n-aí,** *one of the two,* 109.

indarbe, n. *expulsion,* 279 ; verb. noun of **ind-arben.**

ind-arben (ind-air-ad-ben-), *expels* ; ipv. pass. **indarbanar,** 101.

indas, n. *state, kind, manner,* 237. **indas (-n-)** *how, as,* 246, 330.

indeb, g. **indib,** n. *wealth,* 59, 151.

indidit, g. **indideto,** *indicative mood,* 44.

indocbál, inducbál (ind-oss-gabāl), g. **indocbále,** f. *glory,* 32, 48, 177.

indráigne, *detriment,* 33.

inducbaide, *glorious,* 72.

ingen, g. **ingine,** f. *daughter,* 326.

in-gor, *impious,* 163.

ingreimm, ingraimm, g. **ingreimme, ingraimme,** n. *persecution,* 48 ; pl. g. **ingramman,** 382 ; verb. noun of **in-greinn,** *persecutes.*

in-medonach, *internal, inward* ; pl. *entrails,* 227.

innunn, *over, to the other side* ; **innúnn,** 207. Mod. Ir. **anonn.**

inonn, inunn, *the same,* 76, 177.

in-reith (ind-reth-), *invades* ; part. pass. **indrisse,** 307.

in-samlathar, -intamlathar, *imitates,* 94, 123, 380, 381.

insce, f. *speech, word,* 140.

inse, *difficult,* 21.

intamail, f. *imitation,* 123, 381 ; *comparison,* 358 ; verb. noun of **in-samlathar.**

int-í (int-hí), m., **ind-í** f., **an-í** n. (art.+stressed **í**) (1) *he, the aforementioned*, **intí Día**, 218. (2) Followed by **sin**: **aní-sin**, *that*, 119, 312; **innahísin**, *those things*, 228; by **siu**: **aní-siu**, *this*, 57, 142; **innahísiu, nahísiu**, *these things*, 87, 93; **isindí-siu**, *in this, herein*, 358. (3) Especially as antecedent to a rel. vb., *he (who), that (which)*, 14, 49, 54, 81, 251, etc. **isindí** as aemulari, 64; so 83, 386. See **airindí, íarsindí**, and **isindí** as conjunctions. For the neut. art. nom. and acc. sg. without **í** see note on 41.

in-tinscanna (ind-to-ind-scann-), *begins*; perf. sg.3 **intindarscan**, 360.

intled, g. **intlide**, f. *snare, ambush*, 105.

intliucht, intśliucht, g. **intliuchto**, m. *sense*, 316.

Iohain, *John*, 53, 360.

Iosofád, *Jehoshaphat*, 291.

irbág, g. **irbáge**, f. *contending, boasting*, 1; verb. noun of **ar-bágim**.

iress, g. **irisse**, f. *faith*, 43, 53, 91.

irnigde, ernigde, f. *prayer*, 177, 257.

irócre (air-fo-oss-gare), n. *command*, 371; verb. noun of **ar-fócair**.

iróin, *irony*, 266.

Hírusalem, *Jerusalem*, 279.

Isaác, Isác, *Isaac*, 292, 365.

ísel, *lowly*, 55.

ísin, *that, those* ⎱ ; after a noun preceded by the article.
ísiu, *this, these* ⎰   30, 229, 328.

isindí (-n-), conj., *in that*, 269.

Ismaíl, *Ishmael*, 365.

Israhél, *Israel*, 234.

Ísu, *Jesus*, 31.

ithe, f. *eating*, 25; verb. noun of **ithid**.

ithid, *eats*, 25.

la, prep. with acc.; with art. **lasin n°-, lasa n°-, lasna**; with rel. **lasa n°-**; with poss. pron. 3 **lia'**, etc. *with*: **do-bertis leu**, 109, cf. 33, 60, 127, 278. *with, among, in* (apud): **la Grécu**, 82, cf. 109, 276. *belonging to*: **ní latt**, *it is not thine*

14. Of the person judging, *in the opinion of*: **is demniu liunn,** *we deem it more certain*, 41, cf. 48, 71, 113, 143, 160, 162, 250, etc. (*pray*) *for*: 172. *by*: 211, 279.

labrad, g. **labrada, labartho, labartha**, m. *speaking, speech,* 111; verb. noun of **labrithir**.

labrithir, *speaks*, 13, 40, 51.

láe, láa, g. **laí**, n. *day*, 93, 187.

laigiu, *less*, 336.

laithe, n. *day*, 300, 386.

la-s(s)e, (**-n-**), *when*, 223, 284.

láthar, g. **láthir**, n. *arrangement, dispensation, device*, 188, 251.

Latindae, *Latin*, 225.

légaid, *reads*, 224.

légend, g. **légind**, n. *reading, study*, 289; verb. noun of **légaid**.

léicid, *leaves, lets go, allows*, 109, 133. **léic úait**, *put from thee*, 87. verb. necess. 311.

léir, *diligent*, 281; equative **lérithir**, ib. **co léir**, *diligently*, 138.

lenaid (**di**), *follows, adheres to*; fut. sg. 3 rel. **liles**, 152; perf. sg. 3 **ro lil**, 257, pl. 3 **ro leldar**, 258.

lére, f. *diligence*, 288.

less, g. **lesso, lessa**, m. *advantage*. **ro-icc less**, with poss. pron. or gen., *needs*, 195.

leth, g. **leith**, n. *half*, 366.

lia, *more*, 132; compar. of **il**.

lie, g. **liacc**, m. *stone*, 54, 126 (see notes pp. 148 and 209).

lige, n. *bed*, 103.

líth, g. **lítho**, acc. pl. **líthu**, m. *festival*, 91.

lobur, *weak*, 177.

loc, g. **luic**, m. *place*, 180, 300, 315.

lóg, lúach, g. **lóge**, n. *price, pay*, 36, 58.

loingthech, *gluttonous* 65; fr. **longid**, *eats*.

londas, g. **londassa**, *indignation*, 207.

longas, g. **loingse**, f. *exile*. **for longais**, *into exile*, 291.

Loth, *Lot*, 256.

lour, *enough*, 24.

-m- : see **Infixed Pronoun** (Paradigms).

ma', *if*, 52, 347 ; neg. **mani**, 348.

macc, g. **maicc**, m. *son*, 46, 93.

Maccidónde, *Macedonian*, 1.

machthad, machdath, *wonder*, 72, 126. **is machthad limm**, *I wonder*, 250.

macthe, *childish, puerile*, 5.

1. **mad-**, *well*. **mad-génatar**, *blessed are*, 301.

2. **mad**, *if it be, if it were* : see **Copula** (Paradigms).

madae, *vain*, 170.

maidid, -maid, -maith, *breaks* (intrans.) 23 ; pres. subj. sg. 3 **-má**, 189 ; fut. sg. 3 **-mema**, 189 ; perf. sg. 3 **ro memaid**, 256. **maidid for nech re neuch**, *some one is defeated by some one*. **for** denotes the vanquished, **re n-** the victor, 23.

maith, *good*, 33. **maith leu**, *they like*, 48. As neut. noun, 280, 364.

maldacht, g. **maldachtae, maldachtan**, f. *curse*, 109, 291.

mám, g. **máma**, *yoke*, **máam, maám**, 250.

manid, *if it is not* 36 : see **Copula** (Paradigms).

mann, g. **mainne**, f. *manna*, 160.

marb, *dead*, 245.

marbaid, *kills*, 240.

masse, f. *beauty*, 34.

mas(s)u', *if it is*, 36, 245 : see **Copula** (Paradigms).

mat, *if they be*, 177 : see **Copula** (Paradigms).

maten, g. **maitne**, f. *morning*, 386.

matinde, *matutinal*, 386.

mé, *I* ; emphatic **messe**, 247.

mebol, mebul, g. **meblae**, f. *shame*. **ni mebul lemm**, *I am not ashamed*, 143.

méit, g. **méite**, f. *size, extent*, 252. **ní hed a méit**, *not only*, 45. See also note on 113.

meldach, *pleasing*, 335.

menmae, g. **menman**, m. *mind*, 182, 270, 386.

mes(s), **messo, messa**, m. *judgement*, 119, 247 ; verb. noun of **midithir**.

mí, g. **mís**, m. *month*, 309.

midithir, *judges* ; pres. ind. sg. 2 **-mitter,** 14 ; ipv. sg. 3
mided, 91 ; subj. sg. 3 **-mestar,** 210 ; fut. sg. 3 rel.
miastar, 209 ; perf. pass. **ro mess,** 295.

milis, *sweet*, 87.

miscuis, *hatred*, 79.

mo', **m',** *my*, 169, 170.

moch, *early*, 386.

mod, g. **muid,** m. *manner*, 362, *mood*, 316.

moídem, g. **moídme,** f. *boasting*, 302 ; verb. noun of **moídid.**

moídid, *boasts*, 8. The verb is in origin transitive, *exalts* ;
hence it takes an infixed reflexive pronoun : **no-m moídim
i n-,** *I boast of* ; **n-a-moídi,** *he boasts* ; etc.

molad, g. **molto,** m. *praise*, 30, 219, 338 ; verb. noun of
molaithir.

molaithir, *praises*, 8, 129, 219.

mór, *great*, 35, 214 ; **mór-chol,** 228 ; equative **móir,** 119

mórálus, m. *morality*, 133.

mos-, *soon* ; only as preverb, 128.

moth, *stupor*, 72.

Moysi, *Moses*, 108.

mug, g. **mogo,** **moga,** m. *slave*, 292.

muinter, **muntar,** g. **muintire,** **muntaire,** f. *household,
folk*, 105, 278.

muir, g. **moro,** **mora,** n. *sea*, 181, 283.

mullach, g. **mullaig,** n. *top*, 291.

1. **-n- :** see **Infixed Pronoun** (Paradigms).
2. **n°,** relative particle. Before specifically relative forms of
simple verbs it is prefixed, e.g. **in tan mberes,** 19, **amal
n-oingter,** 360. But it follows corresponding copula forms,
e.g. **húare as n-,** 24, **a mba n-,** 307, **a mbas n-,** 309.
Otherwise it is infixed, e.g. **in tain no mbeid,** 77, **amal
no-n-da,** 12. Its chief uses are :—

(*a*) It is added optionally to the verb when a relative form
expresses an accusative relation, e.g. 23, 25, 59, 87, 161,
220 (but without **n,** e.g. 7, 64, 170, 177) ; but not when it
expresses a nominative relation, e.g. 54, 81.

(*b*) It has the force of an oblique case of the relative, e.g. **in molad ro mmolastar,** *the praise wherewith he praised,* 219 ; **in déne as mbuidigthi,** *the speed with which thanks must be given,* 310 ; **laithe ro ngénair,** *the day on which he was born,* 300 ; **ní hed a méit no-n chretid-si,** *not only do ye believe it,* 45 : see further 25, 246, 288.

Special instances of (*b*) are the uses of **n** :—

(α) After adjectives of manner, e.g. **is dían do-r-rérachtid,** *it is swiftly that ye have abandoned,* 250; **is lérithir in so no nguidim-se,** *so diligently do I pray,* 281.

(β) After nominal and pronominal conjunctions, e.g. **amal** 12, **a n-** 307, **céne** 314, **in tan** 19, **lasse, óre** 8, **airindí** 300.

(*c*) It is used in reported speech, e.g. **foillsigthir as n-ísel,** *it is made manifest that it is lowly,* 55 : cf. 66, 140, 163, 175.

(*d*) It is used with a dependent subjunctive, e.g. **nád chumaing ara-n-ísar,** *which cannot be found,* 196 : cf. 63, 82, 155, 173, 176, 198.

1. **ná,** *nor,* 251.

2. **ná,** *not.* Used (*a*) with the imperative, e.g. 88, 93 ; (*b*) in relative or dependent negation, e.g. **ná-n°,** 160, **anná-** 306, **aná-** 308. Cf. **arná, conná, forná.**

ná-ba, 2. **ná** with sg. 2 ipv. of the copula, 90.

nach, nom. acc., neut. **na** (geminating), *any,* 20, 22, 64, 134, 200 ; dat. **nach,** 277 ; proclitic forms of **nech,** etc.

nách-, used for 2. **ná** before an infixed pronoun, e.g., 72, 91, 101, 204, etc.

nád, *not,* in relative or dependent negation (it lenites except where it is followed by relative **n**), e.g. 67, 83, 105, 116, 163, 183, 196, 228, 240, 251, etc.

námae, g. **námat,** m. *enemy,* 23, 137, 228.

nammá, *only,* 185 ; **nammáa,** 69.

náte, *nay !* 320.

nech, neut. **ní,** nom. and acc., *some one, anyone, something, anything* ; **fri nech,** 358 ; **fíu ní,** 121 ; g. **neich,** 25 ; d. **neoch, neuch,** 335. Before a relative verb : **do neuch as**

doraid, *concerning whatever is difficult,* 138 ; **do neuch no-d n-eirbea ind,** *to whomsoever shall trust in Him,* 161, cf. 290. **na ní, na nní,** *whatever,* 20, 22.

nechtar, *either of two.* **nechtar n-aíi,** *either of them,* 274.

nem, g. **nime,** n. *heaven,* 65, 166, 340.

neph-chomthetarrachte, *incomprehensible,* 119.

nert, g. **neirt,** n. *strength,* 107.

nertad, g. **nerto, nerta,** m. *strengthening, exhortation,* 175.

neutur, g. **neutair,** n. *neuter,* 83.

-ni, 37, 39, etc. ; see **Emphasizing Pronoun** (Paradigms).

1. **ní :** see **nech.**

2. **ní,** *not* ; in independent negation, 3. See note on 2.

nícon‘,[1] *not* ; in independent negation, 29.

nímu-, see **im(m).**

no, nu, verbal particle. It is used (*a*) regularly with the impf. ind., past subj., and sec. fut. of simple verbs, when they are not preceded by any particle which requires the conjunct form of the verb ; (*b*) under similar conditions, in other parts of the simple verb to infix a personal pronoun or relative **-n-,** 8, 32 ; (*c*) in some parts of the verb in a relative function : see note on 7.

nó‘, *or,* commonly written l.

noch is, *that is to say,* 173.

noíb, *holy, a saint,* 200, 251.

noíbaid, *sanctifies,* 131, 232.

notire, m. *amanuensis,* 117.

nu : see **no.**

núall, n. *cry,* 23.

nú-íadnisse (nue+fíadnisse), n. *New Testament,* gen. **nuíednissi,** 211, 234, **nufíadnissi,** 224.

1. **ó‘, úa‘,** prep. with dat.; with art. **ónd‘,** 289 note, **húan‘,** 98 ; with rel. **hó n°-,** 336 ; **húa n°-,** 98, *from* : **húa Abracham,** 292, cf. 245, 365, 376 ; **ó nach fochunn,** *from any cause,* 308 ; **do-inscanna ó,** *begins with,* 359 ; **glanad ó,** *purification from,* 364. Partitive : **drécht úaib** ,

---

1 In later O. Ir. aiso with nasalization of a dental, Ml. 53ª17.

245, cf. 168. Of instrument or manner: **húa súlib**, *with the eyes*, 41 ; **ó bélib, ó chridiu** 111 ; **húan báas**, *by the death*, 98 ; **húa etrachtai**, *in splendour*, 350 ; **hó aimsir**, *for a time*, 387. Of the agent, *by* : **no oircthe ó popul** 109, cf. 130, 360, 382.

2. **ó'**, conj. (*a*) with perf., *after, when*, 23 ; (*b*) with pret., *from the time that, since*, 230.

oc, prep. with dat. ; with poss. sg. 3 **oca**, 291. *at* : **oc suidiu** 177, **occaib** 338, **oc precept** 147, **oc tuistin** 366, With a verbal noun and the substantive verb it often makes a periphrastic form, e.g. **bíuu-sa oc irbáig**, *I am wont to be boasting*, 1 ; **is oc precept soscéli attó**, *I am preaching the Gospel*, 6.

ocu-ben, -ocman, *touches*, 382 ; fut. pl. 3 **ocu-biat**, pass. sg. 3 **ocu-bether**, 154.

ocus', acus', *and* ; commonly written *et* or ⁊, 8, 14, 22, 55, etc.

oín, óen, *one*, 134 ; in composition, 47, 171, 225, 329.

oínar, *one man*, regularly in dat. with poss. pron. *alone*, e.g. **fuirib for n-oínur**, lit. *on you in your one man*, i.e. *on you alone*, 60.

oís : see 2. **aís**.

ol, *says* ; **ol sí**, *says she*, 301 ; **ol Dauíd**, *says David*, 213.

olc, g. **uilc**, *bad* ; neut. *evil*, 358.

ol-chene : **na n-abstal ol-chene**, *of the rest of the apostles*, 53.

ol-daas, *than*, 41, 53. The second part of the word is the substantive verb, and it is inflected, e.g. **ol-dó**, *than I am* ; **ol-daí**, *than thou art* ; **ol-daas**, *than he is* ; **ol-dáte**, *than they are* ; **ol-mboí**, *than he was* ; **ola-mbieid**, *than ye will be*, etc.

ón : see **són**.

ongid, *anoints* ; pres. pass. pl. 3 **-oingter**, 360 ; perf. pl. 3 **ro oingthea**, 360.

orcaid, orgaid, *slays* ; fut. sg. 2 **-íírr**, 197, 229 ; pass. impf. **no oircthe**, 109.

óre, úa(i)re (-n-), *because*, 15, 24, 379, etc. ; gen. sg. of **ór, úar**, f. *hour*.

Pátricc, *Patrick,* 368.

peccad, g. **pectha,** pl. n. **pecthi, pecdæ,** g. **pecthae,** acc. **pecthu,** m. *sin,* 30, 60 (**pecad,** 109), 131, 221, 234, 255.

pecthach, g. **pecthaig,** *sinful, a sinner,* 119.

persan, g. **persine,** f. *person,* 4, 13, 53, 239.

Petur, *Peter,* 53.

popul, g. **popuil,** m. *people,* 109, 144, 234.

precept, g. **precepte,** f. *preaching, teaching,* 6, 58, 132.

preceptóir, g. **preceptóro,** m. *teacher,* 333.

pridchid, *preaches,* 10, 71 ; pres. ind. pl. 3 rel. **pridchite,** 49, **predchite,** 376 ; fut. sg. 3 **pridchibid,** 211.

rádid, *speaks,* 270.

ran-gabál, g. **rangabálae,** f. *participle,* 24, 385.

rann, g. **rainne,** f. *part,* 267.

rath, rad, g. **raith,** n. *grace,* 234, 340, 384.

re n°-, ria n°-, prep. with dat., *before,* 207, 256. **remib,** *before them,* 23.

recht, g. **rechto, rechta,** m. *law,* 28, 91, 137.

remcaissiu (rem-ad-cissiu), g. **remcaissen,** f. *providence,* 212.

remdéicsiu (rem-di-en-cissiu), g. **remdéicsen,** f. *providence,* 228, 251.

remi-epir, *says before,* 374.

remi-tét, *precedes,* 383 ; perf. pl. 3 **-remdechutar,** 384.

renaid, *sells* ; pres. subj. pl. 3 **-riat,** 151.

re-síu, conj. with subj., *before,* 148, 187.

rét, g. **réto, réta,** d. **rét, réit,** n. pl. **réte,** acc. **rétu,** m. *thing,* 72, 177, 195.

rethid, *runs,* 47.

rí, g. **ríg,** m. *king,* 319, 350, 376.

ríagol, f. *rule,* 225.

riam, *before,* 297.

ríar, f. *will.* **fo réir,** *in subjection to,* 57.

ríchtu, f. *coming, arrival,* 128 ; verb. noun of **ro-icc.**

ro, ru, verbal particle. The chief uses of **ro** or its equivalents (see above, p. 154) are as follows :—

(*a*) It changes a preterite to a perfect, e.g. **as-bert,** *he said* ; **as-rubart,** *he has said.*

(*b*) In a dependent clause of a general sentence it gives a present the force of a perfect, e.g. **hó ru maith fora náimtea remib,** *when their enemies have been routed by them,* 23.

(*c*) It expresses possibility, e.g. **at-robair,** *can say it,* 26 ; **cia ru-bé,** *though it can be,* 70 ; **ní rubai,** *it cannot be,* 70 ; **d-a-rigénte,** *ye could have done it,* 165.

(*d*) Sometimes it turns a past subjunctive into a pluper- fect,e.g. **ro-d-scríbad,** 117, **do-rónta,** 126, **ro ṅgenad,** 300.

(*e*) For **ropia,** 166, see note.

(*f*) With sec. fut. of copula it is used instead of **no** : **ro-m-bad,** 140, **robad,** 185.

(*g*) In **ro-fitir** and **ro-cluinethar** it is used only when a deut. form is required.

(*h*) With the subjunctive it is regular :—

    (α) In wishes : **d-a-rolgea,** 68.

    (β) After **acht,** *provided that*: **acht rop,** 71; **acht as- robarthar,** 309 ; **act ní arbarat,** 337.

    (γ) After **co n°-,** *until* : **con ríctar,** 85.

    (δ) After **re-síu,** *before* : **resíu docoí,** 187.

    (ε) Occasionally with other subjunctives, where its usage is less clear : **ara tart** 60, **arná derṅmis** 164, **arná dich** 188, **ce ru samaltar** 84, **con rucca** 69 (perhaps *that he may be able to bring*), **cor-rop** 76, **corru anat** 80.

ro-cluinethar, -cluinethar, *hears,* 29 ; ipv. sg. 2 **cluinte,** 89 ; pres. subj. pl. 1 **ro-cloammar,** 148 ; fut. sg. 3 **ro- cechladar,** 147 ; perf. sg. 2 **ro-cúala,** 270, pl. 2 **ro-cúalid,** 273 ; pass. **ro-clos,** 275.

rodbo—nó, *either—or,* 340.

ro-finnadar : see **ro-fitir.**

ro-fitir (pres. and perf.), **-fitir,** *knows, knew,* 29 ; pres. **ro-finnadar, -finnadar,** *finds out* ; pass. **-fintar,** 105, pl. **ro-finnatar,** 187 ; pres. subj. sg. 3 **-festar,** 208 ; fut. sg. 3 **ru-fiastar,** 207.

ro-icc, ricc, *comes, reaches,* 128, 195. See Paradigms
ro-saig, *reaches* ; fut. pl. 3 -**roisset,** 366.
rosc, g. **roisc,** n. *eye,* 238.
rún, g. **rúne,** f. *mystery,* 10, 182.
rúnde, *mystical,* 81.

-s- : see **Infixed Pronoun** (Paradigms).
1. **-sa, -se,** 1, 10, 12, 75, etc. : see **Emphasizing Pronoun** (Paradigms).
2. **sa** : see **so.**
sacart, g. **sacairt,** m. *priest* ; **sacardd,** 360.
saíbid, *perverts,* 224.
saidid, *sits* ; fut. sg. 3 **seiss,** 211 ; perf. sg. 3 **do-essid,** 211.
sain, *different, special,* 111, 239 ; **sain-bás,** 98, **sain-écoscc,** 376.
sainred, n. *speciality.* **sainriud,** *in particular,* 319.
sáith, *satiety, repletion,* 160.
saíthar, g. **saíthir,** n. *labour,* 120.
salm, g. **sailm,** m. *psalm,* 279, 287.
saml(a)id, *like that, thus,* 69, 177, 319.
samlaidir, *compares,* 56 ; fut. pl. 1 -**samlafammar,** 135.
samthach, g. **samthige,** f. *handle (of an axe),* 283.
sapait, *Sabbath,* 91.
sásad, g. **sásta,** m. *food,* 185.
scaraid (fri), *parts, separates* (intrans. and trans.), 102, 113, 131.
scíath, g. **scéith,** m. *shield,* 358.
scríbaid, *writes,* 117.
scríbend, g. **scríbind,** d. **scríbunt,** 225, n. *writing* ; verb. noun of **scríbaid.**
scrútaid, *investigates,* 212.
-se : see **Emphasizing Pronoun** (Paradigms).
se, *this,* neut. acc. in **ar-se, co-sse, la-sse** ; dat. see **síu** and **re-síu.** See also **int-í.**
1. **sech,** prep. with acc., *past, differing from,* 98.
2. **sech,** conj., *yet, although.* **sech is,** in explanation, *that is.*
sechithir, *follows,* 93.
sechmadachte, *past,* 385.

sechmall, g. **sechmaill,** n. *passing by,* 25 ; verb. noun o
  sechmo-ella.
sechmo-ella, -sechmalla, *passes by,* 138 ; with **ó,** *lacks,* 385.
Semei, man's name, 291.
sémigud, m. *extenuation,* 221.
sen, *old* ; **sen-Gréc,** 225.
séns, m. *sense,* 133, 353.
serc(c), g. **serce,** f. *love,* 72, 79.
-si, sg. 50, pl. 1, etc. : see **Emphasizing Pronoun** (Paradigms).
sib *you,* 52.
side, sidi : see **suide.**
síl, g. **síl,** n. *seed,* 331, 365.
sillab, sillabae, f. *syllable,* 362.
1. **sin,** *that,* indeclinable. (1) stressed, 4, 317 ; referring to
  a poss. pron., 118 ; after a prep. 19 ; with art., 162, 212 ;
  iss ed laithe in sin, *that is the day,* 300 ; after prep.+
  suff. pron. **samlid in sin,** *like that,* 193, **airi in sin,**
  on account of that, 270. (2) enclitic, after noun preceded
  by art., 10, 18, 111, etc. ; after **(h)í,** 30, 328.
2. **sin,** *here,* 357.
Sïón, *Zion,* 279.
sís, *below,* 275.
síu, *here, in this world* (ἐνθάδε), 207, often contrasted with **tall,**
  yonder, in the other world (ἐκεῖ).
slíab, g. **slébe,** n. *mountain,* 119, 227, 291.
slóg, slúag, g. **slóig,** m. *host,* 20.
smacht, g. **smachta,** m. *sway, command, institute,* 91, 211.
-sn- : see **Infixed Pronoun** (Paradigms).
sní, *we,* 221.
so, *this, these,* indeclinable. (1) stressed, with art., 7, 177, 196,
  etc. (2) enclitic (also written **sa,** and after palatal **se**) following
  a noun preceded by art., 27, 46, 72, 162, etc. Cf. **se.**
sochude, sochaide, f. *multitude,* 134, 363.
Sodaim, *Sodom,* 256.
sodin, sodain : see 1. **suide.**
soïd, *turns* ; fut. sg. 2, **-soífe,** 374.
soilse, f. *light,* 93, 96, 319.
sóinmech, *prosperous* ; neut. pl. **inna sóinmecha,** *prosperity,*
  119, 163.

sóinmige, f. *prosperity,* 163.

soírad, g. **soírtha,** m. *deliverance,* 169 ; verb. noun of **soíraid.**

soíraid, *delivers,* 139.

-som, 11, 25, 109, etc.: see **Emphasizing Pronoun** (Paradigms).

són, ón, *that* :—as subject : 62, 69, 118, 180, 266, 281 ; often in explanation, *that is to say* : 20, 39, 63, 67, 173, 175, 192, 200, 258, 266, 342, 343 ; as object : 64, 177, 298.

soscéle, g. **soscéli,** m. *Gospel,* 6, 250.

spirut, g. **spiurto,** m. *spirit,* 27, 177.

stoir, g. **stoir,** f. *history, literal sense,* 133, often contrasted with **rún,** *mystical sense.*

-su, -siu, 64, 66 : see **Emphasizing Pronoun** (Paradigms).

súaichnid, súaignid, *well-known,* 131, 250.

1. **suide,** an anaphoric pronoun, *he, the last-mentioned, the latter.*

    The forms are in part enclitic, in part accented.

    (*a*) Enclitic :—

    (α) nom. sg. m. **side, sede,** f. **ade, ede, side,** n. **side ;** pl. **sidi, side, adi, ade.** These forms serve either as the subject of a verb, or they are attached to the pron. **é,** e.g. **é-side, sí-ade ;** is **preceptóir-side,** 333.

    (β) Similar forms attached to a verb, and going with an infixed pron., e.g. **cota-óei-ade,** 340.

    (γ) gen. m. n. **sidi, side, adi, ade,** f. **ade, adi, sidi,** pl. **side, sidi, ide, adi.** These forms are attached to a noun preceded by a poss. pron., e.g. **a guth-sidi,** 148, **a leth-adi,** 366.

    (*b*) Accented :—

    The dat. and acc. are accented and inflected regularly, save that **sodin** serves as acc. neut. They are used with prepositions and after the comparative, e.g. **hi suidiu,** 13, **oc suidiu,** *herein,* 177, **amal sodin,** 38, 52.

2. **suide,** n. *sitting, seat* ; verb. noun of **saidid. inna suidiu,** *seated,* 182.

suidigidir, *places, fixes,* 213. 215.

súil, g. **súlo, súla,** f. *eye,* 41, 77.

sund, sunt, *here,* 3, 30, 44.

suth(a)in, *lasting.* **issa suthin,** *for ever,* 387.

-t- : see **Infixed Pronoun** (Paradigms).

tabart, g. **tabairte, tabartae,** f. *giving, putting, taking,* 18, 57, 237 ; verb. noun of **do-beir.**

tairchechuin : see **do-airchain.**

táirciud, m. *effecting,* 328 ; verb. noun of **do-áirci.**

tairmorcenn (tairm-forcenn), g. **tairmorcinn,** n. *termination* 347-8.

tairmthechtas, *transition,* 239 ; fr. **tarmi-tét.**

tairngere, n. *promise,* 115 ; verb. noun of **do-airngir.**

tan, f. *time* ; in **tain,** in **tan** (-n-), *when,* 13, 19, 177.

-tan- : see **Infixed Pronoun** (Paradigms).

tánaise, *second,* 13.

tar, dar, prep. with acc., *over* ; with verbs of swearing, *by* ; with poss. pron. sg. 1 **tarm,** 86, 3 m. **dara'** 167, pl. 2 **dar far** n°- 1, 149, 3 **dara** n°-, 150, **tra** n°-, 193 ; with rel. **tarsa** n°-, 358, **tara** n°-, 280. See **cenn** and **éiss.**

tech, g. **tige, taige,** n. *house,* 319.

techt, g. **techtae,** f. *going,* 207 ; verb. noun of **téit.**

techtaid, *possesses,* 64, 124.

téchte, *fitting, right.* **inna théchtu,** *in its proper order,* 92.

te(i)ched, g. **techid,** n. *flight,* 97 ; verb. noun of **techid,** *flees.*

teilciud, m. *throwing,* 148 ; verb. noun of **do-léci,** *throws.*

téit, *goes* ; *goes to,* 20, 37. See Paradigms.

temel, g. **temil,** *darkness,* 105.

tempul, g. **tempuil,** n. *the Temple,* 211.

tengae, g. **tengad,** m. *tongue,* 40.

testas, g. **testassa,** m. *testimony,* 122.

testimin, g. **testimin,** m. *text,* 216.

Tíamthe, *Timothy,* 286.

timmorte, *shortened* (correptus), 355 ; part. pass. of **do-immuirc** (to-imm-org-).

timthirthid, m. *servant,* 301.

tinfeth, g. **tinfith,** *inspiration, aspiration,* 225 ; verb. noun of **do-infet.**

Tit, *Titus,* 286, 289.

titul, g. **tituil,** m. *title, superscription,* 329.

tochmarc (to-com-arc-), g. **tochmairc,** n. *wooing,* 292.

todlugud, tothlugud, m. *asking, demanding,* 160 ; verb. noun of **do-tluchethar.**

todochide, *future,* 169.

toíb, g. **toíb,** m. *side,* 227.

toimtiu, g. **toimten,** f. *thought, opinion,* 183, 293 ; verb. noun of **do-moinethar.**

toirsech, *sad,* 90.

toísech, *first* ; compar. **toísegu, toísigiu,** *prior,* 53, 148.

tol, g. **tuile,** f. *will, desire,* 36, 77.

-tomnad : see 114, note.

tomil : see **do-meil.**

tongid, *swears* ; past subj. sg. 3 **-tóissed ;** perf. sg. 3 **do-cuitig,** 280.

torad, g. **toraid,** n. *fruit,* 25, 96, 120.

torb(a)e, n. *profit,* 61, 69, 248 ; cf. **do-ror-ban,** *profits.*

torbatu, g. **torbatad,** m. *utility,* 241.

toschith, *sustenance,* 58.

tossach, g. **tossaig,** n. *beginning.* **i tos(s)uch, i tossug,** *at first,* 57, 214, 287.

tossogod, m. *beginning,* 288.

trá, *then,* 57, 177.

tremfeidligud, m. *lasting, continuance,* 387 ; verb. noun of **tremi-feidligedar.**

tremi-beir, *transfers* ; pass. **trimi-berar,** 386.

tremi-feidligedar, *remains permanently,* 387.

tremi-tét, *transgresses,* 274.

trén, *strong,* 214.

trete, traite, f. *quickness,* 250 ; fr. **trait,** *quick.*

tri', tre', prep. with acc., *through,* 31, 180, 333 ; with art. **trisin,** 123 ; with poss. sg. 3 **tria,** 299, 363 ; **trea,** 340.

trócaire, f. *mercy,* 207.

trógae, f. *misery,* 246, 382.

trom, *heavy,* 60.

trop, g. **truip,** m. *figure of speech,* 358.

tú, *thou,* 21 ; emphatic **tussu,** 59.

túailṅge, f. *ability* ; gen. id., 42.

túare, f. *food,* 120, 337.

túath, g. **túaithe,** f. *people, laity,* 371.

tuistiu, g. **tuisten,** f. *generation, creation,* 366 ; verb. noun of **do-fuisim.**

tuus, *leading, first place.* **ar thuus,** *at the beginning, first,* 313.

úa' : see 1. **ó'.**

úall, g. **úaille,** f. *pride,* 118.

úare : see **óre.**

úasal, *noble* ; compar. **úaisliu,** 280.

ucut, *yonder, yon,* with substantive preceded by the article, 225.

u(i)le, *all.* With neut. art. **isind huiliu,** 40, **inna huli,** 374 ; **rethit huili,** 47, cf. 252 ; **cenaib huli,** 70 ; before noun 85 ; *whole,* 349.

uisse, *fitting,* 84, 331.

ADDENDA

PARADIGMS

p. 25 : l. 1, add : Attached to adj. following such a noun, e.g. **cluinte mo chneit trúaig-se,** *hear my wretched groan,* Félire Óengusso.

p. 33 : l. 4, after **for**[1] add *f.* **fuiri.**

p. 38 : Note 4. In all verbs, in all moods and tenses in which the 3 sg. personal ending is normally a spirant **-d,** this comes from an older **-th (berith, gaibith,** etc.). The same applies to the 2 pl. conjunct. The **-th** is still common, especially in archaic texts. When the preceding vowel is syncopated, the voiceless ending remains : **beirthi, gaibthi,** etc., delenited in **ittius, sástum, bent(a)i,** etc. Cf. the perf. pass. (a nominal form) **ro marbad** and **ro marbath,** pl. **ro marbtha ; do-rónad** and **do-rónath,** pl. **do-rónta.**

Note 5. The **t** (from original *nt*) in the ending of the 3 pl. is in all cases pronounced **d.** Hence the variant spellings **-bentar, -bendar,** etc. Except when final, the sound is often expressed by **dd** in the S. Gall Glosses, e.g. **ad-cuireddar,** *they return,* **remi-suidigddis,** *they used to set before.*

Note 6. While the relative ending in the 3 sg. and pl., **beres, bertae,** etc., may express the subject or object of the verb, in the 1 pl. it never refers to the subject : **aní bermae,** *that which we bear,* **in tan mbermae,** *when we bear,* but **is sní beres,** *it is we who bear.* See Selections, note on 52.

p. 68 : l. 16, after **at-tá** add **atá.**

NOTES

14. Possibly **in cách** here before the rel. vb. means *the one, the person*=**intí**; cf. Wb. 12ᶜ46. This meaning is well attested in Mid. Ir. Cf. **inmain cāch isa c[h]orp so,** *dear was he whose body this is*, LB 275a17, and several examples of (**in**) **cách** in Táin Bó Cúalnge, ed. Windisch.

21. **ní tú no-d n-ail,** *it is not thou that nourishest it*, lit. *(that) which nourishes it is not thou.* In Irish the word following the copula is the predicate; cf. 52. Note that the pronouns **-d n-** and **hé** are masc., though the Latin *radix* is fem., and the O. Ir. **frén** (later **frém**) apparently neut.; see ZCP xii. 409.

38. **do**=**di.**

40. Add: Cf. **fou . . . fon chéill,** 216.

41. **an ro-** see 226. Cf. 69 and 208.

52. Add: **ata** (in later spelling **ada**) 3 pl. rel. of copula, is not to be confused with **atá, 3** sg. of substantive vb.

63. Add: The subj. with rel. **n-** is regularly used to translate the Latin infinitive, except after verbs of saying and thinking.

72. Add: **corathar** is here impersonal; lit. *that it may not put him*, i.e. *that he may not fall.* **dia seirc,** *from love of them.* The **a** in **di-a** is an objective gen.; cf. 79.

78. **comalnit.** Note the act. form beside **-comalnammar,** 73. Even in the O. Ir. period the deponent flexion is giving place to the active. Cf. **feidligte, tremfeidliget,** 387.

· 105. One would expect **ind fortgidiu** or **ind fortgidid** (*f*=*ḟ*). The **-d** of the art. is usually retained before a vowel, *ḟ, l, n,* and *r.*

119. After first line add : It is not as a rule followed by a
rel. clause, hence **amal ní-** 121.   Cf. **amal do-berrthe,**
as though she were shorn, Wb. 11ᶜ12.   The example with rel.
-n- cited in l. 10 is exceptional.

126. Add : Or it may be an early example of the gen. **liac**
used as dat. ; cf. Corm. 1059 and *Ériu* xii. 217.

131. Add : When a vb. in the ind. after **cia,** etc. is accom-
panied by an inf. pron., this has as a rule the ordinary form :
cini-n fil, 33 ; **ma nu-m gaibi,** *if thou takest me,* Wb.
32ª16 ; **ma nu-b baitsim,** *if I baptize you,* 8al ; **ce no-s
labratar,** *though they speak them,* 12ᵈ28.   But the 3 sg. m.
and n. has the form **d (id)** ; cf. **ci as-id-roilliset,** 229.   The
use of **dub** (Class C) for the 2 pl. in 52 is peculiar.

158. l. 5.   There are few O. Ir. examples of **fo bíthin** as
conj., but doubtless it originally had the same construction
as **fo bíth.**   Cf. **fu bíth do-n-gníat cercol,** *because they
make a circle,* Bcr. 18ᵈ2.

177. Add : **con-ic,** like other compounds of **-ic,** can take
a direct object, e.g. **cia con-icc ní dúun,** *who can do aught
unto us ?* Wb. 4ᵇ11.   The object may be a verb. noun, **con-ic
dígail forib,** *he can punish you,* 6ª17, or a dependent subjunctive, **cun-ic du-n-ema,** *it can protect,* Ml. 74ᵇ14.   See 196.

196. See also note on 177.   The dependent subj. is required
to express the passive.

212–302, p. 154, l. 17, read : **com-,** when the followinɡ
part of the verb begins with a consonant).   l. 19, after **con
aitecht** add : (But **con-rótaig (con-utaing),** *has built*
l. 26, after Vocabulary, add : and Paradigms.

216.   **fou :** see note on 40.

234. The voc. **a popuil** occurs in Ml. 103ᵃ4.

290. Alternatively the form may be analysed thus: **fo-rro-r-congrad,** a variant spelling of **fo-ro-r-congrad,** the **rr** marking the gemination of the element following a proclitic preposition ending in a vowel when there is no rel. infix. Cf. **do-rrigéni** Wb. 30ᵈ22; **fo-rruim,** *he put,* Thes. Pal. ii. 242, 8; **du-bbert** 241, 15.

291-2. **luid, luide :** see **téit** (Paradigms).

328. Over **obtimi** (*sic* MS.) is the gloss: **ba doig bed n-ingcert in testimin so,** *probably this text is uncertain.* The glossator takes *meriti* as nom. pl. In the facsimile of Ml. the last letter of **foircimi** is doubtful.

336. **ar-roét :** Perhaps we should divide **ar-ro-ét,** with unstressed **ro.** Cf. sg. 1 **arroiéit.** 236, 3 **arroéit,** Wb. 28ᵈ28, rel. **araroiat,** Ml. 24ᵈ28, but **ar-roít,** 268.

339. **ar-i-n-d-chrin, as-i-n-d-bail.** Note that the **-n-** is always infixed before the **-d-** of Class C.

INDEX TO THE NOTES

ba, negative *níbu*, with modal sense, 113.
bíid implying use and wont, 30.
boí with modal sense, 302

cách, 14 (Add.)
cenid, *ce no-d*, 131.
co forming adverbs, rarely used in O. Ir., 138.
co' and *co n-*, 111.
co n- introducing consecutive clause, followed by indicative. 56.
cognate accusative, 37, 134.
coibnesta, later form of *coibnestae*, 24.
com-, perfective use of, p. 154.
com- in verbal composition, 340-8.
con-ic, 177, 196 (Add.).
copula, no forms for imperfect indicative as distinguished from preterite, 103.
cot- for *com-* before infixed personal pronoun, p. 141.
cum- for *com-*, p. 162.

-d'-, infixed neut. pronoun, Class C., lost between certain consonants, 45, 227.
-d'- (*id'*) inserted after *cia*, *ceni*, *ma*, *mani*, followed by indicative, 131.
-d'- expressing subject relative, 119.
dative plural for accusative, 80.
di-, *de-*, in verbal composition, 349-56.
do-, *du-* (earlier *di-*) in verbal composition, p. 163 ; when leniting, 41.
do-, *du-* (earlier *to-*) in verbal composition, p. 163 ; when leniting, 41.
do with logical subject when predicate is not a noun or adjective, 289.
dó, proleptic, 112.
do-cuitig, ' has sworn ', p. 154.
do-essid, ' has sat ', p. 154.
do-tét for, ' touches upon ', 183.
dual subject with plural verb, 109.

en-, a shorter form of *ind-*, used before perfective *-com-*, 238.
-enggnatar, 196.
equative followed by the accusative, 119
ess- in verbal composition, 316-23.
ess- in perfective function, p. 154.
etymological spelling, 20, 316.

long vowel spreads analogically in verbs, 361, 363.
-ll- for *-ln-* in later O. Ir., 310.

mad, ' well ', with preterite, p. 154 ; 301.
ma no-d, mani-d, 131.
méite, 113.
miastar, 209.
modal sense of *ba*, 113 ; of *boí*, 302.
móir, ' as great as ', 119.

na n- = *inna n-*, 15.
nách, dependent negative form of copula after *ocus*, 22.
nách before a verb implies an infixed personal pronoun, 72.
nach mór, 277.
námmin, 114.
narrative tense, p. 154.
nasalization of tenuis expressed in writing, 252.
ní, ' not ', followed by lenition, implying an infixed neuter pronoun, 64.
ní, ' is not ', 2.
nípí, 34.
no prefixed to verbs used relatively, 7 ; serves to infix pronouns, 8.
nominative used out of construction, 54 ; for vocative, 234.

ó, ' since ', with preterite, p. 154.
oc-, ocu-, in verbal composition, 382-7.
(h)óre, (h)úare, followed by relative form of verb, 15 ; with relative
    -n-, 8, 10, 24.

pluperfect sense given to past subjunctive by *ro*, 117.
possessive pronoun with verbal noun, 291.
predicate a prepositional phrase, 32.
predicative genitive, 42.
present indicative with *ro* in sentences of a general type, 23.
pronouns suffixed to verbs, 22.

relative usage of verb, 7, 8 ; form used in deponent and passive, 28 ;
    when verb of relative clause is in 3 sg., 52 ; irregular use, 225, 262.
relative *-n-*, when used, 8, 10, 24, 158 ; when not used, 8 ; not espressed
    in writing, 10, 13 ; gradually lost in Mid. Ir., 158.

CORRIGENDA

p. 7, l. 24, *for* **dá blíadnaib** *read* **dá blíadnae**

p. 13, l. 19, *for* a *read* a.

p. 24, l. 16, *for* eclipse *read* *nasalize*

p. 26, l. 25, *for* rel. is subject *read* the non-rel. takes Class **A**

p. 27, l. 23, *for* **nib** *read* **níb**

p. 28, note 2, *read* pl. 1 **ro-n-ánaic**, 2 **ro-b-ánaic**

p. 65, l. 6, *for* Perfec *read* Perfect

p. 68, l. 17, *for* **-tathar** *read* **-táthar**

p. 72, l. 8, *for* **condam'** *read* **condan'**

p. 73, l. 1, *for* **ropo** *read* **ropo'**

p. 75, l. 13, *for* **érbaraid** *read* **-érbaraid**

p. 80, l. 14, *for* **do-uchtar** *read* **do-ucthar**

p. 81, l. 12, *for* **do-bertais** read **do-bértais**

l. 19, *for* **tabrath** *read* **-tabrath**

p. 85, l. 12, *for* **do-róntai** *read* **do-róntais**

l. 25, *for* **-dergenat** *read* **-dergénat**

l. 30, *for* **-digenta** *read* **-digénta**

l. 32, *for* **-digente** *read* **-digénte**

p. 86, ll. 16 ff. *for* **-digensam** *read* **-digénsam**, *etc.*